Estimating Products

During the big holiday sale, Brewster's Shirt Shop sold 876 shirts. Estimate the amount of money taken in from the sale of shirts.

We need to estimate how much money the store took in from the sale of shirts.

We know there were _876_ shirts sold, and each cost _$11.79_.

To find the amount of money received, we multiply the number of shirts sold, by the cost of each shirt. Since we want an estimated product, we round each factor to its greatest place value. Then we multiply the rounded numbers.

$$\underline{876} \times \underline{\$11.79}$$

number sold   **cost of shirt**

$$\underline{900} \times \underline{\$12.00} = \underline{\$10,800.00}$$

rounded   **rounded**

The shirt shop took in about _$10,800.00_.

Getting Started

Estimate the products.

1. 486 × 33

    _15,000_

2. 615 × 295

    _180000_

3. 79 × 3,415

    _249000_

4. 350 × 7,968

    _2800000_

5. 415 × $18.75

    _$8,00080_

6. 563 × $203.40

    _12000000_

Copy and multiply.

7. 375 × $86

    $3 22 50

8. 916 × 493

    451588

9. 56 × 5,042

47

Practice

Estimate the products.

1. 476×83

_____

2. 42×356

_____

3. 58×472

_____

4. 396×67

_____

5. $83 \times \$9.68$

_____

6. $\$6.87 \times 412$

_____

7. $95 \times 6,296$

_____

8. $5,065 \times 128$

_____

9. $7,967 \times 684$

_____

10. $396 \times \$41.56$

_____

11. $787 \times 4,973$

_____

12. $850 \times \$78.45$

_____

13. $3,907 \times 218$

_____

14. $\$25.83 \times 896$

_____

15. $\$286.36 \times 476$

_____

16. $526 \times 9,738$

_____

17. $\$321.15 \times 610$

_____

18. $721 \times 8,801$

_____

Copy and Do

19. $\$85.63 \times 48$

20. 681×757

21. $9,008 \times 62$

22. $7,042 \times 508$

23. $\$4,983 \times 78$

24. $2,389 \times 236$

25. $98 \times 6,473$

26. 746×815

27. $\$589.56 \times 36$

Apply

Solve these problems.

28. One square unit on the map at the planetarium shows 2,315 stars. Estimate how many stars 89 square units will show.

29. Each share of Ace Airlines stock sells for $7.87. Estimate how much 48,976 shares will cost.

30. Each container on a cargo ship can hold up to 28,475 pounds of freight. Estimate the maximum weight the cargo ship can carry in 985 containers.

31. In March, the record store sold 3,885 sale albums at $11.79 each. The shop also sold 2,956 full-price albums at $13.49 each. About how much did the shop make from the sale of these albums?

48

Multiplying by a 1-digit Factor

On Saturday, there are 5 shows at the movie theater. The ushers clear the theater after each show. Last Saturday, the theater was full for all performances. How many people saw the movie?

We want to find the total movie attendance for Saturday.

We know that _____ people saw the movie at each

showing, and there were _____ shows.

To find the total attendance, we multiply the number of viewers of each showing by the number of times

the film was shown. We multiply _____ by _____.

Multiply the ones. Rename if needed.	Multiply the tens. Add any extra tens. Rename if needed.	Multiply the hundreds. Add any extra tens. Rename if needed.

$$\begin{array}{r} \overset{4}{3\,4\,8} \\ \times\ \ \ 5 \\ \hline 0 \end{array}$$

$$\begin{array}{r} \overset{2\ 4}{3\,4\,8} \\ \times\ \ \ 5 \\ \hline 4\,0 \end{array}$$

$$\begin{array}{r} \overset{2}{3\,4\,8} \\ \times\ \ \ 5 \\ \hline 1{,}7\,4\,0 \end{array}$$

The total Saturday attendance was _____ people.

Getting Started

Multiply.

1. $\begin{array}{r} 94 \\ \times\ 7 \\ \hline \end{array}$

2. $\begin{array}{r} 467 \\ \times\ 4 \\ \hline \end{array}$

3. $\begin{array}{r} 307 \\ \times\ 6 \\ \hline \end{array}$

4. $\begin{array}{r} 59 \\ \times\ 8 \\ \hline \end{array}$

5. $\begin{array}{r} 915 \\ \times\ 3 \\ \hline \end{array}$

Write >, < or = between the numbers.

6. 79×3 ___ 248

7. 8×576 ___ 4,600

8. 7×340 ___ 2,380

Copy and multiply.

9. 39×4

10. 6×705

11. 657×8

49

Practice

Multiply.

1. $\begin{array}{r} 73 \\ \times\ 6 \\ \hline \end{array}$	2. $\begin{array}{r} 118 \\ \times\ 7 \\ \hline \end{array}$	3. $\begin{array}{r} 296 \\ \times\ 3 \\ \hline \end{array}$	4. $\begin{array}{r} 56 \\ \times\ 4 \\ \hline \end{array}$	5. $\begin{array}{r} 708 \\ \times\ 5 \\ \hline \end{array}$
6. $\begin{array}{r} 296 \\ \times\ 7 \\ \hline \end{array}$	7. $\begin{array}{r} 49 \\ \times\ 9 \\ \hline \end{array}$	8. $\begin{array}{r} 375 \\ \times\ 8 \\ \hline \end{array}$	9. $\begin{array}{r} 961 \\ \times\ 2 \\ \hline \end{array}$	10. $\begin{array}{r} 90 \\ \times\ 8 \\ \hline \end{array}$
11. $\begin{array}{r} 352 \\ \times\ 6 \\ \hline \end{array}$	12. $\begin{array}{r} 58 \\ \times\ 7 \\ \hline \end{array}$	13. $\begin{array}{r} 496 \\ \times\ 8 \\ \hline \end{array}$	14. $\begin{array}{r} 749 \\ \times\ 3 \\ \hline \end{array}$	15. $\begin{array}{r} 80 \\ \times\ 9 \\ \hline \end{array}$

Write >, < or = between the numbers.

16. 59×3 ___ 180

17. 6×184 ___ 1,104

18. 159 ___ 22×7

19. 9×16 ___ 18×8

20. 7×125 ___ 109×8

21. 9×189 ___ 4×426

22. 6×47 ___ 32×9

23. 4×156 ___ 140×5

24. 8×282 ___ 5×415

Copy and Do

25. 15×7

26. 8×139

27. 6×47

28. 573×3

29. 219×8

30. 9×307

31. 6×98

32. 43×2

33. 439×4

34. 518×5

35. 6×847

36. 8×78

Apply

Solve these problems.

37. Harry collects stamps. Each stamp book holds 248 stamps. How many stamps does Harry have in 6 books?

38. Josie works in a biology laboratory making microscope slides. She has 695 slides to make for one project. She makes 85 slides a week. By the end of 6 weeks, how many slides does she have left to make?

39. Mr. Li's office is 26 miles from his house. How many miles does Mr. Li drive to and from work, in a 5-day week?

40. A newspaper columnist wrote a weekly article for 8 years. How many columns did she write?

Multiplying Larger Numbers

The students at Hamilton High School sold 3,416 raffle ticket books to raise money for band instruments. Each ticket cost $2.35, and there are 6 tickets in each book. How many raffle tickets were sold? How much did each book cost?

We want to know the number of raffle tickets sold altogether. We know the students sold _____ books; there are _____ tickets in each book, and each ticket costs _____.

To find the total number of tickets, we multiply the number of tickets in each book by the number of books. We multiply _____ by _____.

Multiply the ones.	Multiply the tens.	Multiply the hundreds.	Multiply the thousands.
$\begin{array}{r} {\scriptstyle 3} \\ 3,41\,6 \\ \times \quad 6 \\ \hline 6 \end{array}$	$\begin{array}{r} {\scriptstyle 3} \\ 3,4\,16 \\ \times \quad 6 \\ \hline 96 \end{array}$	$\begin{array}{r} {\scriptstyle 2} \\ 3,\,416 \\ \times \quad 6 \\ \hline 496 \end{array}$	$\begin{array}{r} {\scriptstyle 2} \\ 3,416 \\ \times \quad 6 \\ \hline 20,496 \end{array}$

The students sold _____ raffle tickets.

To find the total cost of one book, we multiply the cost of one ticket, by the number of tickets in the book. We multiply _____ by _____.

✔ Multiply money the same way you multiply whole numbers. Remember to place the dollar sign and decimal point in the product.

$$\begin{array}{r} \$2.35 \\ \times \quad 6 \\ \hline \end{array}$$

Each book of tickets costs _____.

Getting Started

Multiply.

1. $\begin{array}{r} \$9.27 \\ \times \quad 5 \\ \hline \end{array}$

2. $\begin{array}{r} \$567.25 \\ \times \quad 4 \\ \hline \end{array}$

Copy and multiply.

3. $9 \times 592,403$

4. $6 \times \$19.56$

51

Practice

Multiply.

1. 1,738 × 4	2. $9.57 × 7	3. 8,406 × 3	4. $46.37 × 9	5. $125.36 × 6
6. 52,640 × 8	7. $247.48 × 2	8. 87,396 × 5	9. $312.60 × 7	10. 43,257 × 4
11. 126,348 × 9	12. $3,274.13 × 8	13. 509,412 × 2	14. $421,212 × 6	15. $900.48 × 5
16. 521,465 × 8	17. $9,215.63 × 3	18. 757,462 × 7	19. $983,415 × 5	20. $803.75 × 6

Copy and Do

21. 5 × 7,961

22. $43.46 × 8

23. 3,975 × 2

24. 8,658 × 4

25. 3 × 6,006

26. 9 × $63.47

27. 5 × 16,743

28. 7 × $148.57

29. 83,925 × 8

30. $423.15 × 3

31. 72,456 × 2

32. 6 × $5,246.15

33. 8 × 626,248

34. 4 × $6,247.12

35. 7 × 327,248

36. 9 × 528,751

37. 5 × $8,493.49

38. 6 × 857,489

Apply

Solve these problems.

39. Wimona earns $4.27 an hour. On Saturday, Wimona worked 6 hours. How much did she earn that day?

40. A truck carries 11,746 kilograms of freight each trip. How many kilograms of freight does the truck carry on 6 trips?

41. Sonar waves travel at 1,410 meters per second in water. It takes 9 seconds for sonar waves to travel between two submarines. How far apart are the submarines?

42. Boneless chicken costs $2.16 a pound. Mr. Irons bought 6 pounds of boneless chicken. He gave the clerk a twenty dollar bill. How much change did Mr. Irons receive?

Multiplying by Multiples of 10

Mr. Schwarz is a buyer for a large electronics store. One month he bought 30 television sets. How much did Mr. Schwarz's company pay for the sets?

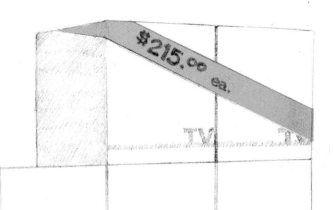

We want to know the total cost of the television sets.

We know each set costs _____, and Mr. Schwarz

bought _____ sets.

To find the total money spent, we multiply the cost of each set by the number of sets.

We multiply _____ by _____.

Write 0 in the ones place.	Multiply by the digit in the tens place.
$\begin{array}{r} \$215 \\ \times\ \ 30 \\ \hline 0 \end{array}$	$\begin{array}{r} \$215 \\ \times\ \ 30 \\ \hline \$6{,}450 \end{array}$

Mr. Schwarz's company paid _____ for the television sets.

Getting Started

Multiply.

1. $\begin{array}{r} 76 \\ \times 20 \\ \hline \end{array}$
2. $\begin{array}{r} 84 \\ \times 30 \\ \hline \end{array}$
3. $\begin{array}{r} 176 \\ \times 70 \\ \hline \end{array}$
4. $\begin{array}{r} \$2.20 \\ \times\ \ 50 \\ \hline \end{array}$
5. $\begin{array}{r} 74{,}368 \\ \times\ \ \ \ \ 40 \\ \hline \end{array}$

Copy and multiply.

6. 93×60
7. $40 \times 9{,}127$
8. $\$12.06 \times 90$

53

Practice

Multiply.

1.	2.	3.	4.	5.
27 × 40	89 × 70	217 × 30	$8.67 × 90	615 × 20

6.	7.	8.	9.	10.
276 × 50	$9.08 × 80	630 × 60	3,728 × 30	$49.26 × 90

11.	12.	13.	14.	15.
526 × 40	$8.57 × 20	750 × 70	4,382 × 50	$92.64 × 80

Copy and Do

16. 30 × 68

17. 57 × 80

18. 39 × 20

19. 156 × 60

20. 50 × 214

21. 90 × $6.15

22. 856 × 40

23. $8.58 × 70

24. 324 × 60

Apply

Solve these problems.

25. Mr. James earns $9.26 per hour for the first 40 hours he works each week. For every additional hour, he earns $14.45. Last week he worked 46 hours. How much did he earn?

26. A box contains 16 shirts. Each shirt costs $20. How much will 5 boxes cost?

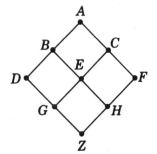

EXCURSION

Start at A. Find all paths to Z. You cannot retrace a line.

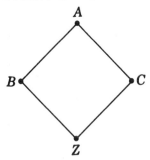

1. ABZ

2. _____

Start at A. Find all paths to Z.

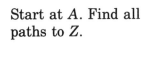

1. ABDGZ

2. _____

3. _____

4. _____

5. _____

6. _____

7. _____

8. _____

Multiplying by a 2-digit Factor

Jumbo jets make 26 daily flights
between Los Angeles and Chicago.
If all the seats are occupied on
each flight, how many passengers
fly between the two cities each day?

We want to know the total number of passengers
flying between Chicago and Los Angeles each day.

We know each jumbo jet has a capacity of _____

passengers, and there are _____ daily flights.

To find the total number of passengers, we multiply
the number of passengers on each flight by the

number of flights. We multiply _____ by _____.

Multiply by ones.	Multiply by tens.	Add the products.

$$
\begin{array}{r}
{\scriptstyle 5\,4} \\
3\,8\,7 \\
\times\ \ 2\,6 \\
\hline
2\,3\,2\,2 \leftarrow 6 \times 387
\end{array}
$$

$$
\begin{array}{r}
{\scriptstyle 1\,1} \\
3\,8\,7 \\
\times\ \ 2\,6 \\
\hline
2\,3\,2\,2 \\
7\,7\,4\,0 \leftarrow 20 \times 387
\end{array}
$$

$$
\begin{array}{r}
3\,8\,7 \\
\times\ \ 2\,6 \\
\hline
2\,3\,2\,2 \leftarrow 6 \times 387 \\
7\,7\,4\,0 \leftarrow 20 \times 387 \\
\hline
10{,}062 \leftarrow 26 \times 387
\end{array}
$$

If all the seats are occupied, _____ passengers fly
between the two cities.

Getting Started

Multiply.

1.	57 × 34	**2.**	80 × 47	**3.**	309 × 74	**4.**	$4.80 × 68
5.	3,724 × 53	**6.**	6,839 × 72	**7.**	4,786 × 29	**8.**	$137.12 × 28

Copy and multiply.

9. 37 × 428   **10.** 46 × $9.51   **11.** 29 × 53,267

55

Practice

Multiply.

1. $\begin{array}{r} 79 \\ \times\ 53 \\ \hline \end{array}$

2. $\begin{array}{r} 96 \\ \times\ 48 \\ \hline \end{array}$

3. $\begin{array}{r} 783 \\ \times\ 86 \\ \hline \end{array}$

4. $\begin{array}{r} \$8.09 \\ \times\ 72 \\ \hline \end{array}$

5. $\begin{array}{r} \$6.53 \\ \times\ 28 \\ \hline \end{array}$

6. $\begin{array}{r} 385 \\ \times\ 36 \\ \hline \end{array}$

7. $\begin{array}{r} 1,215 \\ \times\ 66 \\ \hline \end{array}$

8. $\begin{array}{r} \$15.35 \\ \times\ 92 \\ \hline \end{array}$

9. $\begin{array}{r} 4,763 \\ \times\ 81 \\ \hline \end{array}$

10. $\begin{array}{r} 9,009 \\ \times\ 45 \\ \hline \end{array}$

11. $\begin{array}{r} \$212.17 \\ \times\ 73 \\ \hline \end{array}$

12. $\begin{array}{r} 9,228 \\ \times\ 59 \\ \hline \end{array}$

Copy and Do

13. 29×48

14. 67×36

15. 52×88

16. 436×29

17. $39 \times \$2.12$

18. 476×76

19. 51×285

20. 709×96

21. $\$9.37 \times 68$

22. $93 \times 1,475$

23. $28 \times 6,208$

24. $4,800 \times 43$

25. $\$49.56 \times 82$

26. $75 \times 8,272$

27. $37 \times \$29.86$

Apply

Use the chart to solve these problems.

Robin's 18-Day Travel Budget	
Air Fare	$425
Motel	$ 43 per day
Meals	$ 15 per day
Recreation	$ 20 per day
Miscellaneous	$ 18 per day

28. How much did Robin budget for recreation altogether?

29. How much did she budget for motels and meals altogether?

30. At the end of 12 days, Robin had spent $252 on miscellaneous items. According to her budget, how much did she have left in this category?

Multiplying by Multiples of 100

Workers at Sunstar Automobile Company work 300 days a year. In one year, the company produced its quota of cars every working day. How many cars did Sunstar produce that year?

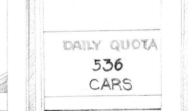

We want to know the total number of cars produced.

We know the company produced _____ cars each

working day, and there were _____ working days.

To find the total number of cars, we multiply the number of cars produced each day by the number of

working days. We multiply _____ by _____.

Write a zero in the ones place.	Write a zero in the tens place.	Multiply by the digit in hundreds place.

```
    536              536              536
  × 300            × 300            × 300
  ─────            ─────            ───────
      0               00          160,800
```

Sunstar Motors produced _____ cars in one year.

Getting Started

Multiply.

1. 239	2. $6.87	3. 57,138	4. $16.50
× 400	× 600	× 700	× 300

Copy and multiply.

5. 428 × 200

6. 500 × $157.86

7. 800 × 3,975

8. 356 × 700

9. 400 × $189.78

10. 600 × 4,539

57

Practice

Multiply.

1.	84	2.	156	3.	782
	× 200		× 700		× 500

4.	$6.37	5.	2,475	6.	$73.49
	× 300		× 400		× 600

7.	8,400	8.	11,365	9.	$458.73
	× 500		× 200		× 600

Copy and Do

10. 400 × 96

11. 54 × 700

12. 138 × 900

13. 465 × 500

14. 200 × $3.76

15. $14.56 × 600

Apply

Solve these problems.

16. The music store pays $6.25 for each cassette ordered. How much does the store pay for 600 cassettes?

17. A plane ticket for a peak time flight is $426.50. The same ticket for a night flight is $283.25. What is the price difference if 300 passengers exchange the more expensive ticket for the less expensive one?

EXCURSION

Lattice multiplication is a special way to multiply two numbers. Study this lattice multiplication of 785 by 84.

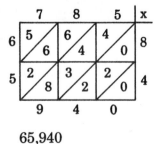

65,940

Use lattice multiplication to multiply 693 by 75.

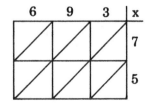

_____

Multiplying by a 3-digit Factor

National Discount Company keeps track of sales of cameras, computers and cassettes in all of its stores. If each of these items continues to sell at its average rate, how many cassettes should be sold in one year?

Item	Daily Sales Average
Cameras	210
Cassettes	859
Computers	767

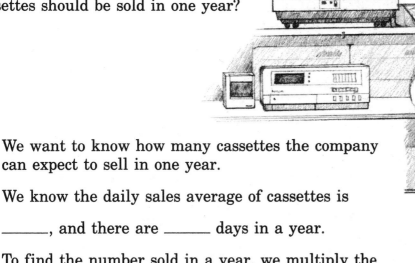

We want to know how many cassettes the company can expect to sell in one year.

We know the daily sales average of cassettes is

_____, and there are _____ days in a year.

To find the number sold in a year, we multiply the number of cassettes sold in one day, by the number of days in a year. We multiply _____ by _____.

Multiply by the ones.	Multiply by the tens.	Multiply by the hundreds.	Add the products.

```
    859              859              859              859
  × 365            × 365            × 365            × 365
  ─────            ─────            ─────            ─────
   4295             4295             4295             4295   ← 5 × 859
                   51540            51540            51540   ← 60 × 859
                                   257700           257700   ← 300 × 859
                                                    ───────
                                                    313,535  ← 365 × 859
```

The company expects to sell _____ cassettes in one year.

Getting Started

Multiply.

1. 586
   × 349

2. $18.26
   ×   730

3. 42,659
   ×   508

Copy and multiply.

4. 901 × 756

5. $76.14 × 523

6. 56,312 × 764

59

Practice

Multiply.

1.	647 × 453	**2.**	981 × 276	**3.**	$14.29 × 855	**4.**	$2,585.50 × 693
5.	3,708 × 436	**6.**	9,512 × 693	**7.**	16,245 × 781	**8.**	365,812 × 215
9.	5,649 × 843	**10.**	8,933 × 745	**11.**	18,302 × 912	**12.**	655,308 × 163

Copy and Do

13. 429 × 587

14. 321 × 853

15. 750 × 926

16. 398 × $7.36

17. 854 × 576

18. 973 × 187

19. 2,349 × 147

20. $44.36 × 210

21. 666 × 7,394

22. 861 × 2,764

23. 6,208 × 427

24. 468 × $82.39

25. 3,770 × 289

26. 727 × $39.95

27. 6,943 × 806

28. 15,362 × 639

29. $394.57 × 950

30. 525 × $615.05

Apply

Solve these problems.

31. An average of 384 people shop in Metroland each day. How many people will shop in Metroland in 185 days?

32. Ham's Burgerie sold 3,814 hamburgers last month. Each cost $1.95. Across the street, McTavish's sold 5,956 hamburgers at $1.80 apiece. How much more did McTavish's make from the sale of hamburgers than did Ham's Burgerie?

33. Mr. Ryan earns $12.85 each hour. In December, Mr. Ryan worked 168 hours. How much did he earn?

34. A factory buys small wheels for $8.67 and large wheels for $13.35. How much will the factory manager pay for 256 small wheels and 483 large wheels?

Looking for a Pattern

Simon is designing a number triangle
to quiz his classmates. If he continues
the pattern, what will be in the sum
of the numbers in the tenth row?

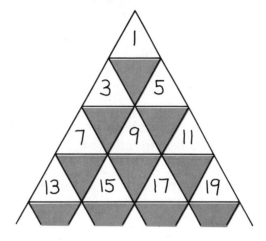

★ **SEE**

We want to find the sum of the numbers in the tenth
row. By studying the diagram, we can see that

consecutive odd numbers are used, and each row has _____
more number than the preceding row.

★ **PLAN**

We can add the numbers on the part of the triangle that
is shown. By putting the results of our work in a table,
we can look for a pattern. We can extend the pattern
to find the sum of the numbers in the tenth row.

★ **DO**

Row	Sum	Row	Sum
1	1	6	_____
2	8	7	_____
3	_____	8	_____
4	_____	9	_____
5	_____	10	_____

The sum of the numbers in the tenth row is _____

★ **CHECK**

We can check by drawing the extended triangle to find
the numbers that will appear in the tenth row. We can
then find the sum of these numbers.

Apply

Look for patterns to help you solve these problems.

1. Consider the four numbers 1, 2, 4 and 8. A game is played in which on the first turn the 1 is the only number not covered. On the second turn only the 2 is uncovered. On the third turn both the 1 and 2 are uncovered. On the fourth turn the 4 is uncovered. What numbers are uncovered on the fourteenth turn?

2. John is lining up marbles in the following patterns:
First turn: OO
Second turn: OOOOOOO
Third turn: OOOOOOOOOOOO
How many marbles should be in the eighth turn?

3. Dumbo the elephant went on a diet and wanted to lose 90 pounds. Dumbo lost 20 pounds the first week, 18 pounds the second week and 16 pounds the third week. If Dumbo continued to lose weight in this fashion, how many weeks would it take for Dumbo to lose the 90 pounds?

4. The pattern for building a 3-step staircase is shown below:
O
OO
OOO
How many markers would be required to build a pattern for a 10-step staircase?

5. Tom Encherri wants to rent a car. One choice is to pay $159.95 for 5 days plus $39.95 for each additional day. Another choice is to pay $39.95 a day. What conditions would make one choice better than the other?

6. Alexis Acura uses her calculator to find this sum: 235 + 457 + 518. However, she discovers that her [5] button does not work. How might she use her calculator anyway to find the sum?

7. Greg's Great Grocery sells Coo-Coo Cola at 3 cans for $1.00. If you buy fewer than 3 cans, they charge you 34¢ for 1 can and 67¢ for 2 cans. Explain why the store does this.

8. Barney Bubble's Bike Shop sells bicycles and bicycles with training wheels. Write a problem where there are 56 wheels and the answer is 9 bikes with training wheels.

Using a Calculator with an Order Form

Nancy is the purchasing agent for the college athletic department. During one month, she placed two orders for baseballs. The first order was for 2 boxes and the second order was for 8 boxes. How much did the baseballs cost?

Baseball Price List	
1 box	$80
2 boxes	$155
3 boxes	$221
Each additional box	$70

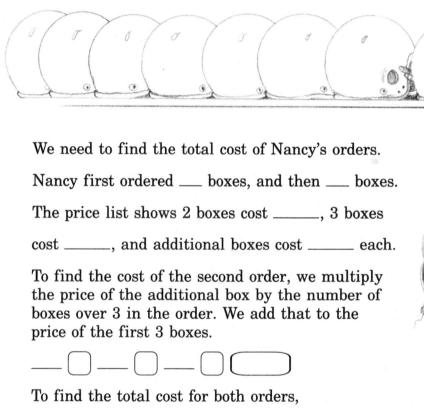

We need to find the total cost of Nancy's orders.

Nancy first ordered ___ boxes, and then ___ boxes.

The price list shows 2 boxes cost _____, 3 boxes

cost _____, and additional boxes cost _____ each.

To find the cost of the second order, we multiply the price of the additional box by the number of boxes over 3 in the order. We add that to the price of the first 3 boxes.

__ ◯ __ ◯ __ ◯ ⬭

To find the total cost for both orders,

we add _____ and _____. The total

cost is _____.

This problem can be worked with one code.

[C] __ ◯ __ ◯ __ ◯ __ = ⬭

Use a calculator to solve the problems. Use estimation to check the answers.

1. 6,394
    × 856

2. 16,584
    × 396

3. $3,749.53
    × 714

4. How much more would Nancy have to pay if she bought all 10 boxes at the single box rate?

5. How much would Nancy save if she bought all 10 boxes at one time?

63

Practice

Use a calculator to multiply. Use estimation to check your answer.

1.
$$\begin{array}{r} 5{,}409 \\ \times \quad 83 \\ \hline \end{array}$$

2.
$$\begin{array}{r} 8{,}976 \\ \times \quad 786 \\ \hline \end{array}$$

3.
$$\begin{array}{r} \$49.95 \\ \times \quad 603 \\ \hline \end{array}$$

4.
$$\begin{array}{r} 36{,}459 \\ \times \quad 584 \\ \hline \end{array}$$

5.
$$\begin{array}{r} \$3{,}967.15 \\ \times \quad 384 \\ \hline \end{array}$$

6.
$$\begin{array}{r} 92{,}359 \\ \times \quad 721 \\ \hline \end{array}$$

Use a calculator to solve these problems.

7. $249 \times 236 - 49{,}385$

8. $(2{,}346 + 5{,}375) \times 625$

9. $(47{,}868 - 46{,}913) \times 658$

10. $98 \times 43 \times 79 - 232{,}978$

Apply

Use a calculator to solve these problems.

Willie is an account manager with Sun Magazine. He is responsible for 2 pages of ads each month. Use the Sun rates to solve 11 through 13.

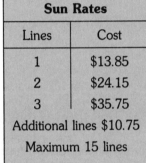

Sun Rates	
Lines	Cost
1	$13.85
2	$24.15
3	$35.75
Additional lines $10.75	
Maximum 15 lines	

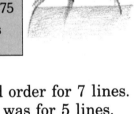

11. What would a maximum length ad cost?

12. If an advertiser has to pay the single line rate for 10 lines, how much extra does it cost?

13. Willie took an ad order for 7 lines. His second order was for 5 lines. How much more did he receive for the first order?

EXCURSION

Find the missing digits.

1.
$$\begin{array}{r} \square\,9\,8 \\ \times \quad 2\,\square \\ \hline 2\,7\,8\,6 \\ 7\,\square\,6\,0 \\ \hline 10{,}7\,\square\,6 \end{array}$$

2.
$$\begin{array}{r} 8\,\square\,6 \\ \times \quad \square\,2\,5 \\ \hline 4\,0\,3\,0 \\ 1\,\square\,1\,2\,0 \\ 2\,\square\,1\,8\,0\,0 \\ \hline 2\,6\,1{,}9\,\square\,0 \end{array}$$

3.
$$\begin{array}{r} 1\,9\,\square \\ \times \quad \square\,4 \\ \hline 7\,7\,\square \\ \square\,8\,6\,0 \\ \hline 4{,}6\,\square\,\square \end{array}$$

Multiply. Use estimation to check the answers.

1.	89 × 6	2.	53 × 9	3.	136 × 4	4.	809 × 7
5.	72 × 8	6.	69 × 5	7.	195 × 6	8.	307 × 3
9.	3,924 × 8	10.	$68.96 × 2	11.	$379.58 × 5	12.	692,453 × 3
13.	4,839 × 6	14.	$82.14 × 3	15.	$525.72 × 4	16.	897,465 × 2
17.	75 × 24	18.	$7.46 × 78	19.	358 × 67	20.	3,849 × 43
21.	63 × 82	22.	$9.56 × 87	23.	477 × 54	24.	6,589 × 75
25.	639 × 276	26.	1,276 × 638	27.	36,758 × 439	28.	$708.15 × 743
29.	498 × 651	30.	3,492 × 563	31.	75,847 × 698	32.	$903.47 × 843

Circle the letter of the correct answer.

1
```
   7
   2
 + 4
```
a 13
b 14
c 15
d NG

2 $7 + 8 = n$
$n = ?$
a 13
b 14
c 15
d NG

3 $17 - 9$
a 7
b 8
c 9
d NG

4 $n + 7 = 13$
$n = ?$
a 5
b 9
c 21
d NG

5 8×8
a 54
b 56
c 64
d NG

6 $7 \times 0 = n$
$n = ?$
a 0
b 1
c 7
d NG

7 $6\overline{)48}$
a 7
b 8
c 9
d NG

8 $n \times 9 = 36$
$n = ?$
a 3
b 4
c 5
d NG

9 $15 + 10 \div 5 = n$
$n = ?$
a 5
b 17
c 30
d NG

10 What is the place value of the 0 in 4,702,931?
a hundreds
b thousands
c ten thousands
d NG

11
```
  42,698
+ 46,853
```
a 88,451
b 89,551
c 90,551
d NG

12
```
  5,086
- 3,994
```
a 1,092
b 1,192
c 2,112
d NG

13 397×5
a 1,455
b 1,585
c 1,985
d NG

score

66

DIVISION OF WHOLE NUMBERS

Using Division Patterns

On the planet Numera, the entrance to the capitol has 5,400 steps. Numerarians can jump 6 steps at a time. How many jumps would a Numerarian take to get to the top of the steps?

We want to know how many jumps it would take for a Numerarian to climb all the steps.

We know that there are _____ steps, and a

Numerarian can jump _____ steps at a time.

To find the number of jumps needed, we divide the total number of steps, by the number of steps

climbed in each jump. We divide _____ by _____.
Consider the pattern in these division sentences.

$54 \div 6 = 9$
$540 \div 6 = 90$ **CHECK**

$5,400 \div 6 =$ _____   _____ $\times 6 = 5,400$

A Numerarian could reach the top of the steps

in _____ jumps.

Getting Started

Complete the pattern.

1. $35 \div 7 =$ _____

      $350 \div 70 =$ _____

    $3,500 \div 70 =$ _____

   $35,000 \div 70 =$ _____

Write each quotient.
Check using mental math.

2. $800 \div 4 =$ _____

3. $6,300 \div 90 =$ _____

4. $21,000 \div 70 =$ _____

Practice

Complete each pattern.

1. $48 \div 6 =$ _____

   $480 \div 60 =$ _____

   $4{,}800 \div 60 =$ _____

   $48{,}000 \div 60 =$ _____

2. $45 \div 9 =$ _____

   $450 \div 90 =$ _____

   $4{,}500 \div 90 =$ _____

   $45{,}000 \div 90 =$ _____

3. $40 \div 8 =$ _____

   $400 \div 80 =$ _____

   $4{,}000 \div 80 =$ _____

   $40{,}000 \div 80 =$ _____

Write each quotient. Check using mental math.

4. $350 \div 5 =$ _____

5. $3{,}200 \div 4 =$ _____

6. $540 \div 9 =$ _____

7. $3{,}600 \div 40 =$ _____

8. $2{,}800 \div 70 =$ _____

9. $1{,}800 \div 90 =$ _____

10. $4{,}200 \div 60 =$ _____

11. $45{,}000 \div 50 =$ _____

12. $32{,}000 \div 40 =$ _____

Apply

Solve these problems.

13. Mrs. Santana drove 270 miles on Sunday. She used 9 gallons of gasoline. How many miles did Mrs. Santana travel on each gallon of gas?

14. Bob said that he has worked for 36,000 seconds. How many hours has Bob worked?

EXCURSION

Multiplication and division are **inverse operations.**
To solve the equation $n \times 9 = 18$, we divide the product by the known factor.

$18 \div 9 = n \qquad n =$ _____

To solve the equation $n \div 4 = 9$, we multiply the quotient by the divisor.

$9 \times 4 = n \qquad n =$ _____

Use the inverse operation to solve these problems.

1. $n \times 6 = 36 \qquad n =$ _____

2. $n \div 8 = 7 \qquad n =$ _____

3. $n \times 30 = 2{,}100 \qquad n =$ _____

4. $n \div 40 = 800 \qquad n =$ _____

Dividing by a 1-digit Divisor

Daniel has been saving quarters for over a year to buy a guitar. How many dollars will Daniel receive in exchange for his savings?

We want to know how many dollars Daniel will get for his quarters.

We know that Daniel has _____ quarters and one

dollar is worth _____ quarters.

To find the number of dollars, we divide the total number of quarters by the number of quarters equal

to one dollar. We divide _____ by _____.

Divide the hundreds.	Divide the tens.	

There are not enough hundreds. We move to the ten's place.

Divide the tens.

$$\overset{2}{4\overline{)11}}$$
Divide.   4)11
Multiply. $4 \times 2 = 8$
Subtract. $11 - 8 = 3$
Compare. $3 < 4$
Bring down the ones.

Divide.   4)38
Multiply. $4 \times 9 = 36$
Subtract. $38 - 36 = 2$
Compare. $2 < 4$
Write the remainder.

$$4\overline{)118}$$

$$\begin{array}{r} 2 \\ 4\overline{)118} \\ 8\downarrow \\ \hline 38 \end{array}$$

$$\begin{array}{r} 29\,R2 \\ 4\overline{)118} \\ 8 \\ \hline 38 \\ 36 \\ \hline 2 \end{array}$$

Daniel will receive _____ dollars, and have _____ quarters left over.

CHECK

$$\begin{array}{r} 29 \\ \times\ 4 \end{array} \quad +\ 2$$

Getting Started

Divide and check.

Copy and divide.

1. 3)72

2. 8)969

3. $309 \div 4$

4. $203 \div 9$

69

Practice

Divide and check.

1. 3)93

2. 7)115

3. 2)326

4. 9)585

5. 6)848

6. 5)935

7. 8)889

8. 9)672

9. 3)956

10. 8)734

11. 4)734

12. 6)834

13. 2)847

14. 7)359

15. 5)275

16. 3)537

Copy and Do

17. $417 \div 5$

18. $912 \div 6$

19. $653 \div 2$

20. $721 \div 9$

21. $95 \div 4$

22. $108 \div 8$

23. $536 \div 3$

24. $815 \div 7$

25. $715 \div 6$

26. $963 \div 3$

27. $847 \div 5$

28. $235 \div 8$

Apply

Solve these problems.

29. Roberta ran 784 meters in 4 minutes. How far did Roberta run in 1 minute?

30. Mr. Davis works 6 hours each day. One month he worked 162 hours. How many days did Mr. Davis work?

31. The sixth grade is renting vans for a science field trip. The charge for each van is $35.25. Each van can carry 9 students. How much will it cost to rent enough vans to take 132 students on the field trip?

32. Mark bought 192 marbles. They were in bags of 8 each. If each bag of marbles cost $1.19, how much did Mark pay?

Working with Larger Quotients

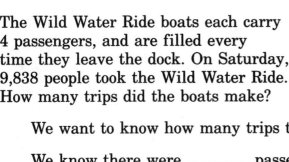

The Wild Water Ride boats each carry
4 passengers, and are filled every
time they leave the dock. On Saturday,
9,838 people took the Wild Water Ride.
How many trips did the boats make?

We want to know how many trips the boats made.

We know there were _____ passengers on the boats

and every boat held _____ people.

To find how many trips were made, we divide the
total number of passengers by the number of

passengers in each boat. We divide _____ by _____.

✔ Remember to divide, multiply, subtract, compare
and bring down.

Divide the thousands.	Divide the hundreds.	Divide the tens.	Divide the ones.

```
     2            2 4           2 4 5          2 4 5 9 R2
4)9,838       4)9,838       4)9,838        4)9,838
  8             8 ↓            8              8
  ─             ───           ─              ─
  1             1 8           1 8            1 8
                1 6           1 6            1 6
                ───           ───            ───
                  2           2 3            2 3
                              2 0            2 0
                              ───            ───
                                3            3 8
                                             3 6
                                             ───
                                               2
```

Because the remainder is _____, another trip was

needed. The boats made _____ trips.

Getting Started

Divide and check.

1. 6)2,368   2. 3)117,886   3. 8)955,656

Copy and divide.

4. 9,631 ÷ 7   5. 503,246 ÷ 4   6. 3,421,523 ÷ 9

71

Practice

Divide and check.

1. 7)2,494

2. 2)3,658

3. 5)6,786

4. 8)7,490

5. 4)26,288

6. 9)32,859

7. 6)37,734

8. 5)327,263

9. 3)652,702

Copy and Do

10. 3,869 ÷ 4

11. 8,346 ÷ 8

12. 9,375 ÷ 2

13. 2,023 ÷ 7

14. 3,196 ÷ 5

15. 7,593 ÷ 6

16. 37,791 ÷ 3

17. 56,241 ÷ 9

18. 50,620 ÷ 8

19. 52,344 ÷ 6

20. 93,857 ÷ 4

21. 81,396 ÷ 5

22. 307,185 ÷ 2

23. 836,459 ÷ 7

24. 1,763,829 ÷ 9

Apply

Solve these problems.

25. A machine sorts apples into bags of 5 apples each. How many bags does it take to store 2,643 apples?

26. The Jogging Club held an 11,168-meter relay on Saturday morning. Each of 8 joggers ran the same distance. How far did each jogger run?

27. Six new movie theaters opened at the shopping mall. Each theater has 242 seats. For one show, half the theaters were full, and half the theaters were half full. How many people were at the movies?

28. A jet plane flew 4,575 kilometers from New York to Los Angeles in 5 hours. What was the plane's average speed per hour?

Dividing with Zeros in the Quotient

Nancy bought new tires for her
bicycle. She spent $21.50. How much
did Nancy pay for each tire?

We want to know the cost of each tire.

We know that Nancy bought _____ tires

and she paid a total of _____.

To find the cost of each tire, we divide the total

cost by the number of tires. We divide _____

by _____.

Divide the dollars.	Place the decimal point above the one in the dividend.	Divide the dimes and cents. Write the dollar sign.

$$\begin{array}{r} 1\,0 \\ 2\overline{)\$2\,1\,.5\,0} \\ \underline{2}\downarrow \\ 1 \end{array}$$

$$\begin{array}{r} 1\,0\,. \\ 2\overline{)\$2\,1\,.5\,0} \\ \underline{2} \\ 1 \end{array}$$

$$\begin{array}{r} \$1\,0\,.7\,5 \\ 2\overline{)\$2\,1\,.5\,0} \\ \underline{2}\quad\downarrow\,| \\ 1\,5\quad| \\ \underline{1\,4}\downarrow \\ 1\,0 \\ \underline{1\,0} \\ 0 \end{array}$$

✔ Remember, for every digit brought down, there
must be a digit in the quotient.

Each tire costs _____.

Getting Started

Divide and check.

1. 5)$85.20

2. 9)$90.36

3. 4)8,031

4. 6)$183.66

5. 3)91,529

6. 7)840,147

Copy and divide.

7. 407,315 ÷ 4

8. 363,230 ÷ 7

9. $636.18 ÷ 6

73

Practice

Divide and check.

1. 6)6,248

2. 4)8,032

3. 8)9,653

4. 2)7,810

5. 9)18,541

6. 5)$952.35

Copy and Do

7. 3,623 ÷ 6

8. 6,539 ÷ 5

9. 9,360 ÷ 8

10. $45.09 ÷ 9

11. 9,017 ÷ 3

12. 8,205 ÷ 2

13. 15,238 ÷ 4

14. 49,035 ÷ 7

15. $515.25 ÷ 5

Apply

Solve these problems.

16. Mr. Shima bought 4 new tires for his car. He paid $563.40 for the tires. How much did each one cost?

17. The greatest known depth of the Pacific Ocean is 35,820 feet. A computerized bathysphere descended to this depth at a speed of 3 feet per second. How many seconds did it take to get to the bottom?

EXCURSION

Divisibility rules for 2, 5, 3, 6 and 9 state: a number is

- divisible by 2 if it ends in 0, 2, 4, 6 or 8.
- divisible by 5 if it ends in 0 or 5.
- divisible by 3 if the sum of the digits is divisible by 3.
- divisible by 6 if it is divisible by 2 and 3.
- divisible by 9 if the sum of the digits is divisible by 9.

Apply the divisibility rules for 2, 5, 3, 6 or 9 by writing which of these numbers is a divisor for the given number.

1. 80 _____

2. 75 _____

3. 342 _____

4. 207 _____

5. 711 _____

6. 113 _____

7. 435 _____

8. 876 _____

Using Short Division

Bjorn works in the school cafeteria.
His check for one week was $24.92.
How much does Bjorn earn per hour?

Bjorn's Time Card	
Monday	2 hours
Wednesday	2 hours
Friday	3 hours
	7 hours

We want to know Bjorn's hourly wage.

We know that he worked _____ hours

last week, and he earned _____ .

To find the amount he earned each hour, we divide
his total wages by the number of hours he worked.

We divide _____ by _____ .

Divide the dollars. Place the decimal point. Think of the remainder next to the dimes.	Divide the dimes. Think of the remainder next to the cents.	Divide the cents. Place the dollar sign.

$$3.\ \overparen{39\ dimes}$$
$$7)\overline{\$24.92}$$

$$3.5\ \overparen{42\ cents}$$
$$7)\overline{\$24.92}$$

$$\$3.56$$
$$7)\overline{\$24.92}$$

CHECK

$$\begin{array}{r} \$3.56 \\ \times\quad 7 \\ \hline \end{array}$$

Getting Started

Divide and check.

1. $7)\overline{1,645}$

2. $4)\overline{9,687}$

3. $2)\overline{\$495.46}$

4. $8)\overline{75,463}$

5. $6)\overline{109,544}$

6. $9)\overline{326,475}$

7. $5)\overline{1,243,675}$

8. $3)\overline{\$5,246.10}$

Copy and divide.

9. $291.12 ÷ 6

10. 729,562 ÷ 8

11. $4,921.95 ÷ 5

Practice

Divide and check.

1. 8)2,368

2. 5)3,646

3. 7)$73.15

4. 6)15,651

5. 4)$256.84

6. 2)39,753

7. 3)$3,316.53

8. 5)689,243

9. 8)2,139,728

Copy and Do

10. 5,295 ÷ 7

11. 56,032 ÷ 8

12. 28,645 ÷ 3

13. $421.38 ÷ 9

14. $152.94 ÷ 6

15. 676,885 ÷ 4

16. 445,731 ÷ 2

17. $3,276.35 ÷ 5

Apply

Solve these problems.

18. Raffi is a serious baseball fan who has collected 1,140 baseball cards. He displays the cards in a 150-page book, putting 8 cards on each page. How many more cards does Raffi need to fill the book?

19. Marcia buys furniture for the E-Z Chair Store. She paid $2,282.40 for 9 chairs. How much did each chair cost?

EXCURSION

Here are two more divisibility rules.
- A number is divisible by 4 if the last 2 digits are divisible by 4.
- A number is divisible by 8 if the last 3 digits are divisible by 8.

Apply the divisibility rules for 4 and 8 by writing which of these numbers is a divisor for the given number.

1. 9,704 _____

2. 6,400 _____

3. 13,120 _____

4. 10,250 _____

5. 26,215 _____

6. 31,884 _____

7. 57,684 _____

8. 95,008 _____

Finding Averages

Onida took 4 spelling tests in March to prepare for the national spelling bee. What was her average score?

MARCH–AVERAGE SCORES
ONIDA | 96 | 90 | 87 | 91

We want to know Onida's average score.

We know that she took _____ tests and her test scores

were: _____, _____, _____ and _____.

To find the average, we add the scores, and divide

by the number of tests. We add _____, _____, _____

and _____ and divide the sum by _____.

| Add the numbers. | | Divide by the number of addends. |

```
    9 6
    9 0
    8 7
  + 9 1
  _____
```

$\overline{)}$

Onida's average spelling score was _____.

Getting Started

Find the average.

1. 521, 672, 970, 153

2. 83, 75, 92, 106, 94

3. 1,952, 1,683, 2,068

4. 13,725, 16,490, 12,862

Practice

Find the average.

1. 646, 783, 914, 853

2. 324, 278, 96, 153, 524

3. 15,987, 18,273, 17,856

4. 87, 68, 83, 74, 75, 81

5. 26, 35, 33, 44, 57

6. 519, 231, 117, 86, 57

7. 864, 651, 865, 372

8. 54, 44, 34, 38, 36, 40

9. 14, 12, 6, 2, 31

10. 5,015, 1,196, 7,343

11. 65, 75, 73, 71

12. 1,015, 362, 1,428, 207

Apply

Use the chart to solve problems 13 and 14.

City Basketball League Total Points				
Game	Nanda	Peg	Carla	Bev
1	11	7	15	12
2	9	14	18	Abs.
3	8	13	9	15
4	6	17	12	14
5	12	9	16	19
6	8	12	14	15

13. How much higher is Peg's average than Nanda's?

14. Bev missed one of the games. Compare her average points with Carla's average.

Use the chart to solve problems 15 and 16.

Robert Jones Weekly Sales Expense	
Day	Amount
Monday	$36.84
Tuesday	$29.16
Wednesday	$24.30
Thursday	$31.82
Friday	$24.53

15. What is Mr. Jones' average daily expense?

16. Which days did Mr. Jones spend more than his average daily expense?

Dividing by Multiples of 10

Mr. Ellis bought an entertainment system for $1,450. He paid $100 down, and promised to pay the balance in 30 months. How much will Mr. Ellis pay each month?

We want to know the amount of Mr. Ellis' monthly payments.
We know that after his down payment, he must

pay a balance of _____ in _____ months.

To find the monthly payments, we divide the amount to be paid by the number of months. We divide

_____ by _____.

Divide the thousands. 30 > 1	Divide the hundreds. 30 > 13	Divide the tens.	Divide the ones.

$$30\overline{)\$1,350}$$

$$30\overline{)\$1,350}$$

$$
\begin{array}{r}
4 \\
30\overline{)\$1,350} \\
120 \\
\hline
15
\end{array}
$$

$$
\begin{array}{r}
\$45 \\
30\overline{)\$1,350} \\
120\downarrow \\
\hline
150 \\
150 \\
\hline
0
\end{array}
$$

 Remember, the partial dividend must be larger than the divisor for a division to take place.

Mr. Ellis will pay _____ each month.

Getting Started

Divide and check.

1. $40\overline{)4,659}$

2. $50\overline{)3,675}$

3. $30\overline{)\$90.60}$

4. $70\overline{)21,657}$

5. $90\overline{)75,075}$

6. $60\overline{)720,486}$

Copy and divide.

7. $37,968 \div 80$

8. $\$114.40 \div 20$

9. $293,680 \div 70$

79

Practice

Divide and check.

1. $50\overline{)3,984}$

2. $70\overline{)4,765}$

3. $90\overline{)8,263}$

4. $60\overline{)8,455}$

5. $20\overline{)12,685}$

6. $80\overline{)39,756}$

7. $20\overline{)\$735.40}$

8. $40\overline{)729,653}$

9. $30\overline{)695,406}$

Copy and Do

10. $7,365 \div 40$

11. $8,296 \div 70$

12. $10,375 \div 20$

13. $4,283 \div 60$

14. $9,217 \div 30$

15. $15,408 \div 80$

16. $16,751 \div 90$

17. $\$217.50 \div 50$

18. $37,219 \div 60$

19. $75,215 \div 70$

20. $60,351 \div 30$

21. $95,477 \div 40$

22. $216,436 \div 80$

23. $785,381 \div 90$

24. $675,215 \div 50$

Apply

Solve these problems.

25. The countdown began 12,780 seconds before blast-off. How many minutes before blast-off is this?

26. Mrs. Murphy earns $489.60. She works a 40-hour week. What is her hourly wage?

27. Mr. Ikeda had 30 car payments to pay the balance of $9,150 on his new car. How much was each payment?

28. A box of 50 tacks costs $1.25. How much will 16,750 tacks cost?

80

Dividing by 2-digit Divisors

During its special sale, ABC Appliances stayed open around-the-clock. How many days without closing was the store open for the sale?

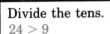

We want to know how many sale days the store was open.

We know ABC Appliances was open ＿＿ hours, and there are ＿＿ hours in one day.

To find the number of days, we divide the total number of hours by the number of hours in one day.

We divide ＿＿ by ＿＿.

Divide the tens. 24 > 9	Not enough tens Think of the dividend as 98 ones.	Round the divisor to the nearest 10. Estimate how many 20s in 98 ones. Think: how many 2s in 9?

$$24\overline{)98}$$

$$24\overline{)98}$$

$$\begin{array}{r} 4\,\textbf{R2} \\ 24\overline{)98} \\ 96 \\ \hline 2 \end{array}$$

CHECK

$$\begin{array}{r} 24 \\ \times\ 4 \\ \hline \end{array} \qquad + \underline{\hspace{2cm}}$$

ABC Appliances was open about ＿＿ days without closing.

Getting Started

Divide and check.

1. $18\overline{)65}$

2. $12\overline{)49}$

3. $39\overline{)165}$

4. $44\overline{)264}$

5. $54\overline{)273}$

6. $36\overline{)285}$

7. $62\overline{)618}$

8. $17\overline{)148}$

Copy and divide.

9. $300 \div 43$

10. $536 \div 77$

11. $581 \div 83$

Practice

Divide and check.

1. $29\overline{)75}$ 2. $24\overline{)75}$ 3. $43\overline{)235}$ 4. $58\overline{)575}$

5. $72\overline{)432}$ 6. $37\overline{)163}$ 7. $68\overline{)308}$ 8. $53\overline{)437}$

9. $49\overline{)304}$ 10. $39\overline{)250}$ 11. $62\overline{)535}$ 12. $85\overline{)743}$

Copy and Do

13. $163 \div 29$ 14. $235 \div 33$ 15. $204 \div 56$ 16. $396 \div 44$

17. $658 \div 72$ 18. $304 \div 34$ 19. $319 \div 52$ 20. $500 \div 68$

21. $372 \div 41$ 22. $437 \div 87$ 23. $205 \div 34$ 24. $260 \div 47$

25. $568 \div 94$ 26. $346 \div 89$ 27. $361 \div 51$ 28. $565 \div 88$

Apply

Solve these problems.

29. The basketball team earned $215 by washing cars. They want to buy basketballs that cost $39 each. How many can the team buy?

30. Mr. Lyons used 248 gallons of hot water during December. How many gallons of hot water did Mr. Lyons use on an average day?

EXCURSION

Find the missing digits.

```
       8 R2_              6 R_               7 R_              9 R____
  6_)5 2 4          _9)5 _ 6           _3)2 _ 5          _1)4 8 1
     5_4               _3 4               _3 1              4_9
     2 _                 _                  _              2 _
```

82

Correcting Estimates

A Mercury year is the same as 59 Earth days. If you lived on Mercury, how much older in Mercury years would you be for each Earth year?

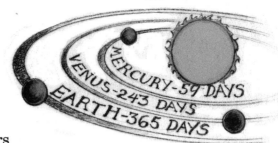

We want to find how many Mercury years are in one Earth year.

We know that one Mercury year is _____ days long, and one Earth year is _____ days long.

To find the Mercury equivalent of an Earth year, we divide the number of days in one Earth year by the number of days in one Mercury year.

We divide _____ by _____.

Not enough hundreds
Not enough tens
Start with 365 ones.

$$59\overline{)365}$$

Think: how many 5s in 36?

$$\begin{array}{r} 6\ \text{R}11 \\ 59\overline{)365} \\ 354 \\ \hline 11 \end{array}$$

CHECK

$$\begin{array}{r} 59 \\ \times\ 6\ + \\ \hline \end{array}$$

Try 7

$$\begin{array}{r} 59 \\ \times\ 7 \\ \hline 413 \end{array}$$
$413 > 365$

Try 6

$$\begin{array}{r} 59 \\ \times\ 6 \\ \hline 354 \end{array}$$
$354 < 365$

In one Earth year there are about _____ Mercury years. On Mercury you would be _____ years old.

Getting Started

Divide and check.

1. $18\overline{)115}$
2. $93\overline{)452}$
3. $73\overline{)495}$
4. $36\overline{)198}$

Copy and divide.

5. $417 \div 87$
6. $252 \div 69$
7. $175 \div 45$
8. $297 \div 35$

83

Practice

Divide and check.

1. 12)86

2. 16)148

3. 49)345

4. 23)180

5. 36)218

6. 75)530

7. 12)110

8. 48)296

9. 86)364

10. 58)355

11. 22)125

12. 28)239

Copy and Do

13. 327 ÷ 42

14. 288 ÷ 48

15. 305 ÷ 37

16. 225 ÷ 43

17. 515 ÷ 66

18. 418 ÷ 44

19. 771 ÷ 84

20. 216 ÷ 36

21. 402 ÷ 83

22. 596 ÷ 71

23. 261 ÷ 63

24. 299 ÷ 35

25. 456 ÷ 56

26. 705 ÷ 86

27. 423 ÷ 57

28. 390 ÷ 78

Apply

Solve these problems.

29. Chef George is baking muffins. He needs to bake 204 muffins for Sunday brunch. How many dozens is this?

30. Kathryn is packing 328 glasses. She puts them in boxes that hold 68 glasses each. How many boxes does she need?

EXCURSION

Use each of the digits 5, 6, 7, 8 and 9 only once to form a division problem.

Find the smallest possible quotient.
Find the largest possible quotient.

Dividing by 2-digit Divisors

I can get 78 bytes on one line.

Computers store information in bytes. One byte is the same as one character on a typewriter. Marcia's computer can store 65,536 bytes. How many lines can Marcia store in her computer?

We want to know the number of lines that can be stored.

We know that the computer can store _____ bytes,

and one line is _____ bytes long.

To find how many lines can be stored, we divide the total number of bytes by the number of bytes in one

line. We divide _____ by _____.

$$7\,8\overline{)6\,5,5\,3\,6}$$ Not enough ten thousands
Not enough thousands
Start with 655 hundreds.

Divide the hundreds.	Divide the tens.	Divide the ones. Write the remainder.

```
       8
7 8)6 5,5 3 6
    6 2 4
    ─────
      3 1
```

```
       8 4
7 8)6 5,5 3 6
    6 2 4↓
    ─────
      3 1 3
      3 1 2
      ─────
          1
```

```
       8 4 0 R16
7 8)6 5,5 3 6
    6 2 4
    ─────
      3 1 3
      3 1 2
      ─────
          1 6
```

Marcia can store just over _____ lines in her computer.

Getting Started

Divide and check.

1. $43\overline{)45,639}$

2. $72\overline{)\$264.24}$

3. $68\overline{)216,450}$

Copy and divide.

4. $537,646 \div 48$

5. $\$1,776.32 \div 32$

6. $82,678 \div 67$

85

Practice

Divide and check.

1. $27\overline{)8,699}$

2. $36\overline{)5,047}$

3. $18\overline{)2,340}$

4. $57\overline{)\$440.04}$

5. $86\overline{)96,475}$

6. $73\overline{)126,475}$

Copy and Do

7. $5,758 \div 46$

8. $6,794 \div 37$

9. $77,659 \div 77$

10. $6,039 \div 12$

11. $15,276 \div 23$

12. $46,745 \div 66$

13. $25,000 \div 16$

14. $57,405 \div 84$

15. $96,214 \div 92$

16. $146,556 \div 58$

17. $207,950 \div 63$

18. $\$1,995.80 \div 85$

19. $216,743 \div 29$

20. $816,321 \div 42$

21. $567,245 \div 73$

Apply

Use the chart to solve these problems.

The 1860 Election Results

Candidate	Popular Vote	Electoral Vote
Lincoln	1,865,593	180
Douglas	1,382,713	12
Breckenridge	848,356	72

22. How many times more electoral votes did Lincoln receive than Douglas?

23. How many more popular votes did Lincoln receive than Douglas?

24. How many times more electoral votes did Breckenridge receive than Douglas?

25. Which of the 3 candidates won a majority of the total popular vote? Of the total electoral vote?

Dividing by 3-digit Divisors

The speed of sound depends upon the material through which the sound waves pass. About how many seconds does it take for sound to travel 2,685 meters through the air?

We want to know how long it takes sound waves to travel a certain distance through the air.

We know sound travels at about _____ meters per second through air, and this sound traveled

_____ meters.

To find the number of seconds it took the sound to travel, we divide the distance the sound traveled by

the speed per second. We divide _____ by _____.

$$335\overline{)2,685}$$

Not enough thousands
Not enough hundreds
Not enough tens
Start with 2,685 ones.

$$\begin{array}{r} 8 \\ 335\overline{)2,685} \\ 2\,680 \\ \hline 5 \end{array}$$

It takes about _____ seconds for sound to travel 2,685 meters through the air.

≡ 335 mps

Getting Started

Divide and check.

1. $237\overline{)1,459}$

2. $118\overline{)\$271.40}$

3. $705\overline{)4,210}$

4. $625\overline{)53,750}$

5. $872\overline{)142,136}$

6. $593\overline{)156,000}$

Copy and divide.

7. $\$272.16 \div 486$

8. $29,675 \div 342$

9. $535,684 \div 701$

87

Practice

Divide and check.

1. 216)1,846

2. 489)$136.92

3. 703)45,896

4. 514)18,236

5. 651)171,513

6. 867)505,260

Copy and Do

7. $128.31 ÷ 329

8. 58,953 ÷ 636

9. 26,412 ÷ 408

10. 51,634 ÷ 750

11. 620,834 ÷ 987

12. $2,109.80 ÷ 548

Apply

Solve these problems.

13. A jumbo jet flies about 596 miles per hour. How many hours will it take for the jet to fly 3,576 miles?

14. The wingspan of a jumbo jet is 198 feet. If 5 jets are parked wingtip to wingtip, what is the total distance across?

15. The 342 pieces of freight on a cargo ship weighed in at 59,850 pounds. What is the average weight of each piece of freight?

16. A test pilot earns $171,900 a year. He makes 15 test flights each month. How much does he earn for each flight?

EXCURSION

Study this problem which shows how to use a calculator to divide large numbers.

6015 [÷] 235 [=] [25.595745]   235 [×] 25 [=] [5875]   6015 [−] 5875 [=] [140]

```
        2 5                    2 5                        2 5 R140
235)6,0 1 5          235)6,0 1 5              235)6,0 1 5
                         5,8 7 5                   5,8 7 5
                                                     1 4 0
```

Use a calculator to find these quotients.

1. 478)9,708

2. 672)90,883

3. 928)79,485

Acting it Out

An explorer wants to cross a desert with
the help of porters. It takes six days
to make the crossing. Each person can
only carry enough food for four days.
How many porters does the explorer need
to take in order to complete the trip?

★ SEE

We want to know how many porters the explorer will
need to take on the trip.

It takes ___ days to cross the desert.

Each person can carry enough food to last ___ days.

★ PLAN

Acting the problem out will help us to think of possible
solutions. We can begin by using one student to act as
the explorer and one student to act as a porter. If
necessary we can add more porters and try again until
we reach a solution.

★ DO

Act the problem out. Answer these questions to help
reach a solution.

How much food does each person have at the end of
the first day?
How many more days will it take to complete the trip?
Is there any way for the explorer to complete the trip
with the help of the porter or porters he presently has?
If a solution cannot yet be reached, continue acting out
the trip adding another porter each time. At the end of
each day go back to answer the same questions until
you find a solution.

The explorer will need to take ___ porters with him.

★ CHECK

A good way to check the solution of this problem is to
explain what will happen on the trip with the required
number of porters.

Apply

Act out these situations to help you solve these problems.

1. It has been said that a rectangular piece of paper can not be folded in half more than eight times. Using several different sizes of paper, attempt to create more than eight such folds. Good luck.

2. Repeat the experiment in problem 1 by cutting a rectangular piece of paper in half. Take one of the one-half sheets and cut that in half. Take one of those half sheets and cut that one in half. Make eight cuts altogether. Approximately how much larger is the original sheet than the final piece of paper?

3. A roll of pennies is worth $0.50. If you agree to pay an employee $0.01 the first day of work, $0.03 the second day, $0.05 the third day, $0.07 the fourth day and so forth, how many rolls of pennies would you need to meet your payroll for five days of work? For 10 days of work?

4. If you agree to pay an employee $0.01 for the first day of work, $0.02 the second day of work, $0.04 the third day, $0.08 the fourth day and so forth, how many rolls of pennies would you need to meet your payroll after 5 days? After 10 days?

5. Nip and Tuck get paid by the hour. They usually get the same amount per hour and work the same number of hours each week. Next week, however, Nip has a special project and will earn twice as much per hour as Tuck, but Tuck will work twice as many hours as Nip. Which one will make more money next week?

6. The Greek Drama Group is discussing how much to charge for tickets to their next play. Members believe that if they charge $14.95 per ticket, they will sell 375 tickets. But if they charge only $11.95 per ticket, they will sell 450 tickets. If you were a member of the group, what would you say to do and why?

7. If m and n represent two whole numbers, which of the following represents the greatest number?
   a. $m \div n$
   b. $(10 \times m) \div n$
   c. $m \div (10 \times n)$

Divide and check.

1. 7)648

2. 5)315

3. 8)896

4. 2)$8.50

5. 7)5,273

6. 4)8,925

7. 6)$61.86

8. 9)16,475

9. 28)230

10. 46)230

11. 75)545

12. 86)643

13. 31)127

14. 37)222

15. 62)191

16. 72)321

17. 12)2,678

18. 96)$18,499.68

19. 83)216,317

20. 911)1,958

21. 315)$6,914.25

22. 723)582,151

23. 49)8,267

24. 53)15,286

25. 67)116,395

Circle the letter of the correct answer.

1 $3 + n = 9$
   $n = ?$

   a 3
   b 6
   c 9
   d NG

2 $8 - n = 3$
   $n = ?$

   a 5
   b 8
   c 11
   d NG

3 $7 \times 9 = n$
   $n = ?$

   a 54
   b 56
   c 63
   d NG

4 $5 \times n = 35$
   $n = ?$

   a 5
   b 7
   c 9
   d NG

5 $48 \div 6 = n$
   $n = ?$

   a 5
   b 7
   c 8
   d NG

6 $5 + 3 \times 4 = n$
   $n = ?$

   a 17
   b 27
   c 32
   d NG

7 What is the place value of
   the 6 in 3,248,653?

   a millions
   b thousands
   c tens
   d NG

8   27,396
     + 42,875

   a 69,161
   b 70,271
   c 71,271
   d NG

9   83,029
     − 47,853

   a 35,176
   b 35,276
   c 44,836
   d NG

10 365×7

   a 2,125
   b 2,555
   c 2,655
   d NG

11     $4.96
     ×   53

   a $39.88
   b $252.88
   c $262.88
   d NG

12   4,659
     ×   468

   a 335,448
   b 2,180,412
   c 2,190,412
   d NG

13 $379 \div 6$

   a 63 R1
   b 6 R19
   c 631
   d NG

 score

NUMBER THEORY AND FRACTIONS

Finding the Least Common Multiple

In a multiplication equation where none of the factors is 0, the product is also called a **multiple** of each factor. What is the least common multiple of 6 and 9? The first six multiples of 6 are 6, 12, 18, 24, 30 and 36.

To name the first four multiples of 9, we think of the non-zero multiplication facts that have 9 as a factor.

$1 \times 9 = 9$ $2 \times 9 = \underline{\quad}$

$3 \times 9 = \underline{\quad}$ $4 \times 9 = \underline{\quad}$

The first four multiples of 9 are ____, ____,

____ and ____.

To name the **least common multiple (LCM)** of 6 and 9, we identify the multiples they have in common.

Multiples of 6:   **6, 12,** 18**, 24, 30,** 36**, . . .**
Multiples of 9:   **9,** 18**, 27,** 36**, . . .**

The first two common multiples of 6 and 9 are

____ and ____.

The **LCM** of 6 and 9 is ____.

Getting Started

Write the first five multiples for each number.

1. 3   2. 8   3. 9   4. 5   5. 10

_____   _____   _____   _____   _____

Write the first three common multiples
for each pair of numbers.

Write the LCM for each
set of numbers.

6. 3, 6   7. 2, 5   8. 6, 8   9. 10, 12   10. 6, 9, 12

_____   _____   _____   _____   _____

Practice

Write the first five multiples for each number.

1. 2   2. 7   3. 12   4. 11   5. 4

_____ _____ _____ _____ _____

6. 12   7. 6   8. 15   9. 20   10. 16

_____ _____ _____ _____ _____

Write the first three common multiples for each pair of numbers.

11. 4, 6   12. 6, 9   13. 4, 8   14. 6, 10   15. 2, 5

_____ _____ _____ _____ _____

16. 9, 12   17. 6, 12   18. 5, 8   19. 3, 10   20. 6, 16

_____ _____ _____ _____ _____

Write the LCM for each set of numbers.

21. 4, 8   22. 5, 7   23. 4, 5   24. 9, 15   25. 7, 8

____ ____ ____ ____ ____

26. 2, 3, 4   27. 3, 4, 5   28. 4, 6, 8   29. 3, 6, 9   30. 8, 9, 12

____ ____ ____ ____ ____

EXCURSION

Multiples of 2 are called **even numbers**. All other counting numbers are called **odd numbers**. Use the words **even** or **odd** to complete each equation. Write an example of each equation.

1. even number + even number = _____ number _____

2. even number + odd number = _____ number _____

3. odd number + odd number = _____ number _____

4. even number × even number = _____ number _____

5. even number × odd number = _____ number _____

6. odd number × odd number = _____ number _____

Finding the Greatest Common Factor

We use multiplication to find the factors of a whole number. The factors of 12 are 1, 2, 3, 4, 6 and 12. What are the factors of 18? What is the **greatest common factor (GCF)** of 12 and 18?

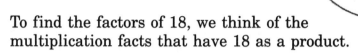

To find the factors of 18, we think of the multiplication facts that have 18 as a product.

$$\underline{\hphantom{xx}} \times 18 = 18$$

$$\underline{\hphantom{xx}} \times 9 = 18$$

$$\underline{\hphantom{xx}} \times 6 = 18$$

The factors of 18 are ____, ____, ____, ____, ____

and ____.

To name the **greatest common factor** of 12 and 18, we identify factors that 12 and 18 have in common.

Factors of 12:   1, 2, 3, 4, 6, 12
Factors of 18:   1, 2, 3, 6, 9, 18

The common factors of 12 and 18 are ____, ____,

____ and ____.

The GCF of 12 and 18 is ____.

Getting Started

Write the factors for each number.

1. 8   2. 9   3. 15   4. 24   5. 36

_____   _____   _____   _____   _____

Write the common factors for each pair of numbers.

6. 4, 6   7. 5, 15   8. 10, 15   9. 12, 24   10. 15, 35

_____   _____   _____   _____   _____

Write the GCF for each pair of numbers.

11. 15, 27   12. 9, 12   13. 6, 24   14. 36, 48   15. 15, 35

_____   _____   _____   _____   _____

95

Practice

Write the factors for each number.

1. 6

2. 10

3. 16

4. 20

5. 26

_____ _____ _____ _____ _____

6. 30

7. 32

8. 45

9. 50

10. 56

_____ _____ _____ _____ _____

Write the common factors for each pair of numbers.

11. 6, 8

12. 10, 15

13. 7, 28

14. 18, 24

15. 20, 50

_____ _____ _____ _____ _____

16. 25, 40

17. 16, 36

18. 36, 48

19. 25, 45

20. 36, 81

_____ _____ _____ _____ _____

Write the GCF for each pair of numbers.

21. 12, 15

22. 8, 36

23. 10, 25

24. 20, 30

25. 25, 50

_____ _____ _____ _____ _____

26. 27, 48

27. 35, 49

28. 36, 96

29. 24, 30

30. 60, 90

_____ _____ _____ _____ _____

EXCURSION

The Greek mathematician Euclid discovered a process to find the GCF by division. The **Euclidean Algorithm** can be used to find the GCF of 12 and 20.

Step 1: Divide the numbers.

$$\begin{array}{r} 1\text{ R}8 \\ 12\overline{)20} \\ \underline{12} \\ 8 \end{array}$$

Step 2: Divide the divisor by the remainder.

$$\begin{array}{r} 1\text{ R}4 \\ 8\overline{)12} \\ \underline{8} \\ 4 \end{array}$$

Step 3: Repeat step 2.

$$\begin{array}{r} 2 \\ 4\overline{)8} \\ \underline{8} \\ 0 \end{array}$$

When the remainder is zero, the divisor is the GCF.
The GCF of 8 and 12 is 4.

Use the Euclidean Algorithm to find the GCF for each pair of numbers.

1. 24, 42 ___

2. 16, 100 ___

3. 17, 46 ___

Identifying Prime and Composite Numbers

A number must be divisible by all of its factors. The number 15 has exactly 4 factors: 1, 3, 5 and 15. What are the factors of 18?

To name the factors of 18, we can use multiplication facts.

$$\underline{\quad} \times 18 = 18$$

$$\underline{\quad} \times 9 = 18$$

$$\underline{\quad} \times 6 = 18$$

The factors of 18 are ____, ____, ____, ____, ____

and ____.

The number 18 has ____ factors. What are the factors of 5?

The factors of 5 are ____ and ____. The number 5 is a prime number. A **prime number** has exactly two different factors: the number 1 and itself. The number 1 is not prime because it has only one factor.

A number greater than 1 that is not prime is a **composite number.** Since 18 has 4 factors, 18 is a

_____ number.

Getting Started

Write all factors for each number.

1. 6   2. 12   3. 20   4. 23   5. 35

_____   _____   _____   _____   _____

Identify each number as **prime** or **composite.**

6. 7   7. 9   8. 32   9. 47   10. 154

_____   _____   _____   _____   _____

Practice

Write all factors for each number.

1. 8

2. 10

3. 21

4. 25

5. 31

_____ _____ _____ _____ _____

6. 36

7. 40

8. 45

9. 57

10. 67

_____ _____ _____ _____ _____

11. 28

12. 42

13. 16

14. 15

15. 29

_____ _____ _____ _____ _____

16. 91

17. 63

18. 21

19. 9

20. 53

_____ _____ _____ _____ _____

Identify each number as **prime** or **composite**.

21. 17

22. 27

23. 49

24. 63

25. 75

_____ _____ _____ _____ _____

26. 87

27. 96

28. 100

29. 120

30. 131

_____ _____ _____ _____ _____

┌─────────── EXCURSION ───────────┐

A Greek mathematician developed a way to find prime numbers. This method is called the Sieve of Eratosthenes. Make a sieve to find all primes less than 201.

- Draw an array from 1 through 200 with 10 numbers in each row.
- Cross out 1. Circle 2. Cross out every second number after 2.
- Circle 3. Cross out every third number after 3.
- Circle the next prime number, 5. Cross out every fifth number after 5.
- Circle the next prime number, 7. Cross out every seventh number after 7.
- Continue this process for 11, 13 and 17.
- Circle all numbers that have not been crossed out.

The circled numbers are the primes less than 201.

Prime Factoring

Any whole number greater than 1 can be written as a product of prime number factors. This is called **prime factoring.** One way to find prime number factors is to make a **factor tree.** There may be different ways to start a factor tree, but the final set of prime factors will always be the same. Use a factor tree to find the prime factors of 24. Use exponents to write this prime factorization.

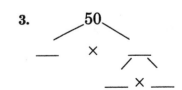

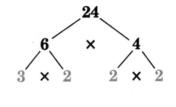

$2 \times 2 \times 2 \times 3$

$2^3 \times 3$

___ × ___ × ___ × ___

___ × ___

✔ Remember, the exponent tells how many times to use the base number as a factor. $2^3 = 2 \times 2 \times 2$

Getting Started

Complete each factor tree.

1. 20
5 × ___
___ × ___

2. 36
4 × 9
___ × ___ ___ × ___

3. 50
___ × ___
___ × ___

Write each prime factorization using exponents if possible.

4. 8   5. 35   6. 48   7. 72   8. 400

_____   _____   _____   _____   _____

Practice

Complete each factor tree.

1.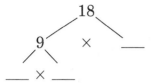

2.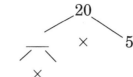

3.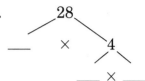

4.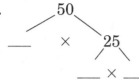

5.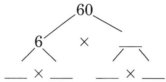

6.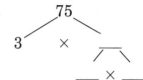

Write each prime factorization using exponents if possible.

7. 10   8. 28   9. 55   10. 64   11. 66

_____   _____   _____   _____   _____

12. 84   13. 100   14. 125   15. 180   16. 225

_____   _____   _____   _____   _____

EXCURSION

1. Primes that differ by 2 are called **twin primes.** 5 and 7 are examples of twin primes. List all the twin primes less than 100.

   _____

2. Primes that have digits that are reversed are called **mirror primes.** 13 and 31 are mirror primes. List all the mirror primes less than 100.

   _____

3. A **perfect number** is a number that is the sum of all of its factors except itself. 6 = 1 + 2 + 3, therefore 6 is a perfect number. List all of the perfect numbers less than 50.

   _____

Naming Fractions

Sol is playing a game of darts.
What part of the dart board is red?
What part of the set of boxes is
filled with darts?

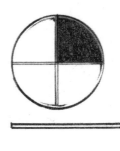

We know that the dart board has ____ equal regions,

and ____ region is red.

To find what part of the dart board is red, we
compare the number of red parts to the total
number of parts.

$$\frac{\text{number of red parts}}{\text{number of equal parts}} = \frac{1}{4} = \frac{\text{numerator}}{\text{denominator}}$$

One fourth or ____ of the dart board is red.

We know there are ____ boxes in the set and ____ of
the boxes are full.

To find what part of the set is filled, we compare
the number of full boxes to the total number of
boxes.

$$\frac{\text{number of full boxes}}{\text{number of boxes}} = \frac{\ \ }{\ \ } = \frac{\text{numerator}}{\text{denominator}}$$

Two thirds or ____ of the boxes are full.

Getting Started

Name each fraction.

1. $\frac{3}{4}$ _____

2. $\frac{1}{5}$ _____

3. $\frac{2}{8}$ _____

Write each fraction.

4. five eighths ____

5. one half ____

6. three fourths ____

Write the fraction that names the shaded part.

7.

8.

9. Write the fraction that shows
what part of the
group is red.

101

Practice

Name each fraction.

1. $\frac{5}{8}$ _____

2. $\frac{1}{3}$ _____

3. $\frac{1}{10}$ _____

4. $\frac{3}{12}$ _____

5. $\frac{7}{8}$ _____

6. $\frac{5}{6}$ _____

Write each fraction.

7. two thirds ____

8. four fifths ____

9. nine tenths ____

10. five twelfths ____

11. zero ninths ____

12. two halves ____

13. three sixteenths ____

14. one fourth ____

15. three sevenths ____

Write the fraction that names the shaded part.

16.

____

17.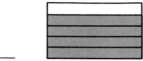

____

18.

____

19.

____

20.

____

21.

____

Write the fraction that shows

22. what part of the group of glasses is full.

 ____

23. what part of the group of apples is *not* red.

 ____

Apply

Solve these problems.

24. There are 9 players on the softball team. Three players are sixth graders. What part of the team is sixth graders?

25. Gerry has 12 coins for a total of 83¢. Seven of the coins are dimes. What part of the coins are nickels?

26. The swim team practices 3 hours a day, 6 days a week. Mort attended practice 7 hours last week. What part of the total practice did he miss?

27. Martin baked a dozen muffins and ate 3 of them. What part of the muffins are left?

102

Finding Equivalent Fractions

Some members of the orchestra arrived early for rehearsal. What fraction of the group are the violinists?

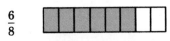

We want to write a fraction that tells what part of the group are violin players.

We know that there are ＿＿ musicians in the group, and ＿＿ of them are violinists.
We compare the number of violinists to the total number of musicians. We say ＿＿ of the musicians are violinists.

We also know there are ＿＿ pairs of musicians, and ＿＿ pair of the musicians are violinists.

We can say, ＿＿ of the musicians are violinists.

$\frac{2}{6}$ and $\frac{1}{3}$ are called **equivalent fractions** because they name the same number.

✔ We find equivalent fractions by multiplying or dividing.

Multiply the numerator and the denominator by the same number.

$\frac{1}{2}$

$\frac{2}{4}$

$$\frac{1}{2} = \frac{1 \times 2}{2 \times 2} = \text{—}$$

Divide the numerator and the denominator by the same number.

$\frac{6}{8}$

$\frac{3}{4}$

$$\frac{6}{8} = \frac{6 \div 2}{8 \div 2} = \text{—}$$

Getting Started

Write a pair of equivalent fractions for the shaded part.

1.
＿＿

2.
＿＿

3.
＿＿

Complete the equation.

4. $\frac{3}{4} = \frac{3 \times}{4 \times} = \frac{9}{12}$

5. $\frac{6}{9} = \frac{6 \div}{9 \div} = \frac{2}{3}$

Complete the equivalent fraction.

6. $\frac{14}{20} = \frac{}{10}$

7. $\frac{3}{8} = \frac{9}{}$

103

Practice

Write a pair of equivalent fractions for the shaded part.

1.

2.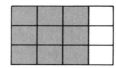

3.

4.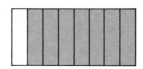

5.

6.

7.

8.

9.

10.

11.

12.

Complete the equation.

13. $\frac{1}{4} = \frac{1 \times}{4 \times} = \frac{5}{20}$

14. $\frac{3}{9} = \frac{3 \div}{9 \div} = \frac{1}{3}$

15. $\frac{5}{10} = \frac{5 \times}{10 \times} = \frac{10}{20}$

16. $\frac{10}{16} = \frac{10 \div}{16 \div} = \frac{5}{8}$

17. $\frac{2}{5} = \frac{2 \times}{5 \times} = \frac{12}{30}$

18. $\frac{4}{8} = \frac{4 \div}{8 \div} = \frac{2}{4}$

19. $\frac{14}{21} = \frac{14 \div}{21 \div} = \frac{2}{3}$

20. $\frac{5}{8} = \frac{5 \times}{8 \times} = \frac{25}{40}$

21. $\frac{4}{11} = \frac{4 \times}{11 \times} = \frac{28}{77}$

Complete the equivalent fraction.

22. $\frac{5}{12} = \frac{}{24}$

23. $\frac{4}{8} = \frac{12}{}$

24. $\frac{6}{18} = \frac{}{9}$

25. $\frac{10}{15} = \frac{2}{}$

26. $\frac{}{3} = \frac{6}{18}$

27. $\frac{12}{16} = \frac{6}{}$

28. $\frac{60}{100} = \frac{}{10}$

29. $\frac{30}{} = \frac{5}{8}$

30. $\frac{}{24} = \frac{5}{8}$

31. $\frac{}{45} = \frac{3}{5}$

32. $\frac{8}{12} = \frac{24}{}$

33. $\frac{16}{20} = \frac{}{100}$

34. $\frac{12}{} = \frac{3}{8}$

35. $\frac{6}{21} = \frac{}{63}$

36. $\frac{}{27} = \frac{6}{9}$

37. $\frac{5}{12} = \frac{}{96}$

Apply

Solve these problems.

38. Zack measured a board to be $\frac{5}{8}$ of an inch thick. How many sixteenths of an inch thick is the board?

39. Sun Li filled $\frac{9}{12}$ of a container with water for a science experiment. How many fourths full is the container?

104

Naming Fractions in Simplest Form

The basketball team is scheduled to play 25 games this season. The team has already played 20 games. What fractional part of the basketball season has been played?

We want to name the fractional part of the season that the team has already played.

We know the team will play a total of ____ games,

and it has already played ____ games.

We compare the number of games played to the total number of games.

The team has played ____ of its games.

What is this fraction in simplest form?

A fraction is in **simplest form** when the greatest common factor of the numerator and denominator is 1.

To write $\frac{20}{25}$ in simplest form:

Find the GCF of 20 and 25.

Factors of 20: **1, 2, 4, 5, 10, 20**
Factors of 25: **1, 5, 25**

The GCF is ____.

Divide the numerator and denominator by their GCF.

$$\frac{20}{25} = \frac{20 \div}{25 \div} = \text{—}$$

$\frac{20}{25}$ named in simplest form is —.

Getting Started

Name in simplest form.

1. $\frac{6}{10} =$ 2. $\frac{10}{25} =$ 3. $\frac{10}{40} =$ 4. $\frac{8}{12} =$

5. $\frac{6}{18} =$ 6. $\frac{9}{12} =$ 7. $\frac{18}{54} =$ 8. $\frac{180}{200} =$

105

Practice

Name in simplest form.

1. $\frac{6}{8} =$ 2. $\frac{12}{18} =$ 3. $\frac{9}{15} =$ 4. $\frac{6}{12} =$

5. $\frac{8}{20} =$ 6. $\frac{25}{30} =$ 7. $\frac{25}{150} =$ 8. $\frac{4}{28} =$

9. $\frac{14}{16} =$ 10. $\frac{15}{18} =$ 11. $\frac{40}{60} =$ 12. $\frac{16}{20} =$

13. $\frac{9}{24} =$ 14. $\frac{14}{21} =$ 15. $\frac{36}{48} =$ 16. $\frac{9}{30} =$

17. $\frac{18}{27} =$ 18. $\frac{25}{75} =$ 19. $\frac{24}{30} =$ 20. $\frac{32}{40} =$

21. $\frac{16}{24} =$ 22. $\frac{42}{63} =$ 23. $\frac{24}{60} =$ 24. $\frac{64}{72} =$

25. $\frac{12}{144} =$ 26. $\frac{32}{120} =$ 27. $\frac{75}{100} =$ 28. $\frac{120}{160} =$

Apply

Use the chart to solve these problems.
Name fractions in simplest form.

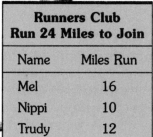

Runners Club Run 24 Miles to Join	
Name	Miles Run
Mel	16
Nippi	10
Trudy	12

29. What part of the distance has Mel run?

30. What part of the distance must Nippi still run?

31. What part of the distance has Trudy run?

32. Mo has run twice as many miles as Nippi. What part of the distance has he run?

EXCURSION

Prime factors can be used to write $\frac{12}{72}$ in simplest form.

Write the prime factors.

$$\frac{12}{72} = \frac{2 \times 2 \times 3}{2 \times 2 \times 2 \times 3 \times 3}$$

2. Circle the common factors. Multiply what is left.

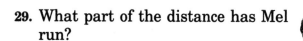

$$\frac{2 \times 2 \times 3}{2 \times 2 \times 2 \times 3 \times 3} = \frac{1}{6}$$

Use prime factors to name these fractions in simplest form.

1. $\frac{15}{50} =$ 2. $\frac{27}{30} =$ 3. $\frac{30}{100} =$

Renaming Mixed Numbers

Casey's hobby is building model ships. Today he cut a mast for a new model schooner. The mast measures $12\frac{1}{4}$ inches. How many quarter inches long is the mast?

We want to know the number of quarter inches in $12\frac{1}{4}$ inches. Numbers such as $12\frac{1}{4}$ are called **mixed numbers.** We need to rename the mixed number as a fraction.

To rename a mixed number, multiply the whole number by the denominator and add the numerator, keeping the denominator the same.

$$12\frac{1}{4} = \frac{(12 \times 4) + 1}{4} = \frac{48 + 1}{4} = \text{---}$$

The mast is ____ quarter inches or ____ inches.

We can also rename a whole number as a fraction

by writing the whole number over 1.

$$2 = \frac{2}{1} \qquad 5 = \frac{\text{---}}{1}$$

Getting Started

Rename each whole or mixed number as a fraction.

1. $3\frac{1}{2} =$

2. $6 =$

3. $4\frac{2}{3} =$

4. $11\frac{1}{9} =$

5. $6\frac{2}{3} =$

6. $5\frac{4}{5} =$

7. $3 =$

8. $109\frac{1}{5} =$

9. $7 =$

10. $3\frac{2}{9} =$

11. $6\frac{7}{10} =$

12. $15\frac{3}{5} =$

13. $7\frac{3}{4} =$

14. $10 =$

15. $103\frac{3}{4} =$

107

Practice

Rename each mixed number as a fraction.

1. $3\frac{1}{4} =$

2. $4 =$

3. $5\frac{1}{2} =$

4. $7\frac{1}{3} =$

5. $9 =$

6. $9\frac{3}{4} =$

7. $2\frac{4}{5} =$

8. $3\frac{4}{9} =$

9. $8\frac{2}{3} =$

10. $9\frac{5}{8} =$

11. $1\frac{7}{12} =$

12. $3\frac{5}{8} =$

13. $7\frac{4}{7} =$

14. $2\frac{5}{9} =$

15. $6\frac{3}{8} =$

16. $5 =$

17. $9\frac{1}{9} =$

18. $4\frac{5}{12} =$

19. $1\frac{7}{16} =$

20. $10\frac{2}{3} =$

21. $15\frac{1}{2} =$

22. $16\frac{3}{4} =$

23. $12\frac{7}{10} =$

24. $100\frac{5}{8} =$

Apply

Solve these problems.

25. A large melon is cut in fourths. How many fourths can be cut from $6\frac{3}{4}$ melons?

26. A gift basket holds 3 grapefruit and four times as many oranges. In simplest form, what fraction of the fruit is oranges?

27. Are $5\frac{2}{3}$ pizzas enough for 16 people if each person eats $\frac{1}{3}$ of a pizza?

28. Pierre was stapling carpet to the floor. He had $4\frac{7}{8}$ inches of carpet left to staple. He stapled every $\frac{1}{8}$ of an inch. How many more staples did he need?

EXCURSION

Cross out the number in each group that does not belong.
Write 5 more members for each set.

1. 54, 16, 18, 72, 63, 9 _____

2. 45, 70, 62, 85, 15, 10 _____

3. 650, 406, 908, 705, 994 _____

4. 36, 93, 75, 67, 84, 72 _____

5. 300, 64, 8, 760, 432, 960 _____

Renaming Improper Fractions

Elaine is sorting bottles in the chemistry lab. She has 14 bottles to put into cartons that hold 4 bottles each. How many cartons will she fill?

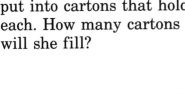

We want to know how many cartons Elaine can fill.

We know that she has ＿＿ bottles, and each carton

holds ＿＿ bottles. To find the number of cartons

Elaine will fill, we divide ＿＿ by ＿＿.

This division can be written as an **improper fraction.**

$$14 \div 4 = \frac{14}{4}$$

Improper fractions can be renamed as whole or mixed numbers.

Divide the numerator by the denominator.	Write the remainder over the divisor.	Rename in simplest form.

$$\begin{array}{r} 3 \\ 4\overline{)1\ 4} \\ \underline{1\ 2} \\ 2 \end{array}$$

$$\begin{array}{r} 3\frac{2}{4} \\ 4\overline{)1\ 4} \\ \underline{1\ 2} \\ 2 \end{array}$$

$$\begin{array}{r} 3\frac{2}{4} = 3\frac{1}{2} \\ 4\overline{)1\ 4} \\ \underline{1\ 2} \\ 2 \end{array}$$

Elaine can fill ＿＿ cartons.

Getting Started

Rename each fraction as a whole or mixed number.

1. $\frac{7}{5} =$ ＿＿

2. $\frac{9}{3} =$ ＿＿

3. $\frac{18}{4} =$ ＿＿

4. $\frac{48}{10} =$ ＿＿

5. $\frac{8}{5} =$ ＿＿

6. $\frac{25}{7} =$ ＿＿

7. $\frac{56}{4} =$ ＿＿

8. $\frac{9}{6} =$ ＿＿

9. $\frac{100}{12} =$ ＿＿

10. $\frac{48}{16} =$ ＿＿

109

Practice

Rename each fraction as a whole or mixed number.

1. $\frac{8}{3}$ = ____

2. $\frac{9}{5}$ = ____

3. $\frac{11}{3}$ = ____

4. $\frac{6}{5}$ = ____

5. $\frac{12}{4}$ = ____

6. $\frac{10}{8}$ = ____

7. $\frac{15}{6}$ = ____

8. $\frac{16}{2}$ = ____

9. $\frac{17}{7}$ = ____

10. $\frac{18}{4}$ = ____

11. $\frac{36}{5}$ = ____

12. $\frac{48}{10}$ = ____

13. $\frac{180}{50}$ = ____

14. $\frac{100}{48}$ = ____

15. $\frac{90}{18}$ = ____

16. $\frac{125}{25}$ = ____

Apply

Solve these problems.

17. Royce is helping to serve at the school picnic. He has 35 hamburgers and is putting 6 hamburgers on a tray. How many trays will Royce need?

18. Mrs. Mencini has 48 liters of lemonade. She wants to put the same amount of liquid in each of 9 containers. How many liters will go into each container?

EXCURSION

We can always find a fraction between 2 fractions. We can use a number line and equivalent fractions to find a fraction between $\frac{2}{5}$ and $\frac{3}{5}$, for example.

$$\frac{2}{5} \qquad\qquad \frac{3}{5}$$

Rename the fractions and find their midpoint.

$\frac{5}{10}$ is the midpoint between $\frac{2}{5}$ and $\frac{3}{5}$.

Find a number between

1. $\frac{5}{7}$ and $\frac{6}{7}$.

_____

2. $\frac{4}{9}$ and $\frac{5}{9}$.

_____

3. $\frac{1}{3}$ and $\frac{2}{3}$.

_____

4. $\frac{3}{4}$ and $\frac{4}{4}$.

_____

5. $\frac{6}{10}$ and $\frac{7}{10}$.

_____

6. $\frac{14}{9}$ and $\frac{15}{9}$.

_____

7. $\frac{3}{49}$ and $\frac{4}{49}$.

_____

8. $\frac{1}{64}$ and $\frac{2}{64}$.

_____

Comparing Fractions

Ronald and Earle ride unicycles. One day, Ronald rode $\frac{3}{4}$ of a mile and Earle rode $\frac{2}{3}$ of a mile. Who rode the farthest?

We want to compare the distances the boys rode.

To compare fractions, we rename them as equivalent fractions with the **least common denominator (LCD)**.

$$\frac{3}{4} = \frac{}{12} \qquad \frac{2}{3} = \frac{}{12}$$

Compare the numerators.

$$\frac{9}{12} \bigcirc \frac{8}{12}$$

✔ Remember, if the denominators are the same, the fraction with the greater numerator is the greater fraction. $\quad \frac{3}{4} \bigcirc \frac{2}{3}$

_____ rode farther than _____ on his unicycle.

Mixed numbers can be compared in the same way. First compare the whole numbers. If they are equal, compare the fractions.

$$2\frac{1}{2} > 2\frac{1}{5} \text{ because } 2\frac{5}{10} > 2\frac{2}{10}.$$

Getting Started

Find the LCD for each pair of fractions.

1. $\frac{2}{3}, \frac{1}{2}$ ____

2. $\frac{1}{2}, \frac{5}{8}$ ____

3. $\frac{7}{12}, \frac{5}{6}$ ____

4. $\frac{5}{6}, \frac{3}{8}$ ____

Write >, = or < between the two numbers.

5. $\frac{3}{4} \bigcirc \frac{1}{2}$

6. $5\frac{6}{8} \bigcirc 5\frac{8}{12}$

7. $3\frac{2}{3} \bigcirc 3\frac{3}{5}$

8. $\frac{1}{2} \bigcirc \frac{4}{8}$

Order the fractions from least to greatest.

9. $\frac{1}{5}, \frac{2}{3}, \frac{1}{2}$ _____

10. $7\frac{3}{8}, 7\frac{1}{4}, 8\frac{5}{6}$ _____

111

Practice

Find the LCD for each pair of fractions.

1. $\frac{3}{4}, \frac{1}{8}$ _____

2. $\frac{2}{3}, \frac{1}{4}$ _____

3. $\frac{3}{4}, \frac{5}{6}$ _____

4. $\frac{3}{5}, \frac{1}{2}$ _____

5. $\frac{3}{8}, \frac{1}{3}$ _____

6. $\frac{5}{6}, \frac{7}{8}$ _____

7. $\frac{2}{3}, \frac{5}{6}$ _____

8. $\frac{3}{4}, \frac{7}{10}$ _____

9. $\frac{3}{7}, \frac{5}{14}$ _____

10. $\frac{3}{8}, \frac{5}{12}$ _____

11. $\frac{5}{6}, \frac{4}{9}$ _____

12. $\frac{1}{4}, \frac{2}{5}$ _____

13. $\frac{3}{8}, \frac{7}{10}$ _____

14. $\frac{5}{16}, \frac{1}{6}$ _____

15. $\frac{7}{10}, \frac{2}{5}$ _____

16. $\frac{1}{11}, \frac{1}{2}$ _____

Write >, = or < between the two numbers.

17. $\frac{3}{4} \bigcirc \frac{1}{8}$

18. $7\frac{2}{3} \bigcirc 7\frac{1}{4}$

19. $\frac{3}{4} \bigcirc \frac{5}{6}$

20. $\frac{3}{5} \bigcirc \frac{1}{2}$

21. $\frac{5}{10} \bigcirc \frac{6}{12}$

22. $\frac{1}{8} \bigcirc \frac{2}{3}$

23. $9\frac{5}{7} \bigcirc 9\frac{3}{4}$

24. $\frac{3}{4} \bigcirc \frac{5}{8}$

25. $6\frac{2}{3} \bigcirc 6\frac{5}{8}$

26. $\frac{5}{9} \bigcirc \frac{1}{2}$

27. $\frac{4}{5} \bigcirc \frac{8}{10}$

28. $\frac{7}{10} \bigcirc \frac{2}{3}$

29. $\frac{1}{7} \bigcirc \frac{1}{3}$

30. $\frac{9}{12} \bigcirc \frac{10}{15}$

31. $1\frac{9}{30} \bigcirc 1\frac{8}{40}$

32. $\frac{3}{15} \bigcirc \frac{4}{10}$

Order the fractions from least to greatest.

33. $\frac{3}{5}, \frac{2}{3}, \frac{1}{6}$

_____

34. $4\frac{1}{4}, 14\frac{5}{8}, 4\frac{2}{3}$

_____

35. $\frac{4}{5}, \frac{2}{3}, \frac{1}{2}$

_____

36. $\frac{5}{8}, \frac{5}{6}, \frac{3}{4}$

_____

37. $2\frac{1}{2}, 1\frac{1}{3}, 2\frac{1}{9}$

_____

38. $\frac{2}{3}, \frac{4}{5}, \frac{3}{4}$

_____

39. $6\frac{3}{4}, 6\frac{1}{2}, 6\frac{2}{3}$

_____

40. $8\frac{4}{5}, 8\frac{5}{6}, 8\frac{2}{3}$

_____

41. $3\frac{3}{10}, 3\frac{4}{15}, 3\frac{1}{6}$

_____

Apply

Solve these problems.

42. Columbus got $\frac{3}{4}$ of the items correct on a math test. His friend Devin got $\frac{4}{5}$ of the items correct. Who had the better score?

43. Diane said she could finish a job in $\frac{5}{8}$ of a day. Gene said he could finish the same job in $\frac{3}{5}$ of a day. Who can finish the job faster?

44. Coleen and Howie ride the bike trail. She rests every 4 miles while he rests every 5 miles. At what point will they stop together?

45. Which bond increased more in value; the city bond up $4\frac{1}{2}$ points or the county bond up $4\frac{2}{7}$?

Making a List or Table

The publisher will use exactly 201 digits in numbering the pages of a book. The book begins with page 1. How many pages will be in the book?

★ SEE

We want to know how many pages will be in the book.

Exactly _____ digits will be used in numbering the pages.

★ PLAN

In order to solve this problem, we can make a table to record the number of digits used in numbering a chosen quantity of pages. This will help break the problem into smaller steps.

★ DO

Pages	Number of Pages	Number of Digits Per Page	Number of Digits Used	Total Digits in Book
1–9	9	1	9	9
10–49	40	2	80	89
50–99	_____	_____	_____	189
100	_____	3	_____	_____
101	_____	_____	_____	_____
102	_____	_____	_____	_____
103	_____	_____	_____	_____

There will be _____ pages in the book.

★ CHECK

We can check our solution by working backwards through the table.

Pages 100–103	4 pages	3 digits each	_____ digits
Pages 10–99	90 pages	2 digits each	_____ digits
Pages 1–9	9 pages	1 digit each	_____ digits

_____ + _____ + _____ = _____ digits.

Apply

1. Ann is offered a job as a bank teller at a starting salary of $10,400 per year. She is told that if her work is satisfactory, her salary will be increased by $1,040 at the end of each year for the next five years. Beth is offered a job at another bank starting at $5,200 for a half year. If her work is satisfactory her half-year salary will be increased by $525 per half year at the end of each half year for the next five years. Who is offered the better paying job?

2. In grade 6 there were 96 students who scored above 80% in the district spelling bee competition. Each grade had only half as many students above 80% as the next grade. That is, the fifth grade had only 48 students score above 80%. How many students altogether scored above 80% in grades 1 through 6?

3. While watching a circus parade, I saw some girls and some horses come by. I counted 46 legs and 15 heads. How many horses and how many girls were in the parade?

4. A triangle has no diagonals, and a rectangle has two diagonals. How many diagonals can be drawn on a STOP sign of eight sides?

5. Rosemary was buying supplies for school. Pencils cost $0.25 and erasers cost $0.15. She spent $1.45. How many pencils and erasers did she buy?

6. Jennifer is preparing for her track meet. She runs one lap around the track the first day, and increases her laps by two per day. On her final day of practice she runs 27 laps. How many days did Jennifer practice?

7. What if the pencils in Problem 5 cost 15¢ and the erasers cost 25¢? Then how many pencils and erasers did Rosemary buy for $1.45?

8. Read Problem 6 again. How would you rewrite the exercise so that the number of days Jennifer practiced was 16 days?

9. Tracy has some nickels, dimes, and quarters. She has $2.25 in all. She has twice as many dimes as nickels and 3 more quarters than nickels. What would be the first step you would take to find how many of each coin she has?

10. Mattie has twice as many dimes as she has nickels. She has $1.75 in all. Ken says, "I think that Mattie has 14 nickels." Arthur says, "No. I think that she has 7 nickels." Tell who is correct, Ken or Arthur, and prove it.

Calculators and Cross Products

All the fractions in the box are equivalent.
Does $\frac{10}{15}$ belong in the box?

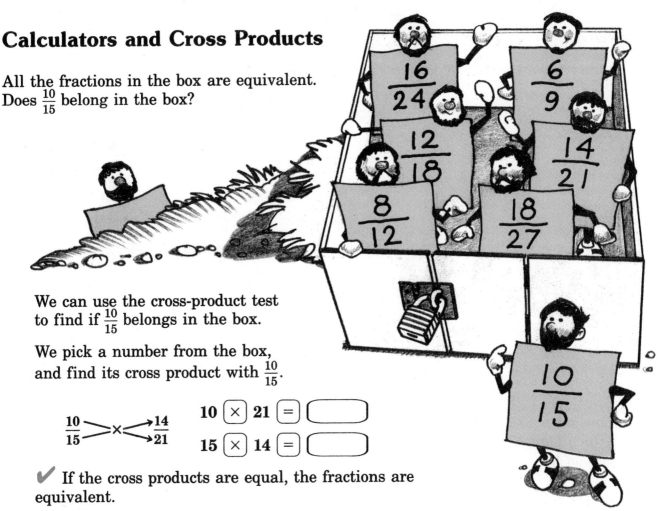

We can use the cross-product test
to find if $\frac{10}{15}$ belongs in the box.

We pick a number from the box,
and find its cross product with $\frac{10}{15}$.

$\frac{10}{15} \!>\!\!\times\!\!<\! \frac{14}{21}$ $10 \;\boxed{\times}\; 21 \;\boxed{=}\; \bigcirc$

$15 \;\boxed{\times}\; 14 \;\boxed{=}\; \bigcirc$

✔ If the cross products are equal, the fractions are equivalent.

Since $10 \times 21 = 15 \times 14$, $\frac{10}{15} \bigcirc \frac{14}{21}$.

We can also use the cross-product test to see which
fraction is larger or smaller.

Cross multiply. Write the product above the fractions.

Compare the products. Write the same sign between the fractions.

$\frac{2}{3} \;?\; \frac{3}{4}$

$\overset{8}{} \qquad \overset{9}{}$
$\frac{2}{3} \!>\!\!\times\!\!<\! \frac{3}{4}$

$8 \;<\; 9$
$\frac{2}{3} \;<\; \frac{3}{4}$

✔ Remember to always multiply the first
numerator by the second denominator, and to write
that product above the first fraction.

Use the cross-product test to compare fractions.
Write <, = or > in each circle.

1. $\frac{5}{6} \bigcirc \frac{2}{3}$

2. $\frac{12}{15} \bigcirc \frac{20}{25}$

3. $\frac{6}{13} \bigcirc \frac{24}{45}$

4. $\frac{1}{5} \bigcirc \frac{7}{12}$

5. $\frac{3}{4} \bigcirc \frac{7}{8}$

6. $\frac{2}{3} \bigcirc \frac{16}{24}$

Practice

Use the cross-products test to compare fractions. Write <, = or > in each circle.

1. $\frac{3}{4}$ ◯ $\frac{15}{18}$

2. $\frac{5}{7}$ ◯ $\frac{11}{15}$

3. $\frac{2}{12}$ ◯ $\frac{5}{30}$

4. $\frac{3}{8}$ ◯ $\frac{5}{14}$

5. $\frac{5}{9}$ ◯ $\frac{8}{15}$

6. $\frac{7}{8}$ ◯ $\frac{14}{17}$

7. $\frac{2}{11}$ ◯ $\frac{1}{6}$

8. $\frac{3}{7}$ ◯ $\frac{5}{11}$

9. $\frac{5}{8}$ ◯ $\frac{7}{12}$

10. $\frac{9}{16}$ ◯ $\frac{15}{24}$

11. $\frac{9}{20}$ ◯ $\frac{13}{30}$

12. $\frac{25}{35}$ ◯ $\frac{15}{21}$

13. $\frac{9}{20}$ ◯ $\frac{7}{16}$

14. $\frac{37}{45}$ ◯ $\frac{21}{25}$

15. $\frac{17}{32}$ ◯ $\frac{24}{45}$

16. $\frac{21}{37}$ ◯ $\frac{11}{19}$

17. $\frac{11}{56}$ ◯ $\frac{19}{100}$

18. $\frac{43}{56}$ ◯ $\frac{37}{48}$

Apply

Solve these problems.

19. Bill made 17 baskets in 25 tries. Ron made 13 baskets in 20 tries. Which player made the greater part of his tries?

20. Marilyn walked $\frac{2}{3}$ of a mile. Betty walked $\frac{7}{12}$ of a mile and Rita walked $\frac{5}{8}$ of a mile. Who walked the farthest?

21. Plunkett High won 3 out of 5 of their games this year. Last year they won 7 out of 10. Which year was better?

22. Which piece is larger; $\frac{4}{32}$ of a pie or $\frac{5}{40}$ of it?

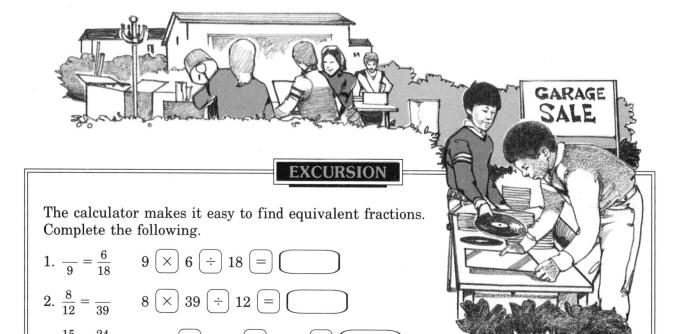

GARAGE SALE

EXCURSION

The calculator makes it easy to find equivalent fractions. Complete the following.

1. $\frac{}{9} = \frac{6}{18}$ 9 ⊠ 6 ÷ 18 = ◯

2. $\frac{8}{12} = \frac{}{39}$ 8 ⊠ 39 ÷ 12 = ◯

3. $\frac{15}{40} = \frac{24}{}$ ___ ⊠ ___ ÷ ___ = ◯

Write the LCM and GCF for each set of numbers.

1. 6, 9

LCM ____

GCF ____

2. 4, 8

LCM ____

GCF ____

3. 5, 7

LCM ____

GCF ____

4. 8, 12

LCM ____

GCF ____

Prime factor each number using exponents.

5. 12 _____

6. 18 _____

7. 50 _____

8. 36 _____

9. 32 _____

10. 49 _____

11. 35 _____

12. 54 _____

Find the equivalent fraction.

13. $\frac{3}{5} = \frac{}{15}$

14. $\frac{3}{} = \frac{12}{32}$

15. $\frac{}{9} = \frac{20}{36}$

16. $\frac{14}{21} = \frac{}{3}$

17. $\frac{12}{16} = \frac{}{4}$

18. $\frac{2}{9} = \frac{}{54}$

19. $\frac{3}{14} = \frac{9}{}$

20. $\frac{}{6} = \frac{32}{48}$

Rename in simplest form.

21. $\frac{15}{18} =$

22. $\frac{25}{35} =$

23. $\frac{10}{12} =$

24. $\frac{24}{48} =$

25. $\frac{36}{72} =$

26. $\frac{35}{60} =$

27. $\frac{14}{42} =$

28. $\frac{50}{75} =$

Write <, = or > in the circle.

29. $\frac{5}{9} \bigcirc \frac{3}{4}$

30. $\frac{2}{3} \bigcirc \frac{5}{8}$

31. $\frac{1}{2} \bigcirc \frac{7}{12}$

32. $\frac{9}{12} \bigcirc \frac{6}{8}$

33. $\frac{4}{7} \bigcirc \frac{2}{9}$

34. $\frac{12}{16} \bigcirc \frac{3}{4}$

35. $\frac{3}{8} \bigcirc \frac{4}{5}$

36. $\frac{3}{14} \bigcirc \frac{1}{5}$

Rename each mixed number as a fraction.

37. $4\frac{3}{5} =$

38. $5\frac{1}{8} =$

39. $1\frac{3}{4} =$

40. $9\frac{7}{10} =$

41. $6\frac{2}{7} =$

42. $10\frac{1}{9} =$

43. $5\frac{4}{5} =$

44. $15\frac{2}{3} =$

Rename each improper fraction as a whole or mixed number.

45. $\frac{11}{3} =$ ____

46. $\frac{9}{6} =$ ____

47. $\frac{20}{5} =$ ____

48. $\frac{37}{4} =$ ____

49. $\frac{54}{9} =$ ____

50. $\frac{18}{12} =$ ____

51. $\frac{90}{10} =$ ____

52. $\frac{75}{6} =$ ____

1 $n + 6 = 13$
$n = ?$

- **a** 6
- **b** 7
- **c** 19
- **d** NG

2 $12 - n = 8$
$n = ?$

- **a** 4
- **b** 8
- **c** 12
- **d** NG

3 $8 \times 7 = n$
$n = ?$

- **a** 49
- **b** 54
- **c** 56
- **d** NG

4 $8 \times n = 32$
$n = ?$

- **a** 4
- **b** 5
- **c** 6
- **d** NG

5 $6 + 8 \div 2 = n$
$n = ?$

- **a** 7
- **b** 10
- **c** 12
- **d** NG

6 What is the place value of the 0 in 427,063?

- **a** thousands
- **b** hundreds
- **c** tens
- **d** NG

7 $136.85
+ 97.48

- **a** $134.33
- **b** $233.33
- **c** $234.33
- **d** NG

8 74,086
$- 15,994$

- **a** 58,192
- **b** 57,192
- **c** 58,092
- **d** NG

9 458×6

- **a** 2,708
- **b** 2,748
- **c** 2,848
- **d** NG

10 $6.29
$\times \quad 47$

- **a** $69.19
- **b** $285.63
- **c** $295.63
- **d** NG

11 $439 \div 7$

- **a** 6 R25
- **b** 62
- **c** 62 R5
- **d** NG

12 $56\overline{)395}$

- **a** 7
- **b** 7 R3
- **c** 73
- **d** NG

13 Complete the equivalent fraction.
$\frac{6}{8} = \frac{?}{24}$

- **a** 2
- **b** 3
- **c** 18
- **d** NG

score

118

ADDITION AND SUBTRACTION OF FRACTIONS

Adding Fractions with Like Denominators

Guido has an overdue book. He decides to drop it off at the library before he bikes to school. How far does Guido bike altogether?

We want to know the distance Guido bikes altogether.

We know that it is _____ miles from his house to the

library, and _____ miles from the library to school.

To find the total distance, we add the distance from the house to the library and the distance from the

library to school. We add _____ and _____.

2$\frac{5}{10}$ miles

1$\frac{3}{10}$ miles

Add the fractions. Write the sum of the numerators over the common denominator.	Add the whole numbers. Simplify the fraction if necessary.

$1\frac{3}{10}$

$+ 2\frac{5}{10}$ 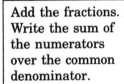 $\;3 + 5 = 8$

$\dfrac{8}{10}$

$1\frac{3}{10}$

$+ 2\frac{5}{10}$

$3\frac{8}{10} = 3\frac{4}{5}$

Guido bikes _____ miles from home to school.

Getting Started

Add. Simplify answers if necessary.

1. $\frac{3}{5} + \frac{1}{5} =$ _____

2. $\frac{4}{9} + \frac{2}{9} =$ _____

3. $\frac{7}{16} + \frac{3}{16} + \frac{5}{16} =$ _____

4. $\quad 4\frac{1}{3}$
$+ 5\frac{1}{3}$

5. $\quad 522\frac{2}{15}$
$115\frac{4}{15}$
$+ 269\frac{6}{15}$

6. $\quad 28\frac{1}{6}$
$+ 17\frac{3}{6}$

7. $\quad 7\frac{5}{12}$
$+ 3\frac{1}{12}$

119

Practice

Add. Simplify answers if necessary.

1. $\frac{5}{8} + \frac{2}{8} = $ _____   2. $\frac{3}{7} + \frac{1}{7} = $ _____   3. $\frac{5}{9} + \frac{1}{9} = $ _____

4. $\frac{3}{10} + \frac{1}{10} + \frac{5}{10} = $ _____   5. $\frac{3}{20} + \frac{9}{20} + \frac{3}{20} = $ _____   6. $\frac{11}{25} + \frac{6}{25} + \frac{4}{25} = $ _____

7. $\begin{array}{r} 5\frac{1}{8} \\ + 2\frac{3}{8} \\ \hline \end{array}$ 8. $\begin{array}{r} 6\frac{7}{15} \\ + 6\frac{3}{15} \\ \hline \end{array}$ 9. $\begin{array}{r} 9\frac{7}{16} \\ + 7\frac{5}{16} \\ \hline \end{array}$ 10. $\begin{array}{r} 21\frac{7}{24} \\ + 13\frac{9}{24} \\ \hline \end{array}$

11. $\begin{array}{r} 3\frac{2}{6} \\ + 8\frac{2}{6} \\ \hline \end{array}$ 12. $\begin{array}{r} 5\frac{7}{15} \\ + 2\frac{3}{15} \\ \hline \end{array}$ 13. $\begin{array}{r} 6\frac{12}{25} \\ + 4\frac{11}{25} \\ \hline \end{array}$ 14. $\begin{array}{r} 17\frac{2}{18} \\ + 22\frac{4}{18} \\ \hline \end{array}$

15. $\begin{array}{r} 3\frac{1}{12} \\ 5\frac{3}{12} \\ + 4\frac{5}{12} \\ \hline \end{array}$ 16. $\begin{array}{r} 15\frac{3}{10} \\ 7\frac{1}{10} \\ + 13\frac{1}{10} \\ \hline \end{array}$ 17. $\begin{array}{r} 17\frac{3}{18} \\ 21\frac{2}{18} \\ + 18\frac{7}{18} \\ \hline \end{array}$ 18. $\begin{array}{r} 135\frac{3}{20} \\ 226\frac{7}{20} \\ + 148\frac{5}{20} \\ \hline \end{array}$

19. $\begin{array}{r} 2\frac{2}{7} \\ 1\frac{3}{7} \\ + 6\frac{1}{7} \\ \hline \end{array}$ 20. $\begin{array}{r} 21\frac{1}{12} \\ 7\frac{4}{12} \\ + 34\frac{1}{12} \\ \hline \end{array}$ 21. $\begin{array}{r} 13\frac{3}{16} \\ 35\frac{3}{16} \\ + 23\frac{6}{16} \\ \hline \end{array}$ 22. $\begin{array}{r} 307\frac{7}{30} \\ 156\frac{13}{30} \\ + 212\frac{5}{30} \\ \hline \end{array}$

Apply

Solve these problems.

23. Paula fastened a board $5\frac{3}{16}$ inches long to a board $\frac{3}{16}$ inches long. How long is the new board?

24. A snack recipe calls for $1\frac{1}{8}$ cups of raisins, $1\frac{1}{8}$ cups of unsalted peanuts and $2\frac{5}{8}$ cups of sunflower seeds. How many cups of ingredients are needed?

25. Bill sleeps 9 hours, goes to school 7 hours, plays 3 hours and does homework for 2 hours. What part of a day has Bill used in these activities?

26. A ribbon is $6\frac{1}{2}$ inches long. Is it possible to cut three ribbons each $2\frac{3}{16}$ inches long from the ribbon?

Adding Fractions with Unlike Denominators

Allison is making fruit punch for the school party. After she mixes the orange juice and lime juice, how many liters of punch will she have?

We want to know the total number of liters of punch.

We know that Allison will mix _____ liters of orange juice, and _____ liters of lime juice.

To find the total amount of punch, we add the amount of orange juice and lime juice.

We add _____ and _____.

Rename the fractions as equivalent fractions with the least common denominator.	Add the fractions.	Add the whole numbers. Simplify the fraction if necessary.
$3\frac{1}{3} = 3\frac{2}{6}$ $+\,4\frac{1}{2} = 4\frac{3}{6}$	$3\frac{1}{3} = 3\frac{2}{6}$ $+\,4\frac{1}{2} = 4\frac{3}{6}$ $\frac{5}{6}$	$3\frac{1}{3} = 3\frac{2}{6}$ $+\,4\frac{1}{2} = 4\frac{3}{6}$ $7\frac{5}{6}$

Allison will have _____ liters of punch.

Sometimes adding two fractions results in an improper fraction which can be simplified as a whole or mixed number.

$$\frac{3}{8} + \frac{5}{8} = \frac{8}{8} = 1 \qquad \frac{2}{3} + \frac{5}{6} = \frac{4}{6} + \frac{5}{6} = \frac{9}{6} = 1\frac{3}{6} = 1\frac{1}{2}$$

Getting Started

Add. Simplify answers if necessary.

1. $\frac{3}{5} + \frac{7}{10} =$ _____

2. $\frac{5}{6} + \frac{7}{8} =$ _____

3. $\frac{2}{3} + \frac{5}{6} + \frac{5}{9} =$ _____

4. $6\frac{1}{2}$ $+\,4\frac{1}{3}$

5. $5\frac{1}{8}$ $+\,4\frac{1}{6}$

6. $11\frac{5}{12}$ $+\,\,9\frac{1}{4}$

7. $12\frac{2}{3}$ $+\,16\frac{1}{5}$

Practice

Add. Simplify answers if necessary.

1. $\frac{1}{3} + \frac{5}{6} =$ ____

2. $\frac{5}{8} + \frac{3}{4} =$ ____

3. $\frac{5}{10} + \frac{1}{2} =$ ____

4. $\frac{5}{8} + \frac{7}{12} =$ ____

5. $\frac{5}{6} + \frac{5}{9} =$ ____

6. $\frac{3}{4} + \frac{5}{8} + \frac{9}{16} =$ ____

7. $\frac{3}{7} + \frac{2}{3} =$ ____

8. $\frac{3}{4} + \frac{11}{12} =$ ____

9. $\frac{11}{16} + \frac{2}{4} + \frac{7}{8} =$ ____

10. $5\frac{3}{5}$
$+ 3\frac{3}{15}$
_____

11. $7\frac{3}{4}$
$+ 6\frac{1}{8}$
_____

12. $9\frac{3}{8}$
$+ 9\frac{4}{16}$
_____

13. $7\frac{3}{4}$
$+ 8\frac{1}{6}$
_____

14. $12\frac{1}{4}$
$+ 7\frac{5}{12}$
_____

15. $10\frac{2}{3}$
$+ 15\frac{1}{5}$
_____

16. $9\frac{1}{3}$
$+ 16\frac{1}{2}$
_____

17. $14\frac{2}{9}$
$+ 8\frac{1}{6}$
_____

18. $16\frac{5}{12}$
$+ 10\frac{3}{8}$
_____

19. $21\frac{3}{10}$
$+ 36\frac{1}{2}$
_____

20. $47\frac{1}{3}$
$+ 39\frac{3}{8}$
_____

21. $28\frac{7}{15}$
$+ 82\frac{3}{10}$
_____

Apply

Solve these problems.

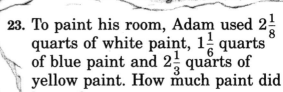

22. Marti went cross-country skiing. She passed the first checkpoint at $\frac{7}{10}$ of a mile and the second checkpoint $\frac{9}{10}$ of a mile later. She stopped at the third checkpoint after $\frac{8}{10}$ of a mile more. How far had Marti skied?

23. To paint his room, Adam used $2\frac{1}{8}$ quarts of white paint, $1\frac{1}{6}$ quarts of blue paint and $2\frac{1}{3}$ quarts of yellow paint. How much paint did he use?

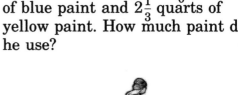

EXCURSION

Find the missing numbers. None of the fractions are improper.

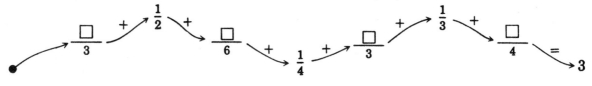

Adding Mixed Numbers with Regrouping

Sidney's goal is to improve his study habits. He kept track of the time he spent on homework last week. How many hours did he spend on his homework?

We want to know the number of hours Sidney worked.

We know that on Monday he worked ____ hours; on

Tuesday, ____ hours; and on Wednesday, ____ hours.

To find his total homework time, we add the

number of hours he worked each day. We add ____,

____ and ____.

Rename the fractions as equivalent fractions with the least common denominator.	Add the fractions.	Add the whole numbers.	Simplify the answer.
$2\frac{3}{4} = 2\frac{3}{4}$ $1\frac{1}{2} = 1\frac{2}{4}$ $+\, 3\frac{1}{2} = 3\frac{2}{4}$	$2\frac{3}{4}$ $1\frac{2}{4}$ $+\, 3\frac{2}{4}$ $\overline{\frac{7}{4}}$	$2\frac{3}{4}$ $1\frac{2}{4}$ $+\, 3\frac{2}{4}$ $\overline{6\frac{7}{4}}$	$\frac{7}{4} = 1\frac{3}{4}$ $6\frac{7}{4} = 6 + 1\frac{3}{4} = 7\frac{3}{4}$

Sidney spent ____ hours on his homework.

Getting Started

Add. Simplify answers if necessary.

1. $3\frac{2}{3}$
$+\, 4\frac{1}{3}$

2. $5\frac{3}{5}$
$+\, 6\frac{2}{3}$

3. $3\frac{1}{2}$
$4\frac{2}{3}$
$+\, 5\frac{1}{4}$

4. $9\frac{2}{3}$
$6\frac{3}{4}$
$+\, 5\frac{1}{6}$

Copy and add.

5. $3\frac{4}{5} + 8\frac{2}{3}$

6. $7\frac{5}{6} + 15\frac{3}{8}$

7. $25\frac{1}{2} + 29\frac{3}{5} + 52\frac{3}{4}$

Practice

Add. Simplify answers if necessary.

1. $4\frac{1}{2}$
   $+ 5\frac{1}{3}$

2. $5\frac{3}{4}$
   $+ 7\frac{1}{4}$

3. $6\frac{3}{4}$
   $+ 4\frac{5}{8}$

4. $8\frac{2}{3}$
   $+ 6\frac{5}{8}$

5. $17\frac{5}{8}$
   $15\frac{5}{6}$
   $+ 4\frac{3}{4}$

6. $21\frac{2}{3}$
   $8\frac{1}{2}$
   $+ 5\frac{5}{6}$

7. $26\frac{3}{8}$
   $14\frac{5}{6}$
   $+ 23\frac{3}{4}$

8. $18\frac{7}{8}$
   $46\frac{5}{6}$
   $+ 38\frac{3}{4}$

Copy and Do

9. $7\frac{5}{8} + 9\frac{3}{4}$

10. $6\frac{7}{12} + 9\frac{5}{6}$

11. $8\frac{2}{3} + 9\frac{1}{2}$

12. $9\frac{7}{12} + 8\frac{5}{8}$

13. $8\frac{3}{8} + 5\frac{2}{3}$

14. $11\frac{9}{16} + 12\frac{7}{8}$

15. $25\frac{7}{9} + 18\frac{11}{12}$

16. $27\frac{2}{5} + 14\frac{2}{3}$

17. $21\frac{6}{7} + 83\frac{4}{5}$

18. $9\frac{1}{6} + 5\frac{3}{4} + 8\frac{1}{2}$

19. $12\frac{2}{3} + 8\frac{3}{4} + 9\frac{1}{6}$

20. $42\frac{1}{2} + 29\frac{5}{8} + 47\frac{5}{6}$

Apply

Solve these problems.

21. The world's longest piece of spaghetti was $2\frac{3}{4}$ feet. Mr. O'Malley made a piece of spaghetti $3\frac{1}{2}$ feet longer. How long is the new spaghetti?

22. A recipe for whole grain bread uses $3\frac{3}{5}$ cups of wheat flour and $2\frac{3}{4}$ cups of rye flour. How much flour is used in the recipe?

23. A railroad crew repaired $3\frac{1}{4}$ miles of track on Monday, $5\frac{2}{3}$ miles on Wednesday and $2\frac{5}{6}$ miles on Friday. How many miles of track did the crew repair during the week?

24. Mr. Peterson fills his car with gasoline each Monday. How many gallons of gasoline did he buy in December?

Monday, December 6 $11\frac{3}{10}$ gallons

Monday, December 13 $10\frac{2}{5}$ gallons

Monday, December 20 $12\frac{7}{10}$ gallons

Monday, December 27 $11\frac{3}{5}$ gallons

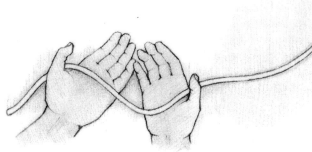

Subtracting Fractions with Like Denominators

Tashiki is preparing a snack for the all-day hike. He has only $1\frac{1}{8}$ pounds of pretzels. How many more pounds will he need?

Nuts	$2\frac{2}{8}$ pounds
Pretzels	$3\frac{3}{8}$ pounds
Raisins	$\frac{3}{8}$ pounds

We want to know how many more pounds of pretzels Tashiki needs.

We know that he needs ____ pounds for the Trail

Mix, and that he has only ____ pounds.

To find the amount he still needs, we subtract the amount he has from the amount required by the

recipe. We subtract ____ from ____.

Subtract the fractions. Write the difference over the denominator.	Subtract the whole numbers. Simplify the fraction if necessary.

$$3\frac{3}{8}$$
$$\underline{-\,1\frac{1}{8}}$$
$$\frac{2}{8}$$

$3 - 1 = 2$

$$3\frac{3}{8}$$
$$\underline{-\,1\frac{1}{8}}$$
$$2\frac{2}{8} = 2\frac{1}{4}$$

Tashiki needs ____ more pounds of pretzels.

Getting Started

Subtract. Simplify answers if necessary.

1. $\frac{5}{9} - \frac{3}{9} =$ ____

2. $\frac{7}{12} - \frac{3}{12} =$ ____

3. $\frac{3}{4} - \frac{1}{4} =$ ____

4. $\quad 6\frac{5}{6}$
$\quad \underline{-\,4\frac{1}{6}}$

5. $\quad 59\frac{7}{10}$
$\quad \underline{-\,26\frac{2}{10}}$

6. $\quad 17\frac{2}{3}$
$\quad \underline{-\,8\frac{1}{3}}$

7. $\quad 527\frac{7}{16}$
$\quad \underline{-\,214\frac{3}{16}}$

Practice

Subtract. Simplify answers if necessary.

1. $\frac{9}{16} - \frac{7}{16} =$ _____

2. $\frac{5}{7} - \frac{3}{7} =$ _____

3. $\frac{5}{9} - \frac{2}{9} =$ _____

4. $\frac{19}{24} - \frac{15}{24} =$ _____

5. $\frac{5}{6} - \frac{1}{6}$ _____

6. $\frac{9}{10} - \frac{5}{10} =$ _____

7. $\begin{array}{r} 8\frac{3}{4} \\ - 3\frac{1}{4} \\ \hline \end{array}$

8. $\begin{array}{r} 12\frac{7}{8} \\ - 7\frac{3}{8} \\ \hline \end{array}$

9. $\begin{array}{r} 16\frac{7}{10} \\ - 9\frac{2}{10} \\ \hline \end{array}$

10. $\begin{array}{r} 13\frac{4}{5} \\ - 6\frac{3}{5} \\ \hline \end{array}$

11. $\begin{array}{r} 35\frac{11}{12} \\ - 12\frac{5}{12} \\ \hline \end{array}$

12. $\begin{array}{r} 42\frac{14}{16} \\ - 29\frac{4}{16} \\ \hline \end{array}$

13. $\begin{array}{r} 39\frac{17}{20} \\ - 26\frac{2}{20} \\ \hline \end{array}$

14. $\begin{array}{r} 71\frac{5}{8} \\ - 46\frac{3}{8} \\ \hline \end{array}$

15. $\begin{array}{r} 123\frac{2}{3} \\ - 97\frac{1}{3} \\ \hline \end{array}$

16. $\begin{array}{r} 206\frac{9}{10} \\ - 167\frac{3}{10} \\ \hline \end{array}$

17. $\begin{array}{r} 614\frac{17}{20} \\ - 246\frac{9}{20} \\ \hline \end{array}$

18. $\begin{array}{r} 531\frac{22}{24} \\ - 345\frac{5}{24} \\ \hline \end{array}$

Apply

Solve these problems.

19. Dan spends $3\frac{1}{6}$ hours working in his garden every Saturday. During the week, he works $10\frac{5}{6}$ hours in his garden. How much longer does Dan work in his garden during the week than on Saturday?

20. The largest pumpkin at the country fair weighs $56\frac{7}{8}$ pounds. The smallest weighs $7\frac{5}{8}$ pounds. How much heavier than the smallest pumpkin is the largest pumpkin?

Use the chart to answer questions 21 and 22.

21. How much farther does Angie run than Margo?

22. Lola runs $3\frac{1}{10}$ miles farther than Margo. How much less than Pat does Lola run?

Running Distances	
Pat	$26\frac{3}{10}$ miles
Margo	$18\frac{5}{10}$ miles
Angie	$25\frac{7}{10}$ miles

Subtracting Fractions with Unlike Denominators

Duncan is feeding the chickens on his uncle's farm. When he started there were $4\frac{1}{2}$ buckets of chicken feed. How much feed has he used?

We want to know how much chicken feed Duncan has used. We know that he started

with ____ buckets of feed, and he has ____

buckets left.

To find the amount used, we subtract the amount left from the original amount.

We subtract ____ from ____.

| Rename the fractions as equivalent fractions with the least common denominator. | Subtract the fractions. | Subtract the whole numbers. Simplify the fraction if needed. |

$$4\frac{1}{2} = 4\frac{2}{4}$$
$$-1\frac{1}{4} = 1\frac{1}{4}$$

$$4\frac{1}{2} = 4\frac{2}{4}$$
$$-1\frac{1}{4} = 1\frac{1}{4}$$
$$\frac{1}{4}$$

$$4\frac{1}{2} = 4\frac{2}{4}$$
$$-1\frac{1}{4} = 1\frac{1}{4}$$
$$3\frac{1}{4}$$

Duncan has used ____ buckets of feed.

Getting Started

Subtract.

1. $15\frac{5}{8}$
    $-\ 7\frac{1}{3}$

2. $87\frac{2}{3}$
    $-39\frac{1}{6}$

3. $533\frac{3}{4}$
    $-526\frac{3}{5}$

4. $51\frac{5}{6}$
    -17

Copy and subtract.

5. $\frac{7}{8} - \frac{1}{4}$

6. $\frac{5}{6} - \frac{1}{2}$

7. $\frac{9}{10} - \frac{6}{15}$

Practice

Subtract.

1. $9\frac{4}{5}$
   $-6\frac{3}{10}$

2. $11\frac{3}{4}$
   $-5\frac{2}{3}$

3. $14\frac{7}{9}$
   $-7\frac{1}{3}$

4. $17\frac{2}{3}$
   $-9\frac{1}{5}$

5. $26\frac{5}{16}$
   -14

6. $47\frac{9}{10}$
   $-28\frac{5}{6}$

7. $36\frac{2}{3}$
   $-18\frac{5}{12}$

8. $82\frac{5}{6}$
   $-46\frac{7}{12}$

9. $112\frac{2}{3}$
   $-66\frac{3}{5}$

10. $625\frac{5}{6}$
    $-148\frac{5}{12}$

11. $907\frac{2}{3}$
    $-319\frac{3}{8}$

12. $536\frac{45}{100}$
    $-243\frac{3}{25}$

Copy and Do

13. $\frac{5}{8} - \frac{1}{2}$

14. $\frac{8}{9} - \frac{1}{6}$

15. $\frac{7}{8} - \frac{2}{3}$

16. $\frac{7}{10} - \frac{1}{2}$

17. $\frac{5}{6} - \frac{1}{4}$

18. $\frac{2}{3} - \frac{1}{5}$

Apply

Solve these problems.

19. The drill bit is $1\frac{3}{4}$ inches long. How thick is the wood?

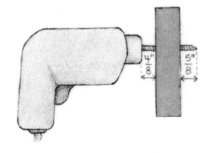

20. This year, workers in the town of Tidyville collected $425\frac{2}{3}$ pounds of newspapers. Last year, they collected $387\frac{1}{4}$ pounds. How much more did the workers collect this year?

EXCURSION

Look for a pattern to help you complete the three problems. Write the next problem in the pattern. Write the answer.

1. $\frac{1}{2} + \frac{1}{4} =$

2. $\frac{1}{2} + \frac{1}{4} + \frac{1}{8} =$

3. $\frac{1}{2} + \frac{1}{4} + \frac{1}{8} + \frac{1}{16} =$

Subtracting Mixed Numbers with Regrouping

Martha is making pottery in art class. She needs $6\frac{1}{4}$ pounds of clay to make six cups. How many more pounds of clay does Martha need?

We want to know how much more clay Martha needs.

We know that she needs _____ pounds of clay, and she has _____ pounds.

To find the difference, we subtract the amount she has from the total amount she needs for the cups.

We subtract _____ from _____.

Regroup the minuend.	Subtract and simplify.

$$6\frac{1}{4} = 5\frac{5}{4}$$
$$-\ 3\frac{3}{4} = 3\frac{3}{4}$$

$$6\frac{1}{4} = 5 + 1 + \frac{1}{4}$$
$$= 5 + \frac{4}{4} + \frac{1}{4}$$
$$= 5\frac{5}{4}$$

$$6\frac{1}{4} = 5\frac{5}{4}$$
$$-\ 3\frac{3}{4} = 3\frac{3}{4}$$
$$2\frac{2}{4} = 2\frac{1}{2}$$

Martha needs _____ more pounds of clay.

Getting Started

Rename each fraction.

1. $7\frac{2}{3} = 6\frac{}{3}$

2. $4\frac{5}{6} = 3\frac{}{6}$

3. $8 = 7\frac{}{4}$

4. $2\frac{1}{2} = 1\frac{}{2}$

Subtract.

5. $\quad 9\frac{3}{8}$
   $-\ 6\frac{5}{8}$

6. $\quad 7$
   $-\ 4\frac{1}{2}$

7. $\quad 23\frac{1}{6}$
   $-\ 17\frac{5}{6}$

8. $\quad 431\frac{1}{7}$
   $-\ 118\frac{5}{7}$

Practice

Subtract.

1. $9\frac{1}{8}$
   $-6\frac{3}{4}$

2. $16\frac{3}{10}$
   $-7\frac{4}{5}$

3. $12\frac{1}{2}$
   $-6\frac{2}{3}$

4. $18\frac{3}{8}$
   $-15\frac{5}{12}$

5. $86\frac{2}{5}$
   $-29\frac{3}{4}$

6. $43\frac{5}{16}$
   $-26\frac{5}{8}$

Copy and Do

7. $7\frac{3}{8} - 2\frac{3}{4}$

8. $24\frac{3}{4} - 9\frac{5}{6}$

9. $28\frac{1}{2} - 19\frac{7}{8}$

10. $1\frac{3}{5} - \frac{3}{10}$

11. $38\frac{2}{7} - 19\frac{3}{5}$

12. $82\frac{1}{3} - 37\frac{3}{4}$

13. $61\frac{1}{2} - 36\frac{2}{3}$

14. $58\frac{1}{9} - 16\frac{5}{12}$

15. $75\frac{3}{8} - 66\frac{5}{6}$

16. $374\frac{1}{5} - 196\frac{2}{3}$

17. $621\frac{2}{3} - 438\frac{7}{8}$

18. $901\frac{4}{15} - 728\frac{7}{10}$

Apply

Solve these problems.

19. Audrey worked $14\frac{1}{2}$ hours one week and $9\frac{3}{5}$ hours the next week. How many more hours did Audrey work the first week than the second?

20. Miguel filled his gas tank with 15 gallons of gas. On Monday, he used $6\frac{2}{3}$ gallons and on Friday, he used another $3\frac{3}{4}$ gallons. How many gallons does Miguel have left?

EXCURSION

Choose a number from each row. Each number must be from a different column.

Find the sum. _____

Choose again. _____

What do you find? _____

Try it again.

Columns

$2\frac{3}{4}$	$2\frac{1}{4}$	2	$2\frac{1}{2}$
$2\frac{1}{4}$	$1\frac{3}{4}$	$1\frac{1}{2}$	2
2	$1\frac{1}{2}$	$1\frac{1}{4}$	$1\frac{3}{4}$
$1\frac{1}{2}$	1	$\frac{3}{4}$	$1\frac{1}{4}$

Rows

Subtracting Mixed Numbers with Regrouping

Chuck is cutting ribbons to make award badges. How much ribbon will be left after he cuts a $3\frac{5}{6}$-inch strip?

We want to know how much ribbon will be left.

We know the ribbon is ____ inches long, and Chuck

needs a strip ____ inches long.

To find the amount left, we subtract the length he cuts from the length he started with. We subtract

____ from ____.

Rename the fractions as equivalent fractions with the least common denominator.	Regroup the minuend.	Subtract.

$$5\frac{1}{4} = 5\frac{3}{12}$$
$$-\;3\frac{5}{6} = 3\frac{10}{12}$$

$$5\frac{1}{4} = 5\frac{3}{12} = 4\frac{15}{12}$$
$$-\;3\frac{5}{6} = 3\frac{10}{12} = 3\frac{10}{12}$$

$$5\frac{1}{4} = 5\frac{3}{12} = 4\frac{15}{12}$$
$$-\;3\frac{5}{6} = 3\frac{10}{12} = 3\frac{10}{12}$$
$$1\frac{5}{12}$$

Chuck will have ____ inches of ribbon left.

Getting Started

Subtract.

1. $\quad 7\frac{1}{3}$
   $-\;4\frac{1}{2}$

2. $\quad 8\frac{3}{8}$
   $-\;3\frac{5}{6}$

3. $\quad 12\frac{1}{9}$
   $-\;6\frac{2}{3}$

4. $\quad 26\frac{1}{8}$
   $-\;18\frac{5}{12}$

5. $\quad 58\frac{3}{4}$
   $-\;23\frac{5}{6}$

6. $\quad 436\frac{3}{5}$
   $-\;189\frac{7}{10}$

Copy and subtract.

7. $9\frac{1}{5} - 2\frac{7}{10}$

8. $60\frac{3}{8} - 27\frac{9}{10}$

9. $703\frac{2}{9} - 677\frac{5}{6}$

131

Practice

Rename each fraction.

1. $6\frac{3}{4} = 5\frac{}{4}$

2. $9\frac{2}{3} = 8\frac{}{3}$

3. $5\frac{5}{9} = 4\frac{}{9}$

4. $6 = 5\frac{}{6}$

5. $7\frac{5}{8} = 6\frac{}{8}$

6. $4\frac{5}{12} = 3\frac{}{12}$

7. $12\frac{5}{7} = 11\frac{}{7}$

8. $1\frac{3}{5} = \frac{}{5}$

Subtract.

9.
$$9\frac{1}{4}$$
$$-\,7\frac{3}{4}$$

10.
$$8$$
$$-\,5\frac{7}{10}$$

11.
$$16\frac{3}{8}$$
$$-\,\,9\frac{5}{8}$$

12.
$$25\frac{2}{5}$$
$$-\,18\frac{3}{5}$$

13.
$$23\frac{1}{3}$$
$$-\,16\frac{2}{3}$$

14.
$$86\frac{5}{11}$$
$$-\,49\frac{7}{11}$$

15.
$$128\frac{1}{16}$$
$$-\,\,92\frac{13}{16}$$

16.
$$309\frac{1}{12}$$
$$-\,153\frac{11}{12}$$

Apply

Solve these problems.

17. At the track meet, Alexa jumped $14\frac{1}{4}$ feet. Marlene jumped $11\frac{3}{4}$ feet. How much farther than Marlene did Alexa jump?

18. Dex wants to collect 100 pounds of aluminum cans. He has made two collection trips. On the first trip he collected $36\frac{3}{8}$ pounds and on the second, he collected $42\frac{5}{8}$ pounds. How many more pounds of aluminum cans does he need to reach his goal?

EXCURSION

Study fraction addition on the clock. Complete the addition table using the clock to help find the sums.

$$\frac{1}{5} + \frac{2}{5} = \frac{3}{5}$$

$$\frac{3}{5} + \frac{4}{5} = \frac{2}{5}$$

$$\frac{2}{5} + \frac{3}{5} = 0$$

+	0	$\frac{1}{5}$	$\frac{2}{5}$	$\frac{3}{5}$	$\frac{4}{5}$
0					
$\frac{1}{5}$					
$\frac{2}{5}$					
$\frac{3}{5}$					
$\frac{4}{5}$					

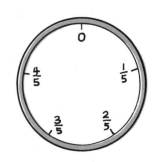

Adding and Subtracting Fractions

Add or subtract. Simplify answers if necessary.

1. $3\frac{1}{4}$
    $+ 4\frac{1}{4}$

2. $8\frac{3}{7}$
    $+ 9\frac{5}{7}$

3. $7\frac{7}{12}$
    $- 5\frac{1}{12}$

4. 8
    $- 2\frac{3}{5}$

5. $12\frac{2}{3}$
    $+ 6\frac{1}{2}$

6. $18\frac{3}{5}$
    $- 11\frac{1}{4}$

7. $62\frac{1}{3}$
    $- 48\frac{2}{3}$

8. $79\frac{3}{4}$
    $+ 26\frac{5}{6}$

9. $61\frac{1}{5}$
    $- 14\frac{3}{10}$

10. $53\frac{2}{3}$
    $- 18\frac{5}{7}$

11. $96\frac{1}{8}$
    $- 48\frac{5}{6}$

12. $43\frac{5}{9}$
    $- 16\frac{5}{6}$

13. $465\frac{1}{2}$
    $- 183\frac{3}{5}$

14. $803\frac{1}{12}$
    $- 675\frac{5}{8}$

15. $721\frac{4}{15}$
    $- 239\frac{7}{10}$

16. $915\frac{2}{3}$
    $- 625\frac{7}{15}$

17. $816\frac{3}{10}$
    $- 177\frac{5}{8}$

18. $279\frac{7}{9}$
    $- 158\frac{4}{5}$

19. $106\frac{3}{8}$
    $- 97\frac{2}{3}$

20. $540\frac{2}{3}$
    $- 215\frac{6}{7}$

Copy and Do

21. $\frac{3}{4} + \frac{2}{3} + \frac{1}{6}$

22. $\frac{1}{2} + \frac{5}{9} + \frac{2}{3}$

23. $\frac{1}{5} + \frac{3}{10} + \frac{7}{15}$

24. $\frac{9}{16} - \frac{1}{6}$

25. $\frac{4}{7} - \frac{2}{5}$

26. $\frac{7}{12} - \frac{3}{16}$

27. $5\frac{2}{3} - 4\frac{3}{5}$

28. $8\frac{7}{8} - 7\frac{1}{6}$

29. $14\frac{1}{3} - 9\frac{4}{5}$

30. $8\frac{1}{2} + 12\frac{5}{8}$

31. $16\frac{2}{9} - \frac{5}{6}$

32. $6\frac{9}{10} + 7\frac{3}{5}$

33. $25\frac{1}{8} - 16\frac{1}{2}$

34. $34\frac{2}{3} - 16\frac{1}{5}$

35. $47\frac{5}{8} + 87\frac{9}{16}$

36. $26\frac{3}{7} + 96\frac{7}{9}$

37. $57\frac{7}{8} - 42\frac{3}{16}$

38. $94 - 87\frac{7}{12}$

39. $124\frac{2}{5} - 86\frac{7}{10}$

40. $836\frac{5}{6} - 429\frac{2}{3}$

41. $415\frac{7}{8} + 329\frac{5}{8}$

42. $607\frac{1}{3} - 498\frac{1}{2}$

43. $943\frac{5}{7} - 485\frac{5}{7}$

44. $821\frac{3}{5} + 468\frac{9}{25}$

133

Apply

Use information from the charts to solve these problems.

Speed in Miles per Hour (MPH)	Miles per Gallon (MPG)
35	24
45	$20\frac{1}{4}$
55	$18\frac{1}{3}$
65	$15\frac{1}{5}$

1. How does the MPG change when the speed is reduced from 45 MPH to 35 MPH?

2. How does the MPG change when the speed is reduced from 65 MPH to 55 MPH?

3. How does the MPG change when the speed is increased from 35 MPH to 65 MPH?

Name of Stock	Yearly High	Yearly Low	Change
ACT	$42\frac{1}{2}$	$36\frac{5}{8}$	?
RPJ	$106\frac{1}{4}$	?	$8\frac{1}{2}$
DCM	$77\frac{3}{8}$	?	$10\frac{3}{4}$
STV	?	$88\frac{7}{8}$	$4\frac{1}{2}$

4. What is the change in ACT stock?

5. What is the yearly low for RPJ stock?

6. What is the yearly low for DCM stock?

7. What is the yearly high for STV stock?

8. How much more did RPJ stock change than STV stock?

9. What is the combined yearly high for both DCM and RPJ stock?

Cases Packed	
Ron	$12\frac{1}{3}$ cases
Al	$9\frac{1}{5}$ cases
Rich	$15\frac{3}{4}$ cases

10. How many cases in all did the boys pack?

11. How many more cases did Rich pack than Al?

12. How many more cases did Al and Rich pack together than Ron?

13. How many more cases did Rich pack than Ron?

Guessing and Checking

Kerry weighs 15 pounds more than Holly. When they step on the scale together, the scale reads 181 pounds. How much does each weigh?

★ **SEE**

We want to know how much Kerry and Holly each weigh.

We know that Kerry is _____ pounds heavier than Holly.

We know that their total weight is _____ pounds.

★ **PLAN**

Using the facts from the problem we can make a guess of Holly's weight. We add 15 to our guess to get Kerry's weight. We can add the weights of the children to check to see if the total is 181 pounds. Making a list will help us to keep a record and to adjust our guesses.

★ **DO**

Holly's Weight	Kerry's Weight	Total Weight
50	65	115
60	——	——
70	——	——
80	——	——
81	——	——
82	——	——
83	——	——

Holly weighs _____ pounds. Kerry weighs _____ pounds.

★ **CHECK**

We can check our solution to see if it fits with the facts of the problem.

Is Holly's weight plus 15 equal to Kerry's weight? _____ + 15 = _____

Do the two weights add up to 181 pounds? _____ + _____ = _____

135

Apply

1. The numbers 2, 4, 6 are a set of 3 consecutive even numbers. Find a set of 3 consecutive even numbers whose sum is 300.

2. Find a set of 4 consecutive odd numbers whose sum is 304.

3. Find a set of 3 consecutive whole numbers whose sum is 303.

4. The sum of Mark's and Bob's ages is 11. Mark is 10 years older than Bob. How old is each boy?

5. In a collection of quarters and nickels there are three more nickels than quarters. How many nickels are there if the collection is worth $2.25?

6. Sarah is four years younger than Joe. In five years Joe will be twice Sarah's age now. How old are they now?

7. Each letter represents a single digit and the same letter represents the same digit each time. Find the value of each digit.

    SEND
    + MORE
    ‾‾‾‾‾‾
    MONEY

8. Pete counted the chickens and pigs in his grandfather's barn. When he counted the heads, he got 20. When he counted the legs, he got 64. How many chickens were in the barn?

9. Write fractions to tell what part of a dollar is represented by a penny, a nickel, a dime, a quarter, and a half-dollar. Without adding the 5 fractions, tell why their sum would be less than 1.

10. Heather has some horses. Take away one half, one fourth, and one fifth of Heather's horses, and she would still have 2 horses left. Explain how you can find how many horses Heather actually has now.

11. The sum of two fractions is $\frac{1}{2}$. What can you tell about the fractions?

12. If each of 2 fractions is less than 1, what is the smallest whole number that is greater than their sum?

Calculators and Formulas

Temperature can be measured on the Celsius and Fahrenheit scales. On the Celsius scale, water boils at 100 degrees. On the Fahrenheit scale, water boils at 212 degrees. These two readings are equal to each other. What is the equivalent Fahrenheit reading for the temperature on the bank?

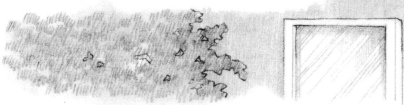

A **formula** is a statement that contains letters that represent numbers. For example, a formula that changes the value of dimes to pennies is written

$$10 \times D = P$$

To find out how many pennies there are in 12 dimes, we replace D by 12 and complete the calculator code.

pennies

$10 \;\boxed{\times}\; 12 \;\boxed{=}\; \boxed{}$

The formula for renaming a Celsius reading to a Fahrenheit reading is written

$$(9 \times C) \div 5 + 32 = F$$

To find out the Fahrenheit equivalent for 20 degrees Celsius, we replace C with 20 and complete the calculator code.

Fahrenheit

$9 \;\boxed{\times}\; \underline{} \;\boxed{\div}\; 5 \;\boxed{+}\; 32 \;\boxed{=}\; \boxed{}$

The temperature at the bank is _____ degrees Fahrenheit.

Getting Started

Use the formula for changing the value of dimes to pennies.

1. 346 dimes =

_____ pennies

2. 457 dimes =

_____ pennies

3. 9,658 dimes =

_____ pennies

Use the formula for changing a Celsius reading to a Fahrenheit reading.

4. 10°C = _____°F

5. 45°C = _____°F

6. 35°C = _____°F

137

Practice

Use the formula for changing the value of dimes to pennies.

1. 808 dimes =

_____ pennies

2. 1,246 dimes =

_____ pennies

3. 7,981 dimes =

_____ pennies

Use the formula for changing a Celsius reading to a Fahrenheit reading.

4. 5°C = _____°F

5. 30°C = _____°F

6. 90°C = _____°F

7. 50°C = _____°F

8. 75°C = _____°F

9. 30°C = _____°F

Apply

Complete each table.

10. Find the distance traveled at 45 miles per hour using the formula rate times time equals distance.

R × T = D distance

45 [×] 2 [=] (90)

T	Time in hours	2	8	15	21	45
D	Distance in miles	90				

11. Find the number of dozens of eggs by dividing the number of single eggs by 12.

S ÷ 12 = D dozens

36 [÷] 12 [=] (3)

S	Number of single eggs	36	144	180	288	768
D	Dozens	3				

EXCURSION

A calculator can help find the sum of two fractions.
Find $\frac{3}{4} + \frac{5}{6}$.
Find the cross products. $3 \times 6 = 18$ $5 \times 4 = 20$
Add. $18 + 20 = 38$
Multiply denominators. $4 \times 6 = 24$
Put the sum over the denominator. $\frac{38}{24}$
Simplify. $1\frac{7}{12}$

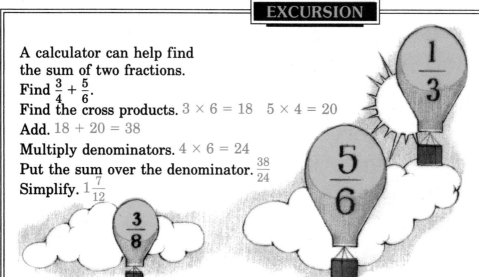

Use a calculator to find these sums.

1. $\frac{1}{2} + \frac{1}{3} =$

2. $\frac{3}{8} + \frac{7}{15} =$

3. $\frac{5}{12} + \frac{5}{6} =$

4. $\frac{9}{16} + \frac{3}{15} =$

Add. Simplify answers if necessary.

1. $\frac{3}{8} + \frac{3}{8} = $ _____

2. $\frac{5}{6} + \frac{4}{6} = $ _____

3. $3\frac{4}{15}$
$+ 5\frac{6}{15}$
_____

4. $9\frac{1}{12}$
$+ 6\frac{5}{12}$
_____

5. $\frac{7}{12} + \frac{3}{4} = $ _____

6. $\frac{2}{3} + \frac{1}{4} = $ _____

7. $8\frac{2}{3}$
$+ 7\frac{1}{5}$
_____

8. $11\frac{2}{9}$
$+ 8\frac{1}{6}$
_____

9. $7\frac{1}{4}$
$+ 8\frac{3}{4}$
_____

10. $16\frac{1}{2}$
$+ 12\frac{3}{4}$
_____

11. $19\frac{2}{3}$
$+ 16\frac{5}{8}$
_____

12. $36\frac{1}{2}$
$18\frac{2}{3}$
$+ 55\frac{3}{4}$
_____

Subtract. Simplify answers if necessary.

13. $\frac{5}{12} - \frac{1}{12} = $ _____

14. $\frac{9}{16} - \frac{7}{16} = $ _____

15. $8\frac{7}{8}$
$- 2\frac{3}{8}$
_____

16. $12\frac{7}{9}$
$- 6\frac{1}{9}$
_____

17. $\frac{5}{16} - \frac{1}{4} = $ _____

18. $\frac{5}{8} - \frac{1}{3} = $ _____

19. $39\frac{4}{5}$
$- 18$
_____

20. $16\frac{2}{3}$
$- 9\frac{5}{8}$
_____

21. $23\frac{1}{5}$
$- 9\frac{3}{5}$
_____

22. 41
$- 16\frac{2}{3}$
_____

23. $79\frac{8}{15}$
$- 48\frac{3}{10}$
_____

24. 63
$- 27\frac{6}{12}$
_____

25. $43\frac{1}{4}$
$- 28\frac{3}{8}$
_____

26. $94\frac{5}{12}$
$- 48\frac{7}{8}$
_____

27. $653\frac{2}{5}$
$- 286\frac{3}{4}$
_____

28. $410\frac{1}{3}$
$- 195\frac{1}{2}$
_____

139

Circle the letter of the correct answer.

1 $n + 9 = 16$
$n = ?$

a 6
b 7
c 8
d NG

2 $n \times 4 = 12$
$n = ?$

a 3
b 8
c 48
d NG

3 $12 \div 4 + 2 = n$
$n = ?$

a 2
b 5
c 11
d NG

4 What is the place value of the 6 in 5,269,384?

a thousands
b ten thousands
c hundred thousands
d NG

5   86,246
   + 64,695

a 140,941
b 150,941
c 151,934
d NG

6 $562.48
   − 296.78

a $265.70
b $267.70
c $334.30
d NG

7 $8.35 × 9

a $72.75
b $74.75
c $75.15
d NG

8   427
   × 38

a 16,226
b 4,697
c 15,226
d NG

9 $440 \div 8$

a 5 R4
b 5 R5
c 50 R5
d NG

10 $28\overline{)7,290}$

a 26
b 26 R1
c 260 R10
d NG

11 $\dfrac{3}{n} = \dfrac{9}{12}$
$n = ?$

a 3
b 4
c 12
d NG

12 Rename in simplest form.
$\dfrac{24}{36}$

a $\dfrac{3}{4}$
b $\dfrac{6}{8}$
c $\dfrac{2}{3}$
d NG

☐ score

140

MULTIPLICATION AND DIVISION OF FRACTIONS

Multiplying Fractions

Margaret is making several batches of biscuits. She will use $\frac{1}{2}$ of the flour in the measuring cup to make the first batch. How much flour will Margaret use in the first batch?

We want to know how much flour Margaret will use.

We know that the measuring cup is _____ full of

flour, and Margaret needs _____ of the flour. To find what part something is of something else, we multiply. The word **of** means times or ×. We multiply to find one half of the amount in the cup.

We multiply _____ by _____.

Multiply the numerators.

Multiply the denominators. Simplify the product if necessary.

$$\frac{1}{2} \times \frac{3}{4} = \frac{1 \times 3}{} = \frac{3}{}$$

$$\frac{1}{2} \times \frac{3}{4} = \frac{1 \times 3}{2 \times 4} = \frac{3}{8}$$

Margaret will use _____ of a cup of flour.

Getting Started

Multiply.

1. $\frac{2}{3} \times \frac{3}{4} =$ _____

2. $\frac{1}{5} \times \frac{3}{8} =$ _____

3. $\frac{5}{6} \times \frac{2}{3} =$ _____

4. $\frac{9}{10} \times \frac{5}{8} =$ _____

5. $\frac{3}{8} \times \frac{3}{5} =$ _____

6. $\frac{1}{2} \times \frac{4}{7} =$ _____

7. $\frac{3}{5} \times \frac{2}{5} \times \frac{1}{2} =$ _____

8. $\frac{1}{3} \times \frac{1}{3} \times \frac{1}{3} =$ _____

Practice

Multiply.

1. $\frac{2}{3} \times \frac{1}{2} =$ _____

2. $\frac{3}{5} \times \frac{4}{7} =$ _____

3. $\frac{3}{8} \times \frac{1}{5} =$ _____

4. $\frac{7}{8} \times \frac{5}{9} =$ _____

5. $\frac{3}{4} \times \frac{3}{8} =$ _____

6. $\frac{3}{8} \times \frac{7}{9} =$ _____

7. $\frac{2}{11} \times \frac{5}{6} =$ _____

8. $\frac{4}{5} \times \frac{3}{10} =$ _____

9. $\frac{1}{10} \times \frac{1}{10} =$ _____

10. $\frac{5}{6} \times \frac{2}{3} =$ _____

11. $\frac{9}{10} \times \frac{1}{3} =$ _____

12. $\frac{1}{4} \times \frac{4}{9} =$ _____

13. $\frac{3}{7} \times \frac{7}{8} =$ _____

14. $\frac{5}{10} \times \frac{4}{5} =$ _____

15. $\frac{6}{7} \times \frac{7}{8} =$ _____

16. $\frac{3}{8} \times \frac{1}{6} =$ _____

17. $\frac{3}{5} \times \frac{4}{7} =$ _____

18. $\frac{5}{8} \times \frac{4}{5} =$ _____

19. $\frac{3}{4} \times \frac{4}{9} =$ _____

20. $\frac{8}{9} \times \frac{5}{7} =$ _____

21. $\frac{2}{3} \times \frac{5}{6} \times \frac{3}{5} =$ _____

22. $\frac{1}{5} \times \frac{2}{3} \times \frac{5}{8} =$ _____

23. $\frac{2}{3} \times \frac{2}{3} \times \frac{2}{3} =$ _____

24. $\frac{2}{5} \times \frac{3}{4} \times \frac{5}{6} =$ _____

Apply

Solve these problems.

25. Pat has a ribbon $\frac{3}{4}$ of a foot long. She needs $\frac{1}{3}$ of the ribbon for a decoration. How long a ribbon does she need?

26. North America makes up about $\frac{1}{6}$ of the world's land surface. The United States is about $\frac{2}{5}$ of North America. What part of the world's surface is the United States?

27. Mr. Ling bought $\frac{5}{6}$ of a pound of swiss cheese at the deli. He ate $\frac{3}{4}$ of it. How much was left?

28. A developer bought 20 acres of land. He built a shopping mall on $12\frac{2}{3}$ acres and a parking lot on $5\frac{1}{4}$ acres. How much land was left?

EXCURSION

Complete the first two magic squares. Remember, in a magic square, the sums of each row, column and diagonal are the same. Subtract each fraction in square 2 from the corresponding fraction in square 1. Write the difference in the corresponding place in square 3. What do you notice?

1.

$3\frac{3}{4}$	$\frac{1}{4}$	$2\frac{3}{4}$
___	___	___
___	___	$\frac{3}{4}$

2.

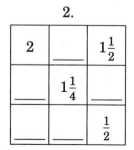

3.

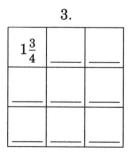

Learning to Factor

Edie was going to walk the $\frac{3}{10}$ of a mile from school to the dentist's office. She stopped at the park to feed the birds. If the park is $\frac{1}{3}$ of the total distance she has to walk, how far is the park from the school?

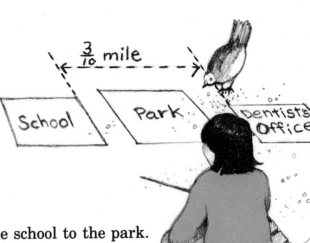

We want to find the distance from the school to the park.

We know that it is _____ of a mile from the school

to the dentist, and it is _____ of this distance from the school to the park. We multiply to find

one third of the distance. We multiply _____ by _____.

We already know one way to multiply fractions. We can take a shortcut by dividing a numerator and a denominator by the same number before we multiply. This is called **factoring.** In this example, we can divide by 3.

$$\frac{\overset{1}{\cancel{3}}}{10} \times \frac{1}{\underset{1}{\cancel{3}}} = \frac{1 \times 1}{10 \times 1} = \frac{1}{10}$$

It is _____ of a mile from the school to the park.

Sometimes we can use the shortcut more than once in a problem.

Factor by 10.	Factor by 3.	Factor by 3 again.

$$\frac{\overset{1}{\cancel{10}}}{21} \times \frac{9}{\underset{3}{\cancel{30}}}$$

$$\frac{\overset{1}{\cancel{10}}}{21} \times \frac{\overset{3}{\cancel{9}}}{\underset{\underset{1}{\cancel{3}}}{\cancel{30}}}$$

$$\frac{\overset{1}{\cancel{10}}}{\underset{7}{\cancel{21}}} \times \frac{\overset{\overset{1}{\cancel{3}}}{\cancel{9}}}{\underset{\underset{1}{\cancel{3}}}{\cancel{30}}} = \frac{1}{7}$$

Getting Started

Multiply. Factor wherever possible.

1. $\frac{4}{5} \times \frac{3}{4} =$

2. $\frac{5}{6} \times \frac{4}{5} =$

3. $\frac{7}{8} \times \frac{4}{9} =$

4. $\frac{2}{3} \times \frac{9}{10} =$

5. $\frac{7}{10} \times \frac{5}{8} =$

6. $\frac{3}{8} \times \frac{7}{12} =$

7. $\frac{9}{16} \times \frac{2}{3} =$

8. $\frac{5}{14} \times \frac{21}{25} \times \frac{10}{15} =$

143

Practice

Multiply. Factor wherever possible.

1. $\frac{4}{5} \times \frac{3}{4} =$
2. $\frac{5}{6} \times \frac{7}{10} =$
3. $\frac{2}{3} \times \frac{9}{10} =$
4. $\frac{5}{8} \times \frac{6}{15} =$

5. $\frac{3}{7} \times \frac{5}{9} =$
6. $\frac{4}{9} \times \frac{3}{10} =$
7. $\frac{6}{15} \times \frac{20}{27} =$
8. $\frac{3}{10} \times \frac{5}{7} =$

9. $\frac{8}{15} \times \frac{9}{10} =$
10. $\frac{3}{4} \times \frac{5}{6} =$
11. $\frac{7}{12} \times \frac{9}{14} =$
12. $\frac{5}{16} \times \frac{8}{9} =$

13. $\frac{5}{8} \times \frac{1}{10} =$
14. $\frac{15}{22} \times \frac{11}{20} =$
15. $\frac{5}{12} \times \frac{8}{15} =$
16. $\frac{10}{21} \times \frac{14}{15} =$

17. $\frac{9}{16} \times \frac{8}{15} =$
18. $\frac{3}{20} \times \frac{15}{21} =$
19. $\frac{5}{18} \times \frac{12}{25} =$
20. $\frac{10}{11} \times \frac{11}{16} =$

21. $\frac{8}{15} \times \frac{7}{20} =$
22. $\frac{1}{5} \times \frac{49}{50} \times \frac{15}{21} =$
23. $\frac{5}{6} \times \frac{18}{75} \times \frac{10}{27} =$
24. $\frac{7}{15} \times \frac{25}{28} \times \frac{49}{100} =$

Apply

Solve these problems.

25. Kimo has planted vegetables in $\frac{2}{9}$ of his garden. Of the vegetables, $\frac{3}{4}$ are carrots. What part of the whole garden is planted with carrots?

26. The milk container was $\frac{9}{10}$ full. Emmy drank $\frac{1}{3}$ of the milk in the container. What part of the milk was left?

27. Tobor the Robot uses $\frac{9}{16}$ of a gallon of oil each day to remove its squeaks. So far today, it has used $\frac{1}{4}$ of a gallon. How much more oil will it use today?

28. Maureen's gas tank was $\frac{7}{8}$ full. When she next looked at the gas gauge, it showed the tank was $\frac{1}{4}$ full. What part of the tank had she used?

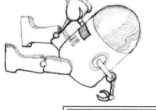

EXCURSION

Use these fractions to make each leg of the magic triangle add up to 1.

$$\frac{1}{20}, \frac{1}{10}, \frac{3}{20}, \frac{1}{5}, \frac{1}{4}, \frac{3}{10}, \frac{7}{20}, \frac{2}{5}, \frac{9}{20}$$

____

____   ____

____   ONE   ____

____   ____   ____

Multiplying Mixed Numbers and Fractions

Mr. Jerome is putting a brick pathway $4\frac{1}{2}$ bricks wide in his yard. Each brick is $9\frac{1}{3}$ inches wide. How wide is the pathway?

We want to know the width of the pathway in inches.

We know that the pathway is ____ bricks wide, and

each brick is ____ inches wide.

To find the total width, we multiply the number of bricks wide the pathway is, by the width of each

brick. We multiply ____ by ____.

Rename the numbers as improper fractions.	Multiply the fractions. Factor wherever possible.

$$4\frac{1}{2} \times 9\frac{1}{3}$$
$$\downarrow \quad \downarrow$$
$$\frac{9}{2} \times \frac{28}{3}$$

$$\overset{3}{\underset{1}{\cancel{\frac{9}{2}}}} \times \overset{14}{\underset{1}{\cancel{\frac{28}{3}}}} = \frac{42}{1} = 42$$

The pathway is ____ inches wide.

Getting Started

Multiply.

1. $\frac{3}{4} \times 3\frac{1}{5} =$ _____

2. $6\frac{1}{4} \times \frac{3}{5} =$ _____

3. $24 \times \frac{2}{3} =$ _____

4. $2\frac{5}{8} \times 1\frac{1}{7} =$ _____

5. $\frac{4}{5} \times 100 =$ _____

6. $5\frac{1}{3} \times 5\frac{1}{4} =$ _____

7. $\frac{3}{8} \times 2\frac{2}{3} \times 93 =$ _____

8. $1\frac{1}{2} \times 5\frac{1}{3} \times 1\frac{1}{8} =$ _____

9. $3\frac{1}{8} \times 6\frac{2}{3} \times 24 =$ _____

Copy and multiply.

10. $\frac{2}{3} \times 150$

11. $4 \times 5\frac{5}{6} \times 3$

12. $2\frac{1}{2} \times 3\frac{1}{3} \times 4\frac{1}{8}$

145

Practice

Multiply.

1. $\frac{5}{6} \times 1\frac{1}{10} =$ _____

2. $4\frac{1}{5} \times \frac{3}{7} =$ _____

3. $\frac{5}{8} \times 64 =$ _____

4. $3\frac{1}{3} \times 1\frac{1}{5} =$ _____

5. $6\frac{1}{4} \times 2\frac{2}{5} =$ _____

6. $9\frac{1}{3} \times 2\frac{1}{4} =$ _____

7. $7\frac{1}{3} \times 2\frac{5}{6} =$ _____

8. $3\frac{1}{8} \times 1\frac{3}{10} =$ _____

9. $3\frac{7}{10} \times 4\frac{1}{6} =$ _____

10. $6\frac{2}{3} \times 4\frac{3}{8} =$ _____

11. $15\frac{3}{4} \times 2\frac{4}{7} =$ _____

12. $2\frac{7}{9} \times 2\frac{7}{10} =$ _____

13. $9\frac{3}{8} \times 5\frac{1}{5} =$ _____

14. $6\frac{3}{10} \times 2\frac{1}{9} =$ _____

15. $3\frac{2}{3} \times \frac{3}{22} =$ _____

Copy and Do

16. $\frac{4}{9} \times 450$

17. $5\frac{1}{4} \times 2\frac{2}{7}$

18. $1\frac{3}{5} \times \frac{10}{11}$

19. $2\frac{1}{4} \times 9\frac{1}{3}$

20. $2\frac{2}{5} \times 2\frac{1}{2}$

21. $6\frac{2}{3} \times 2\frac{5}{8}$

22. $\frac{2}{3} \times 12 \times 2\frac{1}{4}$

23. $3\frac{1}{3} \times 1\frac{1}{8} \times 2\frac{2}{5}$

24. $1\frac{1}{5} \times \frac{7}{10} \times 2\frac{1}{12}$

25. $1\frac{1}{14} \times 1\frac{1}{2} \times 2\frac{2}{3}$

26. $\frac{3}{4} \times 1\frac{7}{9} \times \frac{3}{4}$

27. $6 \times 2\frac{1}{12} \times 8$

28. $1\frac{2}{5} \times 1\frac{5}{28} \times 3\frac{3}{4}$

29. $7\frac{1}{9} \times 1\frac{15}{16} \times \frac{3}{7}$

30. $3\frac{3}{5} \times 1\frac{1}{3} \times 1\frac{7}{8}$

Apply

Solve these problems.

31. The gravity on the moon is $\frac{1}{6}$ of the gravity on the earth. If a person weighs 180 pounds on the earth, how much will that person weigh on the moon?

32. A recipe calls for $2\frac{3}{4}$ cups of white flour and $3\frac{1}{2}$ cups of whole wheat flour. How much flour will be needed to make the recipe $1\frac{3}{5}$ times larger?

33. Mr. Williams earned $2,844 in November. How much did he spend on food and rent?

34. How much more did Mr. Williams spend for rent and other items than on food?

November Pay

146

Using Reciprocals

When the product of two numbers is one, the numbers are called **reciprocals** of each other. What are the reciprocals of $\frac{2}{3}$, $2\frac{1}{4}$ and 5?

To find the reciprocal of a fraction, we exchange the positions of the numerator and the denominator.

Fraction	Reciprocal	Check
$\frac{2}{3}$ $\longrightarrow$	$\frac{3}{2}$	$\frac{2}{3} \times \frac{3}{2} = \frac{6}{6} = 1$

To find the reciprocal of a mixed number or whole number, first name it as an improper fraction.

Mixed Number	Improper Fraction	Reciprocal	Check
$2\frac{1}{4}$ $\longrightarrow$	$\frac{9}{4}$ $\longrightarrow$	$\frac{4}{9}$	$\frac{9}{4} \times \frac{4}{9} = \frac{36}{36} = 1$

Whole Number	Improper Fraction	Reciprocal	Check
5 $\longrightarrow$	$\frac{5}{1}$ $\longrightarrow$	$\frac{1}{5}$	$\frac{5}{1} \times \frac{1}{5} = \frac{5}{5} = 1$

The reciprocals of $\frac{2}{3}$, $2\frac{1}{4}$ and 5 are ____, ____ and ____.

Getting Started

Write the reciprocal.

1. $\frac{5}{8}$
2. $\frac{11}{3}$
3. $2\frac{1}{5}$
4. 9
5. $3\frac{1}{3}$

Write the missing factors.

6. $\frac{3}{8} \times$ ____ $= 1$
7. $4\frac{1}{2} \times$ ____ $= 1$
8. $3 \times$ ____ $\times 5 = 1$

Practice

Write the reciprocal.

1. $\frac{7}{8}$ 　　　　 2. $2\frac{1}{3}$ 　　　　 3. 7 　　　　 4. $4\frac{1}{8}$ 　　　　 5. $\frac{1}{9}$

6. $\frac{5}{9}$ 　　　　 7. 12 　　　　 8. $\frac{17}{100}$ 　　　　 9. 1 　　　　 10. $6\frac{1}{4}$

11. $\frac{5}{3}$ 　　　　 12. $\frac{9}{10}$ 　　　　 13. 8 　　　　 14. $9\frac{3}{8}$ 　　　　 15. 69

16. $\frac{3}{110}$ 　　　　 17. $4\frac{3}{4}$ 　　　　 18. $\frac{15}{4}$ 　　　　 19. 14 　　　　 20. $\frac{3}{17}$

21. 75 　　　　 22. $\frac{19}{2}$ 　　　　 23. $15\frac{2}{3}$ 　　　　 24. $\frac{15}{16}$ 　　　　 25. $6\frac{7}{9}$

Write the missing factors.

26. $\frac{2}{3} \times \underline{\hspace{0.7cm}} = 1$ 　　　　 27. $\underline{\hspace{0.7cm}} \times \frac{4}{5} = 1$ 　　　　 28. $2\frac{1}{2} \times \underline{\hspace{0.7cm}} = 1$

29. $\underline{\hspace{0.7cm}} \times 7\frac{1}{2} = 1$ 　　　　 30. $2\frac{1}{3} \times \underline{\hspace{0.7cm}} = 1$ 　　　　 31. $4\frac{2}{3} \times \underline{\hspace{0.7cm}} = 1$

32. $\underline{\hspace{0.7cm}} \times 6 = 1$ 　　　　 33. $\frac{3}{8} \times \underline{\hspace{0.7cm}} = 1$ 　　　　 34. $\underline{\hspace{0.7cm}} \times \frac{2}{5} = 1$

35. $2\frac{9}{10} \times \underline{\hspace{0.7cm}} = 1$ 　　　　 36. $\underline{\hspace{0.7cm}} \times 15 = 1$ 　　　　 37. $\underline{\hspace{0.7cm}} \times 6\frac{2}{3} = 1$

38. $\frac{3}{4} \times \underline{\hspace{0.7cm}} = 1$ 　　　　 39. $8 \times 7 \times \underline{\hspace{0.7cm}} = 1$ 　　　　 40. $2\frac{1}{3} \times \underline{\hspace{0.7cm}} \times \frac{3}{7} = 4$

41. $7 \times 5 \times \underline{\hspace{0.7cm}} = 1$ 　　　　 42. $3 \times \underline{\hspace{0.7cm}} \times 4 = 1$ 　　　　 43. $\underline{\hspace{0.7cm}} \times \frac{5}{3} \times 6 = 1$

EXCURSION

These cards are face up on a table.

1. Turn over two cards whose difference is $\frac{1}{2}$.

2. Turn over two cards whose sum is $\frac{39}{40}$.

3. Find the product of the two remaining cards.

1. Turn the cards face up again.

2. Turn over two cards whose product is $\frac{3}{7}$.

3. Turn over two cards whose product is less than $\frac{1}{4}$.

4. Find the product of the two remaining cards.

Dividing Fractions

Nick is cutting a board to make book ends. How many pieces $\frac{1}{3}$ of a foot long, can he cut from the board?

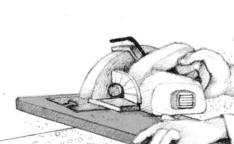

We want to know how many equal-sized pieces Nick can cut.

We know that the length of the board is _____ feet,

and each piece he cuts is _____ of a foot long.

To find the number of pieces, we divide the length of the board by the length of each piece. We divide

_____ by _____.

To divide by a fraction, we multiply the dividend by the reciprocal of the divisor. Remember to factor where possible.

$$\overset{\text{divisor}}{\underset{\text{dividend}}{6}} \div \overset{\downarrow}{\frac{1}{3}} = \frac{6}{1} \times \overset{\text{reciprocal}}{\frac{3}{1}} = 18$$

Nick can cut _____ pieces of wood.

Getting Started

Divide.

1. $\frac{1}{5} \div \frac{2}{3} =$

2. $9 \div \frac{1}{6} =$

3. $7 \div \frac{3}{4} =$

4. $\frac{3}{8} \div \frac{1}{4} =$

5. $\frac{5}{8} \div \frac{1}{2} =$

6. $\frac{7}{12} \div \frac{5}{8} =$

7. $\frac{3}{5} \div \frac{9}{10} =$

8. $\frac{9}{10} \div \frac{3}{5} =$

9. $\frac{7}{11} \div \frac{3}{7} =$

149

Practice

Divide.

1. $\frac{1}{8} \div \frac{2}{3} =$

2. $\frac{5}{8} \div \frac{5}{9} =$

3. $\frac{5}{6} \div \frac{2}{9} =$

4. $25 \div \frac{1}{3} =$

5. $\frac{5}{12} \div \frac{2}{3} =$

6. $\frac{3}{7} \div \frac{6}{7} =$

7. $8 \div \frac{4}{5} =$

8. $\frac{9}{20} \div \frac{6}{15} =$

9. $\frac{9}{16} \div \frac{3}{4} =$

10. $12 \div \frac{8}{9} =$

11. $\frac{5}{6} \div \frac{1}{2} =$

12. $\frac{5}{6} \div \frac{1}{3} =$

13. $\frac{3}{10} \div \frac{11}{15} =$

14. $\frac{5}{12} \div \frac{15}{16} =$

15. $6 \div \frac{2}{3} =$

16. $\frac{3}{8} \div \frac{5}{6} =$

17. $\frac{7}{16} \div \frac{7}{10} =$

18. $\frac{4}{5} \div \frac{8}{9} =$

19. $\frac{4}{15} \div \frac{3}{10} =$

20. $15 \div \frac{5}{8} =$

21. $\frac{4}{9} \div \frac{2}{3} =$

22. $\frac{7}{8} \div \frac{7}{8} =$

23. $\frac{5}{12} \div \frac{7}{16} =$

24. $\frac{5}{24} \div \frac{15}{16} =$

Apply

Solve these problems.

25. Nina works at the Peanut Emporium. She is putting peanuts in $\frac{3}{4}$-pound boxes. How many boxes will Nina need for 18 pounds of peanuts?

26. Henry has 200 baseball cards. He gave $\frac{1}{5}$ of them to his brother. Then he gave $\frac{1}{4}$ of the remaining cards to his sister. How many cards does Henry have left?

27. On a map, each $\frac{3}{8}$ inch represents one mile. If the distance between two towns on the map is $\frac{3}{4}$ inches, how far apart are the towns?

28. One glass of milk fills $\frac{3}{4}$ of a pitcher. How many glasses of milk can 6 pitchers hold?

EXCURSION

What fraction does each letter represent?

A = _____   B = _____   C = _____   D = _____

The rectangle is 1 unit. Find:

A + B   A × B

B − C   C ÷ B

A × C ÷ D

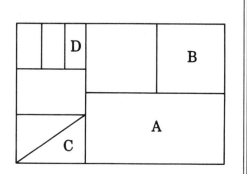

150

Dividing Mixed Numbers

The Continental Railway crew must repair $13\frac{3}{4}$ miles of track this week. If they are to meet this goal, how many miles of track will the crew have to fix each day?

Day	Miles
Monday	
Tuesday	
Wednesday	
Thursday	
Friday	

We want to know how many miles of track should be repaired each day.

We know that the Continental crew must repair

_____ miles of track in _____ days.

To find how many miles the crew will have to repair in one day, we divide the miles of track to be

repaired by the number of days. We divide _____ by _____.

Rename the numbers as improper fractions.	Multiply by the reciprocal of the divisor. Factor wherever possible.

$$13\frac{3}{4} \div 5$$
$$\downarrow \qquad \downarrow$$
$$\frac{55}{4} \div \frac{5}{1}$$

$$\frac{\overset{11}{\cancel{55}}}{4} \times \frac{1}{\underset{1}{\cancel{5}}} = \frac{11}{4} = 2\frac{3}{4}$$

The crew must repair _____ miles of track each day.

Getting Started

Divide.

1. $2\frac{1}{4} \div 1\frac{1}{2} =$ _____

2. $5\frac{1}{3} \div 4 =$ _____

3. $6\frac{1}{4} \div 1\frac{2}{5} =$ _____

4. $6 \div 3\frac{1}{3} =$ _____

5. $\frac{5}{9} \div 1\frac{1}{2} =$ _____

6. $1\frac{3}{4} \div 7 =$ _____

7. $2\frac{1}{3} \div 2\frac{2}{3} =$ _____

8. $1\frac{1}{2} \div 3\frac{2}{3} =$ _____

9. $5\frac{3}{7} \div 1\frac{2}{3} =$ _____

Copy and divide.

10. $2\frac{1}{3} \div 1\frac{2}{5}$

11. $3\frac{3}{8} \div 1\frac{1}{2}$

12. $5 \div 1\frac{3}{7}$

13. $2\frac{1}{4} \div 3\frac{3}{8}$

151

Practice

Divide.

1. $1\frac{3}{8} \div 11 =$ _____

2. $6 \div 3\frac{3}{5} =$ _____

3. $1\frac{1}{7} \div \frac{6}{7} =$ _____

4. $4\frac{1}{2} \div 1\frac{2}{3} =$ _____

5. $4\frac{1}{8} \div 1\frac{4}{7} =$ _____

6. $2\frac{3}{4} \div 2\frac{4}{9} =$ _____

7. $28 \div 3\frac{1}{2} =$ _____

8. $5\frac{1}{3} \div 1\frac{7}{9} =$ _____

9. $2\frac{2}{5} \div 1\frac{2}{3} =$ _____

10. $3\frac{1}{5} \div 3\frac{1}{10} =$ _____

11. $3\frac{2}{3} \div 2\frac{1}{6} =$ _____

12. $4\frac{1}{5} \div 1\frac{8}{13} =$ _____

Copy and Do

13. $5\frac{7}{9} \div 1\frac{1}{3}$

14. $4\frac{2}{3} \div 1\frac{1}{15}$

15. $2 \div 1\frac{1}{7}$

16. $8\frac{1}{4} \div 3\frac{2}{3}$

17. $5\frac{3}{5} \div 14$

18. $1\frac{1}{8} \div 5\frac{1}{4}$

19. $2\frac{7}{16} \div 1\frac{5}{8}$

20. $1\frac{1}{2} \div 2\frac{1}{3}$

21. $7\frac{1}{2} \div 4\frac{1}{5}$

Apply

Solve these problems.

22. Ben is filling a pail that holds $4\frac{1}{2}$ quarts. He is using a dipper that holds $\frac{3}{4}$ of a quart. How many times will Ben fill the dipper?

23. An ant takes $1\frac{1}{4}$ hours to crawl one block. How many blocks can the ant crawl in 10 hours?

24. Doris ran $3\frac{1}{4}$ miles, $1\frac{3}{4}$ miles and $2\frac{1}{2}$ miles on three different days. What is her average daily mileage?

25. The Indianapolis Speedway Track is $2\frac{1}{2}$ miles long. The race is $\frac{1}{4}$ over after 125 miles. How many laps around the track is the race?

EXCURSION

Circle the correct value for each letter to make the equation true.

A = 1

E = 1

B = $\frac{1}{3}$ or $\frac{2}{3}$

F = $\frac{3}{4}$ or $\frac{4}{3}$

C = 2 or $\frac{1}{2}$

G = 3 or 2

D = $\frac{2}{3}$ or $\frac{3}{2}$

H = $\frac{1}{4}$ or $\frac{1}{2}$

$B + D - A = C \times 2 - A$ $(E + F) \times G \times \frac{1}{7} = F - H$

Working with Fractions

The city is designing athletic fields for Highland Park. The city planners are using $\frac{1}{3}$ of the park for soccer fields, and $\frac{1}{8}$ of the park for baseball fields. How many acres will be left open for picnicking?

We want to know how many open acres will be left.

We know Highland Park contains ____ acres, and

____ of it will be used for soccer and ____ of it for baseball.

To find how many acres will be left open, we must add to find what part will be used for the two sports and subtract that fraction from one which stands for the whole park. Then we multiply to find the number of acres left for picnicking.

Find the total part used for fields.	Subtract from 1 which stands for the whole park.	Find $\frac{13}{24}$ of 36.

$$\begin{array}{r} \frac{1}{3} = \frac{8}{24} \\ + \frac{1}{8} = \frac{3}{24} \\ \hline \frac{11}{24} \end{array}$$

$$\begin{array}{r} 1 = \frac{24}{24} \\ - \frac{11}{24} = \frac{11}{24} \\ \hline \frac{13}{24} \end{array}$$

$$\frac{13}{24} \times 36 = \underline{\quad}$$

There are ____ acres left for picnicking.

Getting Started

Compute each problem. Simplify answers wherever necessary.

1. $5\frac{1}{3} + 4\frac{1}{2} =$ ____

2. $5\frac{1}{3} \times 4\frac{1}{2} =$ ____

3. $5\frac{1}{3} - 4\frac{1}{2} =$ ____

4. $5\frac{1}{3} \div 4\frac{1}{2} =$ ____

Copy and compute.

5. $43 - 6\frac{7}{9}$

6. $3\frac{1}{5} \times \frac{3}{8} \times \frac{13}{7}$

7. $3\frac{3}{4} \div 3\frac{1}{8}$

8. $5\frac{1}{2} + 6\frac{2}{3} + 7\frac{3}{4}$

Practice

Compute each problem. Simplify answers wherever necessary.

1. $2\frac{3}{8} + 8\frac{1}{4} = $ _____

2. $5\frac{1}{3} + 2\frac{1}{4} = $ _____

3. $6\frac{1}{2} \times 5\frac{1}{2} = $ _____

4. $7\frac{1}{3} - 2\frac{1}{2} = $ _____

5. $9\frac{1}{4} + 7\frac{2}{3} = $ _____

6. $8\frac{1}{3} \times 4\frac{1}{5} = $ _____

7. $6\frac{3}{8} - 4\frac{1}{7} = $ _____

8. $3\frac{1}{5} + 2\frac{1}{12} = $ _____

9. $4\frac{2}{5} \times \frac{10}{11} = $ _____

10. $8\frac{1}{9} + 16\frac{3}{4} = $ _____

11. $8\frac{2}{3} \div 6 = $ _____

12. $14 - 3\frac{2}{7} = $ _____

13. $12\frac{1}{4} \times \frac{16}{21} = $ _____

14. $10\frac{1}{9} - 4\frac{3}{5} = $ _____

15. $8\frac{2}{5} \div 6 = $ _____

Copy and Do

16. $8\frac{1}{3} + 3\frac{2}{3}$

17. $3\frac{1}{3} \div 6\frac{2}{9}$

18. $6\frac{1}{8} + 7\frac{5}{6}$

19. $4\frac{2}{7} \times 1\frac{4}{10}$

20. $1 \div \frac{2}{3}$

21. $15\frac{1}{4} - 7\frac{5}{6}$

22. $7\frac{3}{10} + 6\frac{9}{15}$

23. $16 - 4\frac{1}{8}$

24. $6\frac{2}{3} \div 1\frac{1}{9}$

25. $\frac{4}{5} \times \frac{7}{8} \times \frac{6}{7}$

26. $2\frac{1}{2} + 5\frac{2}{3} + 6\frac{7}{12}$

27. $2\frac{1}{2} \times 19\frac{5}{9} \times \frac{2}{5}$

28. $3\frac{2}{3} + 5\frac{5}{8} + 2\frac{1}{2}$

29. $7\frac{1}{2} \times 2\frac{2}{35} \times 1\frac{1}{2}$

30. $15 \div 3\frac{4}{7}$

Apply

Solve these problems.

31. Mr. Alison is on a diet of 1,500 calories a day. For lunch, he has $\frac{2}{5}$ of his calories. How many calories can Mr. Alison have for his other meals?

32. Hugh had $3\frac{1}{8}$ quarts of paint. He used $\frac{4}{5}$ of that paint to paint a bookcase. The amount he had left was $\frac{3}{4}$ of what he needed to paint some shelves. How much paint did Hugh need?

33. The library is $\frac{4}{5}$ of a mile from Rick's house. The library is $\frac{2}{3}$ of a mile from Mary's house. How much farther is it from Rick's to the library than from Mary's to the library?

Solving a Simpler But Related Problem

The Big Dipper Ice Cream Store sells 20 different flavors
of ice cream. How many different two-scoop ice cream
cones can be made? A cone with vanilla on the bottom
and chocolate on the top is different from a cone with
chocolate on the bottom and vanilla on the top.

★ SEE

We want to know how many different combinations of
cones with two scoops can be made.

There are _____ different flavors we can use.

★ PLAN

We can solve a simpler problem using fewer flavors.
By recording our results in a table, we can find a
pattern that will help us to solve the problem.

★ DO

Number of Flavors	Combinations	Number of Combinations
1 vanilla	$\frac{v}{v}$	1 (1 × 1)
2 vanilla chocolate	$\frac{v}{c}$ $\frac{c}{v}$ $\frac{c}{c}$ $\frac{v}{v}$	4 (2 × 2)
3 vanilla chocolate strawberry	$\frac{v}{c}$ $\frac{c}{v}$ $\frac{v}{s}$ $\frac{s}{v}$ $\frac{c}{s}$ $\frac{s}{c}$ $\frac{v}{v}$ $\frac{c}{c}$ $\frac{s}{s}$	9 (3 × 3)
4 vanilla chocolate strawberry chocolate chip	$\frac{v}{c}$ $\frac{c}{v}$ $\frac{v}{s}$ $\frac{s}{v}$ $\frac{v}{cc}$ $\frac{cc}{v}$ $\frac{c}{s}$ $\frac{s}{c}$ $\frac{c}{cc}$ $\frac{cc}{c}$ $\frac{s}{cc}$ $\frac{cc}{s}$ $\frac{v}{v}$ $\frac{c}{c}$ $\frac{s}{s}$ $\frac{cc}{cc}$	_____ (_ × _)

Using 20 flavors, we can make _____ different two-scoop ice cream cones.

★ CHECK

We can check by actually listing and counting the possible combinations
of 20 different flavors of ice cream.

Apply

Solve a simpler but related problem to help solve these.

1. How many rectangles are found in this diagram?

2. What is the greatest number of regions you can make by drawing 6 chords through a circle?

3. Find the area of this figure:

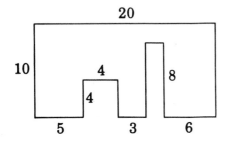

4. How many different squares are in this diagram?

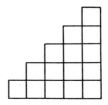

5. How many diagonals can be drawn in a dodecagon?

6. Sally wrote the numbers from 1 to 100. How many times did she write the numeral 5?

7. Everyone at the Student Council meeting shook hands with everyone else exactly once. If there were 105 handshakes exchanged, how many people were at the meeting?

8. All 48 students in the sixth grade class will take place in an elimination checkers tournament. Each student will play a game. The loser is eliminated and the winner will continue to the next round. How many checker games will need to be played in order to determine a champion?

9. What if one more rectangle were added to the diagram in Problem 1? How many rectangles would there be in the diagram then?

10. Look at the geometric figure shown in Problem 3. How could you change the figure so that the area is 184 square units?

11. Silly Willy said that the product of two numbers is always greater than either of the two numbers. Show at least one example that proves Silly Willy is incorrect.

12. The sum of the two whole numbers 2 and 2 is the same as their product. Why is it not possible to find two fractions between 0 and 1 whose sum is the same as their product?

Calculators and Functions

A function can be used to find **input** or **output** numbers. The **function** is an operation with a number written in a circle. An **arrow diagram** is used to show the direction of the function.

Input	Function	Output		Input	Function	Output
6 —— (+3) —→ 9				225 —— (÷5) —→ ___		

Sometimes the output and the function are known. We can use the inverse function to find the input. Notice the change in the arrow's direction.

					Inverse	
Input	Function	Output		Output	Function	Input
? —— (×8) —→ 96				___ ←— (÷8) —— 96		

Multiplication and division
are inverse operations.

Two functions that are used together are called **composite functions.**

		Output 1		
Input 1	Function 1	Input 2	Function 2	Output 2
16 ——— (×3) ——→ 48 ——— (÷4) ——→ ___				

We can find a single function for these two functions.

16 —— $\left(×\frac{3}{4}\right)$ —→ ___

Use a calculator to complete each arrow diagram. Then write a single function to combine the two functions.

1. 12 —(+6)→ ___ —(+4)→ ___   12 —◯→ ___

2. 215 —(−35)→ ___ —(+51)→ ___   215 —◯→ ___

3. 6 —(÷3)→ ___ —(×2)→ ___   6 —◯→ ___

157

Practice

Use a calculator to complete each arrow diagram.

1. 10 ——(×5)—→ ___

2. 16 ——(+25)—→ ___

3. ___ ——(+9)—→ 17

4. 28 ——(÷7)—→ ___

5. ___ ——(×8)—→ 120

6. ___ ——(×9)—→ 72

7. 64 ——(−18)—→ ___

8. ___ ——(×7)—→ 98

9. ___ ——(+38)—→ 76

10. 89 ——(−27)—→ ___

11. 17 ——(×12)—→ ___

12. 300 ——(÷15)—→ ___

13. 53 ——(−15)—→ ___

14. ___ ——(×25)—→ 350

15. ___ ——(+53)—→ 109

16. ___ ——(÷16)—→ 25

17. 9 ——(×7)——(+7)—→ ___

18. 48 ——(×5)——(÷12)—→ ___

19. 34 ——(+9)——(−9)—→ ___

20. 56 ——(÷7)——(×7)—→ ___

Use a calculator to complete each arrow diagram.
Then, write a single function to combine the two functions.

21. 36 ——(×7)——(÷2)—→ ___   36 ——( )—→ ___

22. 306 ——(+5)——(−3)—→ ___   306 ——( )—→ ___

23. 73 ——(−16)——(−10)—→ ___   73 ——( )—→ ___

Use the function to complete the table.

24. Input ——(×12)—→ Output

Input	1	4	6	7	12	16
Output						

25. Input ——(+15)—→ Output

Input	1	9	25	40	62	80
Output						

26. Input ——(×$\frac{2}{3}$)—→ Output

Input	6	12	24			72
Output				20	32	

27. Input ——(×5)——(+3)—→ Output

Input	2	6	8			28
Output	13			53	78	

Multiply. Factor wherever possible.

1. $\frac{2}{3} \times \frac{3}{8} =$

2. $\frac{5}{9} \times \frac{3}{15} =$

3. $\frac{7}{8} \times \frac{4}{5} =$

4. $\frac{5}{6} \times \frac{9}{10} =$

5. $16 \times \frac{3}{4} =$

6. $\frac{5}{8} \times 6 =$

7. $15 \times \frac{3}{10} =$

8. $24 \times \frac{9}{16} =$

9. $6\frac{1}{2} \times 18 =$

10. $2\frac{1}{3} \times 5\frac{1}{7} =$

11. $3\frac{1}{3} \times 2\frac{1}{10} =$

12. $5\frac{1}{7} \times 3\frac{1}{6} =$

13. $3\frac{4}{5} \times 6\frac{1}{4} =$

14. $8\frac{2}{9} \times 5\frac{1}{2} =$

Write the reciprocal.

15. $\frac{2}{3}$

16. $\frac{5}{8}$

17. $2\frac{1}{3}$

18. $4\frac{1}{5}$

19. 18

20. $\frac{17}{5}$

Divide.

21. $\frac{1}{2} \div \frac{3}{4} =$

22. $\frac{5}{8} \div \frac{15}{16} =$

23. $\frac{3}{7} \div \frac{6}{7} =$

24. $\frac{3}{8} \div \frac{5}{6} =$

25. $9 \div \frac{3}{4} =$

26. $\frac{5}{8} \div 10 =$

27. $15 \div \frac{5}{7} =$

28. $\frac{2}{3} \div 18 =$

29. $2\frac{1}{2} \div 1\frac{1}{5} =$

30. $4\frac{2}{3} \div 1\frac{1}{9} =$

31. $7\frac{1}{7} \div 3\frac{1}{3} =$

32. $4\frac{1}{6} \div 6\frac{2}{3} =$

33. $2\frac{5}{11} \div \frac{3}{7} =$

34. $5\frac{5}{6} \div 2\frac{2}{3} =$

Circle the letter of the correct answer.

1 $n \times 3 = 15$
$n = ?$

  a 5
  b 6
  c 45
  d NG

8 $808 \div 7$

  a 12 R4
  b 115
  c 115 R5
  d NG

2 $12 - 6 \div 3 = n$
$n = ?$

  a 2
  b 6
  c 10
  d NG

9 $32\overline{)8,156}$

  a 25 R24
  b 254
  c 254 R28
  d NG

3 What is the place value of the 3 in 682,351?

  a ones
  b tens
  c hundreds
  d NG

10 Complete the equivalent fraction.
$$\frac{5}{9} = \frac{?}{18}$$

  a 5
  b 9
  c 10
  d NG

4 $\$134.56$
  $+ \quad 97.85$

  a $231.41
  b $232.31
  c $232.41
  d NG

11 $3\frac{5}{6}$
  $+ 2\frac{1}{4}$

  a $5\frac{1}{12}$
  b $5\frac{3}{5}$
  c $6\frac{1}{12}$
  d NG

5 $31,052$
  $- 15,785$

  a 15,267
  b 15,367
  c 24,733
  d NG

12 $6\frac{1}{5}$
  $- 3\frac{7}{10}$

  a $2\frac{1}{2}$
  b $3\frac{3}{10}$
  c $3\frac{7}{10}$
  d NG

6 39×5

  a 155
  b 195
  c 1,545
  d NG

7 615
  $\times \quad 34$

  a 4,305
  b 20,810
  c 20,910
  d NG

score

ADDITION AND SUBTRACTION OF DECIMALS

Understanding Decimals as Tenths and Hundredths

Numbers to the left of the decimal point represent whole numbers. Numbers to the right of the decimal point represent a fractional or decimal part of one.

This one region is divided into _____ equal parts. Each part is $\frac{1}{10}$ of the region. The shaded part is $\frac{3}{10}$.

The unshaded part is _____ of the region. Every fraction has a decimal equivalent.

Fraction **Decimal**

$$\frac{1}{10} \quad = \quad 0.1$$

 Remember, the zero in 0.1 says there are no ones in the decimal number.

This region is divided into _____ equal parts. Each

part is _____ of the region. The shaded part is

_____. The unshaded part is _____ of the region.

Fraction **Decimal**

$$\frac{1}{100} \quad = \quad 0.01$$

We can use a place value chart to understand and read decimals.

tens	ones	tenths	hundredths
1	5	2	7

We read 15.27 as **fifteen and twenty-seven hundredths.**

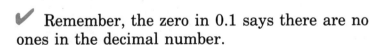 Remember, we say **and** in a number only to represent a decimal point.

Getting Started

Write the decimal.   Write the decimal number in words.

1. $3\frac{25}{100}$ _____   **2.** seven and four tenths _____   **3.** 6.3 _____

Practice

Write the decimal.

1. $7\frac{3}{100}$ _____
2. $6\frac{1}{10}$ _____
3. $28\frac{5}{10}$ _____
4. $39\frac{5}{100}$ _____

5. $4\frac{8}{10}$ _____
6. $12\frac{50}{100}$ _____
7. $36\frac{76}{100}$ _____
8. $52\frac{1}{10}$ _____

9. $116\frac{3}{100}$ _____
10. $203\frac{4}{100}$ _____
11. $91\frac{40}{100}$ _____
12. $57\frac{9}{10}$ _____

13. four and two tenths _____

14. sixteen hundredths _____

15. seventy hundredths _____

16. thirty hundredths _____

17. five tenths _____

18. one tenth _____

19. eighty-seven hundredths _____

20. six and two hundredths _____

Write the decimal numbers in words.

21. 8.43 _____

22. 12.6 _____

23. 29.05 _____

24. 127.38 _____

25. 214.3 _____

26. 576.49 _____

Apply

Solve these problems.

27. Bill had $10. He spent $3. What decimal represents the part of his money Bill spent?

28. Nancy has 100 coins. She has 46 nickels. What decimal represents the part of the coins that are not nickels?

29. If you toss a coin 100 times and it turns up heads 55 of those times, what decimal represents the number of times it turns up tails?

30. Of the 10 people on the bus, 4 are adults and 7 are female. Write a decimal to represent each of the following groups on the bus: adults, children, females, males.

Understanding Decimals as Thousandths

Beth put an odometer on her bike two years ago. The odometer shows the number of miles she has ridden since then. She took the bike to get a license, and had to read the odometer number to the inspector. How many miles had she ridden?

A place value chart helps us read this number.

hundreds	tens	ones	.	tenths	hundredths	thousandths
4	3	1	.	0	4	6

4 hundreds

3 tens ————

1 one ————

0 tenths ————

———— ————

———— ————

The place value of the third digit to the right of the decimal point is _____. The decimal number on Beth's odometer is read

_____

✔ In reading a decimal number, say the number to the right of the decimal point as a whole number followed by the name of the last place value.

Getting Started

Write the decimal.

1. $\frac{86}{1000}$ _____

2. $7\frac{236}{1000}$ _____

3. $12\frac{5}{1000}$ _____

4. nine and fifty-seven thousandths _____

Write the decimal number in words.

5. 8.456 _____

Practice

Write the decimal.

1. $\frac{181}{1000}$ ———

2. $\frac{316}{1000}$ ———

3. $\frac{9}{10}$ ———

4. $\frac{47}{1000}$ ———

5. $\frac{14}{100}$ ———

6. $\frac{5}{1000}$ ———

7. $4\frac{216}{1000}$ ———

8. $4\frac{30}{1000}$ ———

9. $12\frac{75}{1000}$ ———

10. $12\frac{75}{100}$ ———

11. $16\frac{305}{1000}$ ———

12. $15\frac{65}{1000}$ ———

13. nine thousandths ———

14. three and two hundred five thousandths ———

15. four and twelve thousandths ———

16. seventy-two hundredths ———

17. eight and five thousandths ———

18. six hundred thousandths ———

19. two hundred ninety-three and one hundred forty-four thousandths ———

20. one thousand twenty-five and forty-eight thousandths ———

Write the decimal numbers in words.

21. 9.326 ————————————————

22. 5.378 ————————————————

23. 0.896 ————————————————

24. 4.6 ————————————————

25. 6.025 ————————————————

26. 12.34 ————————————————

Apply

Solve these problems.

27. Mr. Ryan drove 1,000 miles on his vacation. On the first day, he drove 312 miles. What decimal represents the part of the whole trip Mr. Ryan drove on the first day?

28. In a poll of 1,000 people, 629 people chose dogs as their favorite pet. What decimal represents the part of all the people that did not choose dogs as their favorite pet?

Understanding Place Value

In his annual physics lecture at the university, Dr. Johnson wrote this number on the chalkboard. Can you read it?

To read the number, we have to understand the decimal place value system.

✔ Each place is 10 times greater than the place on its right.

✔ Each place is $\frac{1}{10}$ of the value of the place on its left.

These principles are the same on both sides of the decimal point.

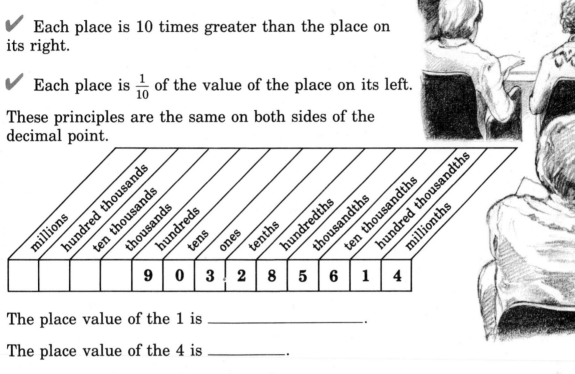

The place value of the 1 is _____.

The place value of the 4 is _____.

We read Dr. Johnson's decimal number as _____

_____.

Decimals that name the same number are called **equivalent decimals.** For example:

    0.5 = 0.50 = 0.500

Getting Started

Write the place value name of 3 in each number.

1. 12.976483 _____ 2. 8.004531 _____ 3. 9.45632 _____

Write the decimal.

4. two hundred and fifty-six ten thousandths _____

Write the decimal number in words.

5. 7.2468 _____

Practice

Write the place value name of 5 in each number.

1. 7.3259 _____

2. 14.56832 _____

3. 136.1245 _____

4. 96.25483 _____

5. 37.291451 _____

6. 139.675148 _____

7. 9.326015 _____

8. 14.63251 _____

Write the decimal.

9. six and five hundred thirty-six hundred thousandths _____

10. thirteen and ninety-eight ten thousandths _____

11. fifty-six millionths _____

12. twelve and one thousand six hundred ten thousandths _____

Write the decimal numbers in words.

13. 6.2439 _____

14. 4.000329 _____

15. 0.47385 _____

16. 2.1806 _____

EXCURSION

Label each point with a fraction. Look for a pattern to help you.

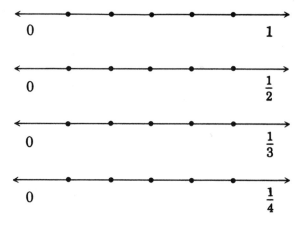

166

Comparing and Ordering Decimals

Abby needs to drill a hole in the bird house she is building. She needs to drill the largest hole that her drill can make. Which drill bit should Abby use?

To find the largest drill bit, we need to compare the three decimal sizes that she has. We compare

————, ——— and ———.

✔ To compare decimals, write them in a column so that the decimal points are aligned. Write zeros to name equivalent decimals.

0.5625
0.6870   0.687 and 0.6870 are equivalent decimals.
0.6250   0.625 and 0.6250 are equivalent decimals.

Start at the left and compare digits. The ones are the same, but the tenths are not.

0.5625   Because **5 < 6,** 0.5625 is the smallest drill bit.
0.6870
0.6250

0.5625

0.687

Next compare hundredths.

0.6870   **2 < 8**   ——— is the middle-sized drill bit.

0.6250   **8 > 2**   ——— is the largest drill bit.

0.625

Abby should use the bit labeled ———.

Getting Started

Write >, < or = between the numbers.

1. 0.2431 ◯ 0.2461   2. 7.19 ◯ 7.190   3. 9.273 ◯ 9.372

Order the numbers from least to greatest.

4. 2.59, 2.493, 2.571   5. 6.1351, 6.13, 6.152, 6.143

——————————   ——————————

Practice

Write >, < or = between the numbers.

1. 5.7 ◯ 5.9

2. 3.26 ◯ 3.260

3. 15.27 ◯ 15.72

4. 0.029 ◯ 0.039

5. 6.8325 ◯ 6.8315

6. 10.03 ◯ 10.030

7. 4.129 ◯ 4.1290

8. 1.0025 ◯ 1.025

9. 4.8317 ◯ 4.9317

10. 29.02 ◯ 29.20

11. 16.157 ◯ 16.15

12. 0.2473 ◯ 0.2437

13. 4.19 ◯ 4.1823

14. 5.9620 ◯ 5.9627

15. 3.2841 ◯ 3.2814

16. 0.003 ◯ 0.0003

17. 13.7 ◯ 13.700

18. 9.2 ◯ 9.199

Order the numbers from least to greatest.

19. 3.26, 3.45, 3.3

_____

20. 5.285, 5.825, 5.582

_____

21. 0.02, 0.002, 0.2

_____

22. 4.15, 4.29, 4.265

_____

23. 8.2416, 8.4261, 8.3416

_____

24. 5.14, 5.1, 5.234, 5.2

_____

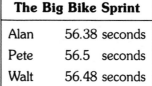

Apply

Solve these problems.

25. Which was the fastest time?

26. List the order of finish from first through fourth.

The Big Bike Sprint	
Alan	56.38 seconds
Pete	56.5 seconds
Walt	56.48 seconds
Paul	56.54 seconds

EXCURSION

Use the digits 6, 7 and 8 to make six different decimal numbers.
Write a check next to the least.
Write an X next to the greatest.

___.___   ___.___   ___.___

___.___   ___.___   ___.___

168

Rounding Decimals

Population density describes the number of people there are in each square mile of an area. Rounded to the nearest hundredth what were the population densities of New York City in 1790 and 1980?

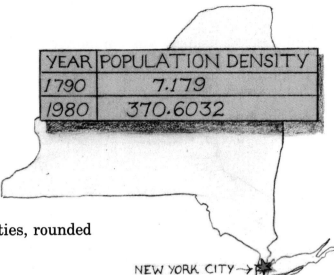

YEAR	POPULATION DENSITY
1790	7.179
1980	370.6032

We want to know the population densities, rounded to the nearest hundredth.

We know the 1790 population density was _____,

and the 1980 density was _____.

To round a decimal number, circle the digit in the place you want to round.

7.1⑦9   3 7 0.6⓪3 2

Look at the digit to the right of the one circled.

NEW YORK CITY →

ONE SQUARE MILE

If the digit is 5 or greater, add 1 to the circled number and drop all digits to the right.

7.1⑦9   9 > 5   7.179 ≈ 7.18

If the digit is less than 5, keep the circled number and drop all digits to the right.

3 7 0.6⓪3 2   3 < 5   370.6032 ≈ 370.60

The sign ≈ is read **is approximately.**

To the nearest hundredth, the population density of

New York was _____ in 1790, and _____ in 1980.

Getting Started

Round to the nearest whole number.

1. 6.437 _____   2. 94.86 _____

Round to the nearest tenth.

3. 11.734 _____   4. 215.963 _____

Round to the nearest hundredth.

5. 7.999 _____   6. 13.534 _____

Round to the nearest thousandth.

7. 0.46581 _____   8. 6.92952 _____

169

Practice

Round to the nearest whole number.

1. 136.29 _____
2. 14.765 _____
3. 9.27 _____
4. 12.565 _____

5. 18.5 _____
6. 37.032 _____
7. 3.8091 _____
8. 116.99 _____

Round to the nearest tenth.

9. 7.39 _____
10. 0.826 _____
11. 25.45 _____
12. 39.06 _____

13. 115.26 _____
14. 59.96 _____
15. 210.53 _____
16. 64.39 _____

Round to the nearest hundredth.

17. 28.735 _____
18. 19.158 _____
19. 37.678 _____
20. 9.241 _____

21. 112.999 _____
22. 7.046 _____
23. 14.393 _____
24. 416.595 _____

Round to the nearest thousandth.

25. 8.53967 _____
26. 0.76463 _____
27. 12.98362 _____
28. 4.58467 _____

29. 16.37995 _____
30. 42.64821 _____
31. 3.54545 _____
32. 7.91659 _____

Apply

Solve these problems.

33. The population density of Colorado is 27.89. What is the density of Colorado, rounded to the nearest tenth?

34. The population density of Kansas is 28.909. What is the density of Kansas rounded to the nearest hundredth?

EXCURSION

Complete the following. Use the pattern set up in the first sentence.

About 3.5 means at least 3.45 and at most 3.54.

About 4.7 means at least _____ and at most _____.

About 18.0 means at least _____ and at most _____.

About 8.32 means at least _____ and at most _____.

About 50¢ means at least _____ and at most _____.

Estimating Sums and Differences

Stan has $920.75 in his savings account. He wants to buy the stereo and speakers while they are on sale. About how much of his savings will Stan have left after his purchase?

We want to know about how much money Stan will have left.

We need to estimate the total cost of the two items.

Then we can find the difference between that total and the amount in Stan's account.

We know the stereo costs _____ and the

speakers cost _____.

To estimate the total cost, we round the two amounts to the nearest $100 and add.

$$\begin{array}{r} \$389.99 \approx \ \$400 \\ 215.50 \approx + \ \ 200 \\ \hline \end{array}$$

To estimate how much will be left in his account, we subtract the estimated total cost from the estimate of his savings.

We subtract _____ from _____.

$$\begin{array}{r} \$920.75 \approx \ \$900 \\ - \ \ 600 \\ \hline \end{array}$$

Stan will have about _____ left in his savings account.

Getting Started

Round to the nearest dollar or whole number and estimate the answers.

1. $50.68
    + 37.26

2. $69.48
    − 14.85

3. $72.50
    − 51.96

4. 18.765
    + 9.213

5. 32.139
    + 16.73

6. 21.5
    − 16.621

Copy and compute. Use estimation to check.

7. 43.5 + 36.73

8. $24.18 − $13.65

9. $501.65 − $287.44

171

Practice

Round to the nearest dollar or whole number and estimate the answers.

1. 17.64
    − 9.85

2. 46.432
    + 15.296

3. 47.896
    + 15.5

4. $38.16
    − 19.39

5. 129.235
    + 16.41

6. $203.75
    − 109.12

7. 83.705
    + 28.9

8. $17.50
    + 12.75

9. 9.2875
    − 6.834

10. $16.42
    + 35.89

11. 5.752
    + 3.948

12. 76.894
    − 62.387

13. $116.99
    − 20.49

14. $49.65
    + 34.81

15. 989
    − 451

Copy and Do

16. 36.5 + 18.91

17. $25.14 − $12.63

18. 4.964 + 8.175

19. $48.36 + $42.15

20. 75.25 + 8.638

21. 39.81 − 16.256

22. 52.43 − 10.71

23. $52.46 − $15.95

24. 109.25 − 78.96

25. 427.81 − 118.04

26. $56.94 + $40.01

27. 3.2985 + 7.216

28. 12.007 + 8.8

29. 8.941 − 8.149

30. $8,210 − $299

31. $87.86 − $36.12

32. $3.95 + $4.01

33. 52.5 + 93.77

Apply

Solve these problems. Round answers to the nearest whole number.

34. Nan weighs 48.36 kilograms and Jan weighs 43.78 kilograms. About how much more does Nan weigh?

35. Mac ran 3.75 kilometers and Hugh ran 7.09 kilometers. About how much farther did Hugh run?

36. A sweater costs $46.87 and a shirt costs $18.95. About how much does it cost to buy both?

37. Mel bought a watch for $26.59 and a ring for $20.59. He gave the clerk $50. About how much change did he receive?

Adding Decimals

Mrs. Garvin uses a pedometer to measure the distance she walks each day. She was surprised by her weekly total, after she recorded that she had walked 2.57 miles on Friday. What was the total distance Mrs. Garvin walked during the week?

	Monday	Wednesday	Friday
Miles	2.16	2.5	2.57

We want to know how many miles Mrs. Garvin had

walked. We know she walked _____ miles on

Monday, _____ miles on Wednesday and _____
miles on Friday.

To find the total mileage, we add the three distances

together. We add _____, _____ and _____.

Write the numbers in a column, aligning the decimal points.	Write equivalent decimals.	Add from right to left. Place the decimal point.
2.16 2.5 + 2.57	2.16 2.50 + 2.57	2.16 2.50 + 2.57 7.23

Mrs. Garvin walked a total of _____ miles.

Getting Started

Add.

1. 5.769
  + 4.243

2. 16.13
  + 29.75

3. 9.275
  + 3.18

4. 8.32
  + 5.7684

Copy and add.

5. 8.762 + 4.38 + 7.323

6. 7.294 + 8.6 + 9.5763

173

Practice

Add.

1.
$$54.9$$
$$+ 16.7$$

2.
$$35.16$$
$$+ 18.25$$

3.
$$29.8$$
$$+ 15.76$$

4.
$$28.57$$
$$+ 16.9$$

5.
$$9.675$$
$$+ 3.429$$

6.
$$25.3$$
$$+ 8.758$$

7.
$$14.2965$$
$$+ 9.9813$$

8.
$$37.4815$$
$$+ 16.39$$

9.
$$29.61$$
$$13.75$$
$$+ 15.83$$

10.
$$13.482$$
$$9.75$$
$$+ 6.824$$

11.
$$6.7$$
$$8.18$$
$$+ 9.964$$

12.
$$0.7384$$
$$0.9248$$
$$+ 0.3956$$

13.
$$80.431$$
$$72.1$$
$$+ 3.007$$

14.
$$12.01$$
$$17.99$$
$$+ 200.472$$

15.
$$86.68$$
$$24.87$$
$$+ 7.26$$

16.
$$143.92$$
$$27.81$$
$$+ 101.79$$

17.
$$28.942$$
$$7.801$$
$$+ 842.55$$

18.
$$38.51$$
$$29.72$$
$$+ 99.004$$

19.
$$501.34$$
$$20.75$$
$$+ 1.09$$

20.
$$22.83$$
$$831.08$$
$$+ 75.29$$

Copy and Do

21. 21.6 + 18.3 + 6.5

22. 12.16 + 8.05 + 7.2

23. 5.943 + 18.976 + 6.1

24. 125.382 + 186 + 59.2

25. 58.2463 + 16.9425

26. 0.2965 + 0.954 + 0.36

27. 47 + 1.96 + 3.3275

28. 19.756 + 0.65 + 8.2903

29. 17.896 + 21.07 + 12.81

30. 486.295 + 211.9094

31. 81 + 201.75 + 821.403

32. 28.714 + 888.28 + 82

Apply

Solve these problems.

33. Bill has three containers. One holds 11.25 liters of water, one holds 9.15 liters and the third holds 8.105 liters. How much water does it take to fill the three containers?

34. A male panda weighs 216.35 kilograms. A female panda weighs 36.5 kilograms more. What is the combined weight of the two pandas?

Subtracting Decimals

The girls 200-meter medley relay team set a new record at the swim meet. How much faster did Lauren swim than Doris?

200-meter Medley Relay		
Amy	50 Backstroke	35.26 seconds
Doris	50 Butterfly	33.7 seconds
Nancy	50 Breaststroke	38.24 seconds
Lauren	50 Freestyle	29.85 seconds

We want to know the difference in times for the two swimmers.

We know Doris swam the 50 butterfly relay in

_____ seconds, and Lauren swam the 50 freestyle

relay in _____ seconds.

To find how much faster Lauren swam than Doris, we subtract Lauren's time from Doris's time. We

subtract _____ from _____.

Write the numbers in a column, aligning the decimal points.	Write equivalent decimals.	Subtract from right to left. Place the decimal point.

$$\begin{array}{r} 33.7 \\ -29.85 \\ \hline \end{array}$$

$$\begin{array}{r} 33.70 \\ -29.85 \\ \hline \end{array}$$

$$\begin{array}{r} 33.70 \\ -29.85 \\ \hline 3.85 \end{array}$$

Lauren swam the 50 freestyle relay _____ seconds faster than Doris swam the 50 butterfly relay.

Getting Started

Subtract.

1. $\begin{array}{r} 6.35 \\ -4.91 \\ \hline \end{array}$

2. $\begin{array}{r} 5.958 \\ -2.68 \\ \hline \end{array}$

3. $\begin{array}{r} 18.21 \\ -3.485 \\ \hline \end{array}$

4. $\begin{array}{r} 7.3408 \\ -1.9659 \\ \hline \end{array}$

Copy and subtract.

5. $18.762 - 9.853$

6. $36 - 7.032$

7. $49.385 - 0.9786$

Practice

Subtract.

1. 9.61
  − 2.35

2. 6.95
  − 2.43

3. 9.671
  − 4.385

4. 1.916
  − 0.187

5. 13.824
  − 2.89

6. 73.508
  − 15.323

7. 18.7659
  − 7.3246

8. 14.683
  − 6.9285

9. 39.392
  − 16.596

10. 128.16
  − 79.3852

11. 13.004
  − 9.7765

12. 25.3
  − 24.965

13. 59.781
  − 21.947

14. 883.01
  − 29.75

15. 175.9291
  − 83.2107

16. 286.1
  − 24.314

Copy and Do

17. 52.7 − 13.8

18. 24.37 − 18.26

19. 51.2 − 13.51

20. 0.679 − 0.296

21. 15.96 − 9.376

22. 48.321 − 19.9681

23. 49 − 3.276

24. 76.423 − 38.9

25. 76.745 − 19.968

26. 15.003 − 14.386

27. 83.76516 − 14.83768

28. 15.3802 − 6.94376

29. 824.39 − 261.22

30. 282.07 − 41.703

31. 12.785 − 4.039

Apply

Solve these problems.

32. From a roll of paper 3.67 meters long, Irv cuts a piece 1.48 meters long. How long is the piece that is left?

33. For a cook-out, Mary bought 4.59 kilograms of swiss cheese and 2.65 kilograms of American cheese. How much cheese did Mary buy?

34. How much longer is the sixth graders' record jump than that of the fifth graders?

35. Gloria is in the sixth grade. Her long jump measured 6.955 meters. How far short of the record is Gloria's jump?

Long Jump Records	
4th Graders	5.3 meters
5th Graders	5.76 meters
6th Graders	7.6 meters

176

Adding and Subtracting Decimals

Randy made a chart to show the average yearly rainfall in different U.S. cities. On the average, how many more inches of rain fall in New York City than in Chicago?

Average Yearly Rainfall

Chicago   39.57 inches
New York City 48.15 inches
Los Angeles   12.23 inches

We want to know the difference in average yearly rainfall in New York City and Chicago. We know

New York averages _____ inches and Chicago

averages _____ inches.

To compare the rainfall in the two cities, we subtract the average Chicago rainfall from the average New York City rainfall.

We subtract _____ from _____.

$$\begin{array}{r} 48.15 \\ -\ 39.57 \\ \hline \end{array}$$

New York City averages _____ more inches of rain than Chicago per year.

Getting Started

Compute.

1.	2.	3.	4.
97.3 − 16.45	32.9 − 16.63	112.476 − 96.789	4.093 + 8.97

Copy and compute.

5. 39.7 + 18.9 − 15.6

6. 5.89 − 3.341 + 14

7. 6.2 + 3.96 + 8.54

8. 24.61 + 18.21 − 3.75

9. 19.61 − 8.75 + 2.95

10. 3.01 + 120.72 − 8.08

177

Practice

Compute.

1. $\begin{array}{r} 16.91 \\ + 15.86 \\ \hline \end{array}$

2. $\begin{array}{r} 37.21 \\ - 19.58 \\ \hline \end{array}$

3. $\begin{array}{r} 32.5 \\ + 18.63 \\ \hline \end{array}$

4. $\begin{array}{r} 75.2 \\ - 17.58 \\ \hline \end{array}$

5. $\begin{array}{r} 126.2 \\ - 97.851 \\ \hline \end{array}$

6. $\begin{array}{r} 52.483 \\ + 78.925 \\ \hline \end{array}$

7. $\begin{array}{r} 89.58 \\ - 23.965 \\ \hline \end{array}$

8. $\begin{array}{r} 49.008 \\ - 15.779 \\ \hline \end{array}$

9. $\begin{array}{r} 156.17 \\ + 28.3954 \\ \hline \end{array}$

10. $\begin{array}{r} 175.43 \\ - 98.7658 \\ \hline \end{array}$

11. $\begin{array}{r} 415.673 \\ - 295.873 \\ \hline \end{array}$

12. $\begin{array}{r} 515.2843 \\ + 329.7689 \\ \hline \end{array}$

Copy and Do

13. $75.2 + 18.6 - 65.3$

14. $82.16 - 13.29 + 16.5$

15. $4.962 + 6.83 - 4.759$

16. $25.371 + 13.7 + 19.651$

17. $39 - 16.28 + 15.75$

18. $96.136 + 48.792 - 63.4248$

Apply

Solve these problems.

19. The maximum weight of a full container is 19.325 kilograms. Into the container, Larry put one object that weighs 9.5 kilograms and another that weighs 7.75 kilograms. How much more weight can Larry put into the container?

20. In one year, 42.8 million passengers passed through O'Hare Airport in Chicago, and 37.9 million passengers went through the Atlanta Airport. The Los Angeles Airport had 4.5 million fewer passengers than did the Atlanta Airport. In all, how many passengers passed through these three airports?

Mr. Martinez kept track of the miles he drove in a car he rented at the airport.

21. How far did Mr. Martinez drive?

22. How much farther did Mr. Martinez drive on Monday and Tuesday than Wednesday and Thursday?

Driving Record	
Monday	365.7
Tuesday	149.35
Wednesday	296.5
Thursday	213.86

Selecting Appropriate Notation

Fred has a blue shirt, a white shirt, a yellow shirt,
a pair of jeans and a pair of black corduroy slacks.
He also has a white jacket and a navy blue jacket.
How many different three-piece outfits can he make?

★ SEE

We want to know how many different three-piece outfits
Fred can make.

It takes a shirt, a pair of slacks and a _____ to make
one outfit.

He has ____ different shirts. He has ____ different kinds

of slacks. He has ____ different jackets.

★ PLAN

Since we have many possible combinations we can use a
tree diagram to show how many outfits Fred can make.

★ DO

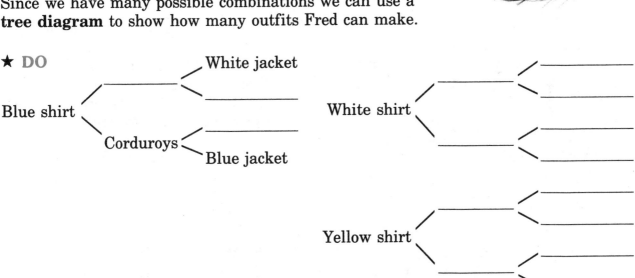

Fred can make ____ different outfits that will use the blue shirt.

He can make ____ outfits with the white shirt and ____ outfits with

the yellow shirt. Fred can make ____ different three-piece outfits.

★ CHECK

We can check our work by being sure we recorded each type
of slacks and each type of jacket with each kind of shirt.

Apply

Select the appropriate notation to help solve these problems.

1. There are 29 sixth graders in Miss Smith's class. Twenty-one students are on the baseball team. Twelve students are on the football team. How many students are on both the baseball and football teams?

2. At Quick Burger you can order a regular burger, a double burger or a giant burger. Side dishes are cole slaw, home fries or salad. Milk shake flavors include vanilla, chocolate, strawberry and banana. How many different meals can you buy that include a sandwich, a side order and a milkshake?

3. Margaret, Fred and Susan all teach at the same school. They teach math, science and social studies. Margaret, who rides a bus to school, teaches in the room next to the math teacher. The social studies teacher gives Susan a ride to school each day. Who teaches what subject?

4. Of the twenty-nine students who take music lessons,
   13 play violin,
   16 play piano,
   8 play trumpet,
   4 play piano and violin,
   1 plays trumpet and violin and
   1 plays all three instruments.
   How many students play only piano? How many play only trumpet?

5. Francis, Linda and Peggy love animals. Their pets are a dog, a cat and a hamster. The pets' names are Daisy, Sasha and Lucky. Peggy feeds Sasha each day before leaving for work. Francis, who owns Lucky, is allergic to cats. Linda walks her dog twice a day. Find the name of each pet and its owner.

6. A scientist has four identical gold nuggets. He knows one is counterfeit. It has a slightly different weight. How can the scientist find the counterfeit nugget using only a balance scale?

7. Malcolm won a prize. He had a choice of receiving $150 right away or a daily payment beginning with $1.50 and doubling each day for 7 days. Which should Malcolm choose and why?

8. The Math Club offers a prize to any person who writes a problem that can be solved using a tree diagram and the answer is 48 choices. What problem would you write?

9. Maria added 3 decimals to get a sum of 5.27. If the sum of the first 2 addends is 3.79, and the sum of the last 2 addends is 3.63, what are the 3 addends added by Maria?

10. You have four addends. Each is a number of dollars and cents. If you round each amount to the nearest whole dollar and add, how far from the actual sum can you be?

180

Calculators and Binary Numbers

The **base ten system** uses ten symbols:
0, 1, 2, 3, 4, 5, 6, 7, 8 and 9. The
base two or **binary system** only uses
0 and 1. We can use a light bulb to
represent binary numbers. If the light
is on, the number is 1. If the light
is not on, the number is 0. What base
ten number is shown on the computer?

Lights	Base 2 Number	Base 10 Number	
○	0	0	$0_{two} = 0_{ten}$
●	1	1	$1_{two} = 1_{ten}$
● ○	10	2	$10_{two} = 2_{ten}$
● ●	11	3	$11_{two} = 3_{ten}$
● ○ ○	100	4	$100_{two} = 4_{ten}$
● ○ ●	101	5	$\underline{}_{two} = \underline{}_{ten}$
● ● ○	110	6	$\underline{}_{two} = \underline{}_{ten}$
● ● ●	111	7	$\underline{}_{two} = \underline{}_{ten}$

The computer shows the base ten number ____.
The number word after the numerals is called a
subscript. It tells what number system the
numerals represent.

✔ In the binary system, each place has a value
2 times the value of the place on the right.
We can use the **binary number reader** to discover
the base ten value of base two numerals.
We enter the base two number into
the binary number reader and use a
calculator to multiply and add.

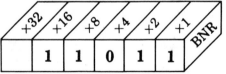

✔ Remember, any number times one
is that number.

$16 + 8 + 0 + 2 + 1 = $ ____$_{ten}$

Use the binary number reader to find the base ten
value of 110101_{two} and 101100_{two}.

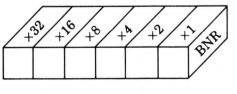

__ + __ + __ + __ + __ + __ = ____$_{ten}$

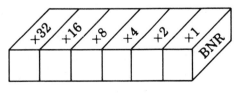

__ + __ + __ + __ + __ + __ = ____$_{ten}$

181

Practice

Use the binary number reader to find the base ten value of the binary number.

1.

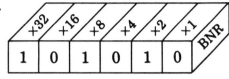

——ten

2.

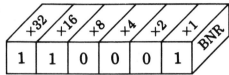

——ten

3.

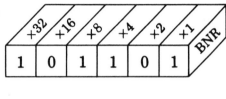

——ten

4.

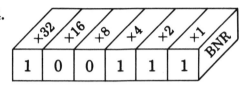

——ten

Change each binary number to a base ten number.

5. 1101010_{two}

———ten

6. 1010111_{two}

———ten

7. 1110011_{two}

———ten

8. 10000000_{two}

———ten

9. 10101010_{two}

———ten

10. 10101111_{two}

———ten

11. 11111111

———ten

12. 100000000_{two}

———ten

Apply

13. Find the binary sum of 1101_{two} and 110_{two}.

14. Find the binary product of 1110_{two} and 11_{two}.

15. Find the binary sum of 11110_{two} and 10001_{two}.

16. Find the binary product of 1_{two} and 101101_{two}.

EXCURSION

Be a mind reader. Try this yourself. Then try it with a friend. Pick a number from 1 to 15. Find all the cards on which the number appears. Add the upper left hand corner numbers on those cards. What do you find?

A		B		C		D	
8	12	4	12	2	10	1	9
9	13	5	13	3	11	3	11
10	14	6	14	6	14	5	13
11	15	7	15	7	15	7	15

What is the place value of the 3 in each number?

1. 6.02031 _____

2. 5.13961 _____

3. 9.24063 _____

4. 3.21 _____

5. 15.3 _____

6. 231.5 _____

Write <, = or > between the decimal numbers.

7. 2.689 ◯ 2.698

8. 4.3216 ◯ 4.321

9. 7.685 ◯ 7.6850

10. 2.613 ◯ 2.631

11. 95.6231 ◯ 95.6223

12. 81.652 ◯ 81.562

Round to the nearest hundredth.

13. 7.9895 _____

14. 4.3861 _____

15. 15.673 _____

Round to the nearest thousandth.

16. 15.6785 _____

17. 14.21849 _____

18. 4.00653 _____

19. 256.2316 _____

20. 38.3672 _____

21. 9.6289 _____

Estimate each sum and difference by first rounding the numbers to the nearest whole number.

22. 42.78
   + 36.12

23. $18.39
   − 9.50

24. 15.372
   − 12.986

25. 12.28
   − 6.428

Add.

26. 14.64
   + 58.97

27. 57.391
   + 16.83

28. 12.241
   + 16.9586

29. 47.3829
   + 25.7883

Subtract.

30. 46.34
   − 18.96

31. 52.385
   − 16.79

32. 24.376
   − 8.9378

33. 75.2418
   − 39.7519

1 $12 - 6 \times 2 = n$
$n = ?$

a 0
b 4
c 12
d NG

2 What is the place value of the 7 in 1,796,851?

a ten thousands
b hundred thousands
c millions
d NG

3 62,412
+ 15,496

a 77,808
b 77,908
c 78,908
d NG

4 46,250
− 38,659

a 7,592
b 12,408
c 17,592
d NG

5 546 × 7

a 3,522
b 3,582
c 3,822
d NG

6 429
× 36

a 3,861
b 15,444
c 16,444
d NG

7 476 ÷ 6

a 7 R56
b 79
c 79 R2
d NG

8 $46\overline{)9,453}$

a 25 R23
b 205
c 205 R23
d NG

9 $3\frac{2}{3}$
$+ 3\frac{1}{6}$

a $6\frac{1}{3}$
b $7\frac{5}{6}$
c $6\frac{5}{6}$
d NG

10 $5\frac{1}{3}$
$- 2\frac{3}{4}$

a $2\frac{7}{12}$
b $3\frac{5}{12}$
c $3\frac{7}{12}$
d NG

11 $1\frac{3}{4} \times 2\frac{2}{3}$

a $\frac{21}{32}$
b $4\frac{1}{2}$
c $4\frac{2}{3}$
d NG

 score

184

MULTIPLICATION AND DIVISION OF DECIMALS

Multiplying by Powers of 10

Complete the patterns to find a shortcut for multiplying by powers of ten.

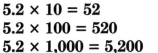

$$10^1 = 10$$
$$10^2 = 100$$
$$10^3 = 1,000$$
$$10^4 = 10,000$$

$5.2 \times 10 = 52$

$5.2 \times 100 = 520$

$5.2 \times 1,000 = 5,200$

$5.2 \times 10,000 =$ _____

$5.2 \times 10^1 = 52$

$5.2 \times 10^2 = 520$

$5.2 \times 10^3 = 5,200$

$5.2 \times$ ___ $=$ _____

$0.8341 \times 10 = 8.341$

$0.8341 \times 100 = 83.41$

$0.8341 \times 1,000 = 834.1$

$0.8341 \times 10,000 =$ _____

$0.8341 \times 10^1 = 8.341$

$0.8341 \times 10^2 = 83.41$

$0.8341 \times 10^3 = 834.1$

$0.8341 \times$ ___ $=$ _____

Multiplying by 10 or 10^1 moves the decimal point ___ place to the right.

Multiplying by 100 or 10^2 moves the decimal point ___ places to the right.

Multiplying by 1,000 or 10^3 moves the decimal point ___ places to the right.

Multiplying by 10,000 or 10^4 moves the decimal point ___ places to the right.

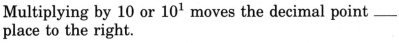 When you multiply by a power of ten, move the decimal point to the right the same number of places as the exponent. Write extra zeros to the right of the number if needed.

Getting Started

Multiply. Use mental math.

1. $7.3 \times 1,000 =$ _____

2. $8.26 \times 10^2 =$ _____

3. $10^4 \times 5.68 =$ _____

4. $10 \times 4.032 =$ _____

5. $4.815 \times 10^4 =$ _____

6. $100 \times 8.265 =$ _____

Write the missing factor in exponential form.

7. $2.5974 \times$ ___ $= 259.74$

8. ___ $\times 5.48 = 5,480$

9. $356.7 \times$ ___ $= 3,567$

Practice

Multiply. Use mental math.

1. $6.451 \times 10^2 = $ _____

2. $1,000 \times 4.275 = $ _____

3. $10^3 \times 19.75 = $ _____

4. $0.0249 \times 10,000 = $ _____

5. $10^2 \times 15.974 = $ _____

6. $5.9 \times 10^2 = $ _____

7. $8.375 \times 10 = $ _____

8. $0.021 \times 10^4 = $ _____

9. $1,000 \times 0.2465 = $ _____

10. $10^3 \times 5.7615 = $ _____

11. $10 \times 0.5 = $ _____

12. $11.751 \times 10^1 = $ _____

Write the missing factor in exponential form.

13. $7.5 \times \underline{\quad} = 750$

14. $\underline{\quad} \times 0.651 = 651$

15. $3.271 \times \underline{\quad} = 327.1$

16. $\underline{\quad} \times 4.61 = 4,610$

17. $17.95 \times \underline{\quad} = 179.5$

18. $\underline{\quad} \times 8.15 = 8,150$

19. $0.4731 \times \underline{\quad} = 47.31$

20. $96.8 \times \underline{\quad} = 96,800$

EXCURSION

Try this unusual way of multiplying.

Row 1	0	1	2	3	4	5	6	7	8	9	10	11	12
Row 2	1	2	4	8	16	32	64	128	256	512	1,024	2,048	4,096

The Row 1 number for 16 is _____.

The Row 1 number for 8 is _____.

The Row 1 number for 128 is _____.

Multiply these numbers.

$$\begin{array}{r} 16 \\ \times\ 8 \\ \hline \end{array}$$

Add these numbers.

$$\begin{array}{r} 4 \\ +\ 3 \\ \hline \end{array}$$

The Row 1 number for 128 is _____.

The Row 1 number for 32 is _____.

The Row 1 number for 4,096 is _____.

$$\begin{array}{r} 128 \\ \times\ 32 \\ \hline \end{array}$$

$$\begin{array}{r} 7 \\ +\ 5 \\ \hline \end{array}$$

Use the Row 1 numbers to find these products.

1. $8 \times 64 = $ _____

2. $512 \times 4 = $ _____

3. $32 \times 32 = $ _____

Multiplying Whole Numbers by Decimals

The shotput can be thrown about 6.1 times farther on the moon than on Earth. What would the Earth's shotput record be on the moon?

We want to know the number of meters the shotput could be thrown on the moon.

We know the shotput record on Earth is ＿＿ meters,

and the shotput can be thrown ＿＿ times farther on the moon.

To find the distance on the moon, we multiply the number of Earth meters by the number of times farther it can be thrown on the moon.

We multiply ＿＿ by ＿＿.

Multiply the same as with whole numbers.	Put as many decimal places in the product as there are in the decimal factor.	Estimate to check the answer.

$$\begin{array}{r} 24 \\ \times\,6.1 \\ \hline 2\,4 \\ 1\,4\,4 \\ \hline 1\,4\,6\,4 \end{array}$$

$$\begin{array}{r} 24 \\ \times\,6.1 \leftarrow 1 \text{ place} \\ \hline 2\,4 \\ 1\,4\,4 \\ \hline 1\,4\,6.4 \leftarrow 1 \text{ place} \end{array}$$

$$\begin{array}{r} 20 \\ \times\;\;6 \\ \hline 1\,2\,0 \end{array}$$

The shotput record on the moon would be ＿＿＿＿ meters.

Getting Started

Place the decimal point in the product.

1. $\begin{array}{r} 79 \\ \times\,2.3 \\ \hline 1\,8\,1\,7 \end{array}$

2. $\begin{array}{r} 3.9 \\ \times\,48 \\ \hline 1\,8\,7\,2 \end{array}$

3. $\begin{array}{r} 2.765 \\ \times\;\;\;87 \\ \hline 2\,4\,0\,5\,5\,5 \end{array}$

4. $\begin{array}{r} 839 \\ \times\,0.44 \\ \hline 3\,6\,9\,1\,6 \end{array}$

Multiply.

5. $\begin{array}{r} 4.7 \\ \times\;\,9 \\ \hline \end{array}$

6. $\begin{array}{r} 27 \\ \times\,0.17 \\ \hline \end{array}$

7. $\begin{array}{r} 9.653 \\ \times\;\;298 \\ \hline \end{array}$

8. $\begin{array}{r} 187 \\ \times\,3.25 \\ \hline \end{array}$

Copy and multiply.

9. 4.503×47

10. 324×8.52

11. 5.39×51

12. 26×4.98

Practice

Place the decimal point in the product.

1.	95 × 5.7 541 5	**2.**	485 × 3.9 1,891 5	**3.**	479 × 4.5 2,155 5	**4.**	396 × 0.123 48 708
5.	2.385 × 12 28 620	**6.**	968 × 1.38 1,335 84	**7.**	12.94 × 168 2,173 92	**8.**	0.9651 × 18 17 3718

Multiply.

9.	2.8 × 7	**10.**	39 × 0.8	**11.**	115 × 2.3	**12.**	7.38 × 12
13.	9.625 × 26	**14.**	592 × 1.58	**15.**	42.6 × 495	**16.**	8,246 × 2.13

Copy and Do

17. 16×4.15

18. 3.02×46

19. 5.198×25

20. 43×1.65

21. 4.3921×6

22. 29×7.246

23. 176×1.09

24. 3.761×24

25. 684.12×28

26. 45×7.207

27. 86×65.826

28. 76×982.1

29. 58.32×95

30. 26.82×19

31. 52×9.65

32. 245×0.5

33. 3.201×77

34. 0.002×69

35. 1.961×84

36. 22.2×881

Apply

Solve these problems.

37. Rhonda weighs 46 kilograms. Earline weighs 1.06 times as much as Rhonda. How much does Earline weigh?

38. Chris jumped 245 centimeters. His cousin Katy jumped 0.45 that distance. Chris's friend, Charlie, jumped 3.7 centimeters less than Katy. How far did Charlie jump?

Multiplying Decimals by Decimals

Mr. Nikomoto and Mr. Allen car pool to work. Mr. Nikomoto's car gets 29.7 miles to a gallon of gasoline. Mr. Allen's car gets 25.3 miles per gallon. How far can Mr. Nikomoto drive on the gas he just purchased?

We want to know how many miles Mr. Nikomoto can drive on a tank of gas.

We know that his car gets _____ miles to a gallon

of gas, and he just bought _____ gallons.

To find the distance he can drive, we multiply the number of miles per gallon, by the number of

gallons. We multiply _____ by _____.

Multiply the same as whole numbers.	Place the decimal point in the product. It has the same number of decimal places as the sum of them in the decimal factors.	Round to whole numbers to check the answer.

$$
\begin{array}{r}
29.7 \\
\times\ \ 8.6 \\
\hline
1782 \\
2376 \\
\hline
25542
\end{array}
\qquad
\begin{array}{r}
29.7 \leftarrow \quad \text{1 place} \\
\times\ \ 8.6 \leftarrow +\text{1 place} \\
\hline
1782 \\
2376 \\
\hline
255.42 \leftarrow \text{2 places}
\end{array}
\qquad
\begin{array}{r}
30 \\
\times\ \ 9 \\
\hline
270
\end{array}
$$

Mr. Nikomoto can drive _____ miles on a tank of gas.

Getting Started

Place the decimal point in the product.   Multiply.

$$
\begin{array}{r}
\textbf{1.}\quad 7.61 \\
\times\ \ 1.5 \\
\hline
11415
\end{array}
\qquad
\begin{array}{r}
\textbf{2.}\quad 9.32 \\
\times\ 0.26 \\
\hline
24232
\end{array}
\qquad
\begin{array}{r}
\textbf{3.}\quad 67.3 \\
\times\ \ 2.7 \\
\hline
\end{array}
\qquad
\begin{array}{r}
\textbf{4.}\quad 4.79 \\
1.05 \\
\hline
\end{array}
$$

Copy and multiply.

5. 5.243×6.76 **6.** 0.37×0.73 **7.** 3.125×0.67

Practice

Place the decimal point in the product.

1.   4.31
  × 1.5
  ———
  6 465

2.   70.3
  × 2.4
  ———
  168 72

3.   1.836
  × 4.9
  ———
  8 9964

4.   6.03
  × 1.25
  ———
  7 5375

5.   4.731
  × 2.54
  ———
  12 01674

6.   6.24
  × 0.73
  ———
  4 5552

7.   14.9
  × 0.075
  ———
  1 1175

8.   7.581
  × 3.18
  ———
  24 10758

Multiply.

9.   4.3
  × 0.6

10.   2.56
  × 1.8

11.   3.246
  × 4.2

12.   9.36
  × 0.8

13.   26.25
  × 7.3

14.   4.96
  × 3.75

15.   4.961
  × 2.37

16.   0.921
  × 0.652

Copy and Do

17. 4.761 × 3.21

18. 0.81 × 0.96

19. 5.134 × 0.25

20. 2.8 × 1.694

21. 2.24 × 2.24

22. 0.68 × 0.47

Apply

Solve these problems.

23. Gasoline costs $0.91 a gallon. How much do 14.6 gallons cost?

24. Alan worked 6.5 hours. If he earns $5.50 an hour, how much did Alan earn?

25. It rained 1.75 centimeters in one hour. How much rain fell in 0.6 of an hour?

26. The length of a garden is 4.25 times as long as the width. If the width is 5.6 meters, how long is the garden?

190

Multiplying with Zeros in the Products

The minicomputer can complete a
command in 0.5 of the time it takes
the microcomputer to do the same job.
How long does it take this minicomputer
to complete an instruction?

We want to know how many seconds it takes the
minicomputer to complete an instruction.

We know that a microcomputer takes _____
seconds to complete a command, and the

minicomputer takes _____ times as long.

To find how long it takes the minicomputer, we
multiply the number of seconds the microcomputer
uses by the number of times as long it takes the

minicomputer. We multiply _____ by _____.

0.0003 SECONDS TO COMPLETE COMMAND

Multiply.

$$
\begin{array}{r}
0.0003 \\
\times \quad 0.5 \\
\hline
1\,5
\end{array}
$$

Write zeros to the left
of the product to get the
correct number of places.

$$
\begin{array}{rl}
0.0003 & \leftarrow \quad 4 \text{ places} \\
\times \quad 0.5 & \leftarrow + 1 \text{ place} \\
\hline
0.00015 & \leftarrow \quad 5 \text{ places}
\end{array}
$$

Check by multiplying
fractional equivalents.

$$\frac{3}{10,000} \times \frac{5}{10} = \frac{15}{100,000}$$

It takes the minicomputer _____ seconds to
complete a command.

Getting Started

Multiply.

1. $\begin{array}{r} 3.26 \\ \times\ 0.01 \\ \hline \end{array}$
2. $\begin{array}{r} 0.003 \\ \times\quad 12 \\ \hline \end{array}$
3. $\begin{array}{r} 0.03 \\ \times\ 0.06 \\ \hline \end{array}$
4. $\begin{array}{r} 4.24 \\ \times\ 0.005 \\ \hline \end{array}$

5. $\begin{array}{r} 0.02 \\ \times\ 0.03 \\ \hline \end{array}$
6. $\begin{array}{r} 9.21 \\ \times\ 0.005 \\ \hline \end{array}$
7. $\begin{array}{r} 0.008 \\ \times\ 0.005 \\ \hline \end{array}$
8. $\begin{array}{r} 6.01 \\ \times\ 0.006 \\ \hline \end{array}$

Copy and multiply.

9. 0.375×0.005

10. $0.07 \times 0.05 \times 0.02$

11. $0.06 \times 0.09 \times 5.8$

191

Practice

Multiply.

1. $$\begin{array}{r} 3.2 \\ \times\ 0.04 \\ \hline \end{array}$$

2. $$\begin{array}{r} 0.006 \\ \times\ \quad 4 \\ \hline \end{array}$$

3. $$\begin{array}{r} 0.02 \\ \times\ 0.02 \\ \hline \end{array}$$

4. $$\begin{array}{r} 4.1 \\ \times\ 0.005 \\ \hline \end{array}$$

5. $$\begin{array}{r} 15.2 \\ \times\ 0.003 \\ \hline \end{array}$$

6. $$\begin{array}{r} 0.006 \\ \times\ 0.008 \\ \hline \end{array}$$

7. $$\begin{array}{r} 0.058 \\ \times\ \ 0.05 \\ \hline \end{array}$$

8. $$\begin{array}{r} 0.009 \\ \times\ \quad 16 \\ \hline \end{array}$$

Copy and Do

9. 0.3×0.3

10. 1.6×0.005

11. 0.002×3.56

12. 0.007×2.3

13. 0.0006×2.21

14. 8.3×0.0041

15. 0.125×0.005

16. 4.04×0.004

17. 0.0047×0.59

18. $0.03 \times 0.04 \times 2.3$

19. $0.9 \times 4.7 \times 0.005$

20. $0.05 \times 0.02 \times 0.06$

Apply

Solve these problems.

21. Each sheet of paper is 0.0025 inch thick. How thick is a stack of 50 sheets?

22. A piece of wire is 0.05 inch wide. How wide is a piece of wire 0.5 as wide?

EXCURSION

Write the missing numbers.

0.7	+		=	1.5
+		+		+
	+	0.4	=	
=		=		=
	+		=	2.5

	−	0.45	=	1.8
−		−		−
1.65	−		=	
=		=		=
	−	0.3	=	

Dividing a Decimal by Whole Numbers

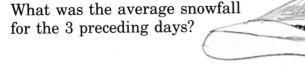

Snowfall	
Friday	6.26 inches
Saturday	4.18 inches
Sunday	5.04 inches

Randi is going skiing this week. What was the average snowfall for the 3 preceding days?

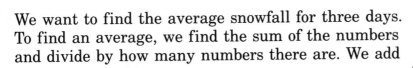

We want to find the average snowfall for three days. To find an average, we find the sum of the numbers and divide by how many numbers there are. We add

_____, _____ and _____.

$$\begin{array}{r} 6.26 \\ 4.18 \\ +\,5.04 \\ \hline \end{array}$$

We divide _____ by _____.

Divide the same as with whole numbers.	Put the decimal point in the quotient, directly above the decimal point in the dividend.	Check.

$$\begin{array}{r} 5\,1\,6 \\ 3\overline{)1\,5\,4\,8} \\ 1\,5\downarrow \quad\; \\ \hline 4\; \\ 3\downarrow \\ \hline 1\,8 \\ 1\,8 \\ \hline 0 \end{array}$$

$$\begin{array}{r} 5.1\,6 \\ 3\overline{)1\,5.4\,8} \\ 1\,5 \\ \hline 4 \\ 3 \\ \hline 1\,8 \\ 1\,8 \\ \hline 0 \end{array}$$

$$\begin{array}{r} 5.1\,6 \\ \times\qquad 3 \\ \hline 1\,5.4\,8 \end{array}$$

The average snowfall for the 3 days was _____ inches.

Getting Started

Divide and check.

1. $6\overline{)140.4}$

2. $9\overline{)11.115}$

3. $23\overline{)143.75}$

Copy and divide.

4. $38.85 \div 5$

5. $501.6 \div 19$

6. $2,677.36 \div 683$

193

Practice

Divide and check.

1. $7)\overline{88.2}$ 2. $3)\overline{16.92}$ 3. $8)\overline{27.616}$

4. $26)\overline{153.14}$ 5. $65)\overline{1,553.5}$ 6. $128)\overline{808.96}$

Copy and Do

7. $3.52 \div 8$ 8. $121.23 \div 9$ 9. $14.668 \div 4$

10. $37.24 \div 14$ 11. $135.2 \div 26$ 12. $313.11 \div 49$

13. $1,515.8 \div 65$ 14. $7,516.8 \div 96$ 15. $3,685.92 \div 56$

16. $1,350.5 \div 365$ 17. $1,842.54 \div 214$ 18. $19,495.25 \div 725$

19. $351.4 \div 25$ 20. $724 \div 1,448$ 21. $5,007.6 \div 963$

22. $6,005 \div 2.5$ 23. $248 \div 0.8$ 24. $296.5 \div 5$

Apply

Solve these problems.

25. A case of 12 bottles of juice contains 16.32 liters. How much does each bottle hold?

26. How far will a car travel in 8 hours if it averages 56.9 miles per hour?

Use the chart to answer 27 and 28.

27. How much more did Morty earn on Friday than on Tuesday?

28. What is Morty's average daily wage?

Morty's Wages	
Monday	$47.23
Tuesday	$42.88
Wednesday	$45.67
Thursday	$48.44
Friday	$50.33

Dividing with Zeros in the Quotients

Marcie is setting up the experiment for today's science class. She has 0.336 liters of sugar water, and is pouring equal amounts into the beakers. How much water will each beaker contain?

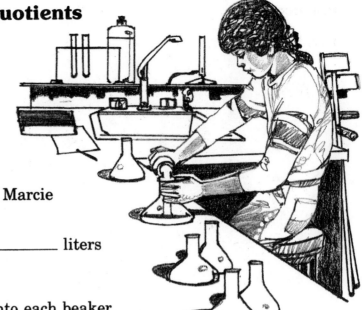

We want to know how much liquid Marcie will pour into each beaker.

We know she is pouring a total of _____ liters

into _____ beakers.

To find how much will be poured into each beaker, we divide the total amount by the number of beakers.

We divide _____ by _____ .

Place the decimal point in the quotient.	Write zeros in the quotient when needed.	Divide.
$6\overline{)0\ 3\ 3\ 6}$	$6\overline{)0\ 3\ 3\ 6}$	$\begin{array}{r} 0.0 \\ 6\overline{)0\ 3\ 3\ 6} \\ \underline{} \\ \\ \underline{} \end{array}$

Remember, every decimal place value in the dividend must be represented in the quotient.

Marcie will pour _____ liters of water into each beaker.

Getting Started

Divide.

1. $8\overline{)0.184}$ 2. $9\overline{)0.054}$ 3. $6\overline{)0.354}$ 4. $15\overline{)1.05}$ 5. $38\overline{)0.304}$

Copy and divide.

6. $0.425 \div 5$ 7. $0.6499 \div 67$ 8. $0.9345 \div 35$

Practice

Divide.

1. $4\overline{)0.144}$

2. $9\overline{)0.576}$

3. $7\overline{)0.0441}$

4. $7\overline{)0.0455}$

5. $16\overline{)0.608}$

6. $29\overline{)0.2494}$

Copy and Do

7. $0.335 \div 5$

8. $0.0156 \div 4$

9. $0.6904 \div 8$

10. $0.888 \div 12$

11. $0.0448 \div 28$

12. $0.0114 \div 19$

13. $0.1323 \div 21$

14. $0.2345 \div 35$

15. $0.1372 \div 49$

16. $3.276 \div 52$

17. $0.6432 \div 67$

18. $6.975 \div 93$

19. $0.02744 \div 49$

20. $20.224 \div 316$

21. $5.7246 \div 658$

EXCURSION

Write the decimals that are:

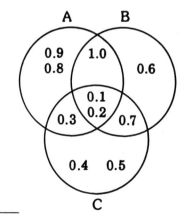

1. in A and B. _____

2. in A or B. _____

3. not in A or B. _____

4. in B and C. _____

5. in A or C. _____

6. in A and B and C. _____

7. in A or B and C. _____

8. not in B and not in C. _____

Dividing by Powers of 10

In an earlier lesson, we found a shortcut
for multiplying by powers of 10. Complete
the pattern to find a shortcut for dividing
by powers of 10.

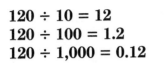

$120 \div 10 = 12$
$120 \div 100 = 1.2$
$120 \div 1,000 = 0.12$

$120 \div 10,000 = 0.012$

$1.6 \div 10 = 0.16$
$1.6 \div 100 = 0.016$

$1.6 \div 1,000 =$ _____

$1.6 \div 10,000 =$ _____

$120 \div 10^1 = 12$
$120 \div 10^2 = 1.2$
$120 \div 10^3 = 0.12$

$120 \div$ ____ $=$ _____

$1.6 \div 10^1 = 0.16$
$1.6 \div 10^2 = 0.016$

$1.6 \div 10^3 =$ _____

$1.6 \div$ ____ $=$ _____

$10^1 = 10$
$10^2 = 100$
$10^3 = 1,000$
$10^4 = 10,000$

Dividing by 10 or 10^1 moves the decimal point ___
place to the left.

Dividing by 100 or 10^2 moves the decimal point ___
places to the left.

Dividing by 1,000 or 10^3 moves the decimal point ___
places to the left.

Dividing by 10,000 or 10^4 moves the decimal point ___
places to the left.

✔ When you divide by a power of 10, move the
decimal point to the left the same number of places
as the exponent in the divisor. Write any extra
zeros needed to the left of the quotient digits.

Getting Started

Divide. Use mental math.

1. $154.89 \div 100 =$ _____

2. $0.063 \div 10^3 =$ _____

3. $14.296 \div 10^1 =$ _____

4. $127.9 \div 1,000 =$ _____

5. $39.58 \div 10^4 =$ _____

6. $4,629.2 \div 10^2 =$ _____

Multiply or divide. Use mental math.

7. $1.5672 \times 10^4 =$ _____

8. $4,893 \div 1,000 =$ _____

9. $0.67 \div 10^2 =$ _____

10. $38.9 \times 10^2 =$ _____

Practice

Divide. Use mental math.

1. $46.9 \div 10 =$ _____

2. $58.16 \div 10^2 =$ _____

3. $459.3 \div 100 =$ _____

4. $5{,}963 \div 10^3 =$ _____

5. $47.24 \div 1{,}000 =$ _____

6. $2{,}941.3 \div 10^2 =$ _____

7. $46.58 \div 10^1 =$ _____

8. $5.76 \div 100 =$ _____

9. $129.7 \div 10^3 =$ _____

10. $54.48 \div 100 =$ _____

Multiply or divide. Use mental math.

11. $81.9 \times 10^2 =$ _____

12. $4.632 \times 1{,}000 =$ _____

13. $129.6 \div 1{,}000 =$ _____

14. $85.26 \div 10^2 =$ _____

15. $19.24 \times 10 =$ _____

16. $48.231 \div 10^2 =$ _____

17. $248.2 \times 1{,}000 =$ _____

18. $3{,}279 \div 100 =$ _____

Apply

Solve these problems.

19. A plant cell measures 0.006 centimeters after it has been magnified 10 times. What was the original size of the cell?

20. A sheet of paper is 0.025 centimeters thick. How thick is a stack of 10,000 sheets of paper?

EXCURSION

Use the powers of 2 to complete the statements.

2	4	8	16	32	64	128	256	512	1,024	2,048	4,096
2^1	2^2	2^3	2^4	2^5	2^6	2^7	2^8	2^9	2^{10}	2^{11}	2^{12}

1. $2^3 \times 2^2 = 8 \times 4 = 32 = 2^5$

2. $2^7 \div 2^3 = 128 \div 8 = 16 = 2^4$

3. $2^4 \times 2^3 =$ _____

4. $2^9 \div 2^4 =$ _____

5. $2^5 \times 2^2 =$ _____

6. $2^{11} \div 2^3 =$ _____

7. $2^6 \times 2^5 =$ _____

8. $2^8 \div 2^5 =$ _____

9. $2^4 \times 2^8 =$ _____

10. $2^{12} \div 2^7 =$ _____

Dividing Decimals by Decimals

The Midtown Bakery is famous for it's bran muffins which the bakers make each morning. They use 3.6 pounds of flour every day. How long will their supply of flour last?

We want to know how many days the flour will last.

We know that the bakers have _____ pounds of

flour, and that they use _____ pounds each day. To find the number of days the flour will last, we divide the total amount by the amount used each day. We

divide _____ by _____.

Multiply the divisor by the power of 10 that makes it a whole number.	Multiply the dividend by the same power of 10, and divide.

$$3.6\overline{)75.6}_{\wedge}$$

Multiply by 10.

$$\begin{array}{r} 2\ 1 \\ 36\overline{)75.6}_{\wedge} \\ 7\ 2 \\ \hline 3\ 6 \\ 3\ 6 \\ \hline 0 \end{array}$$

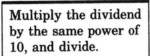
Multiply by 10

✔ We can use a caret (∧) to show where the decimal point has been moved.

The flour will last _____ days.

Getting Started

Put carets in the divisor and dividend to show where the decimal point moves.

1. $4.71\overline{)15.072}$ **2.** $0.6\overline{)215.4}$ **3.** $1.8\overline{)1.1718}$ **4.** $0.025\overline{)0.975}$

Divide.

5. $2.6\overline{)10.14}$ **6.** $0.09\overline{)76.077}$ **7.** $0.008\overline{)5.6584}$

Copy and divide.

8. $9.074 \div 1.3$ **9.** $1.332 \div 1.5$ **10.** $0.1485 \div 16.5$

199

Practice

Put a caret in the divisor and dividend to show where the decimal moves.

1. $6.9\overline{)54.631}$

2. $2.568\overline{)3.81467}$

3. $0.06\overline{)424.2}$

Divide.

4. $0.4\overline{)27.24}$

5. $0.03\overline{)12.852}$

6. $2.7\overline{)0.54}$

7. $0.008\overline{)0.05056}$

8. $1.9\overline{)12.35}$

9. $0.038\overline{)0.23712}$

10. $0.15\overline{)0.00945}$

11. $7.3\overline{)332.88}$

12. $12.5\overline{)156.25}$

Copy and Do

13. $1.52 \div 0.4$

14. $0.01945 \div 0.005$

15. $0.234 \div 0.06$

16. $67.385 \div 0.01$

17. $3.616 \div 0.08$

18. $22.569 \div 0.3$

19. $0.2576 \div 4.6$

20. $1.8375 \div 0.25$

21. $0.09312 \div 0.048$

22. $3.5441 \div 0.083$

23. $8.8038 \div 1.34$

24. $1,855.45 \div 0.215$

Apply

Solve these problems.

25. A human can run 44.76 kilometers per hour. A human can run about 0.38 as fast as a cheetah. How fast can a cheetah run?

26. A box containing ball bearings weighs 635.2 grams. The box weighs 500 grams and each ball bearing weighs 2.6 grams. How many ball bearings are in the box?

200

Dividing with Zeros in the Dividends

Shelby is working at a co-op produce store. She is putting 2.75 kilograms of rice into each sack. How many sacks of rice will Shelby fill from the basket of rice?

We want to know the number of sacks that can be filled with equal amounts of rice.

We know that the basket holds _____ kilograms of

rice, and each sack holds _____ kilograms.
To find how many sacks Shelby can fill, we divide the total amount by the amount in each sack. We

divide _____ by _____.

| Write extra zeros after the decimal point in the dividend. | Multiply to make the divisor a whole number. Multiply the dividend by the same power of 10. | Divide. |

$$2.75\overline{)33.00}$$

$$2.75_\wedge\overline{)33.00_\wedge}$$

$$2.75_\wedge\overline{)33.00_\wedge}$$

✔ Remember, any number of zeros can be written to the far right of a decimal number without changing its value.

Shelby will fill _____ sacks of rice.

Getting Started

Divide.

1. $5.2\overline{)104}$

2. $0.6\overline{)0.3}$

3. $0.09\overline{)1.8}$

4. $1.2\overline{)360}$

5. $0.51\overline{)10.2}$

6. $0.032\overline{)40}$

Copy and divide.

7. $72 \div 1.6$

8. $3.44 \div 0.08$

9. $128 \div 0.8$

201

Practice

Divide.

1. $0.4\overline{)164}$

2. $0.07\overline{)16.1}$

3. $0.005\overline{)210}$

4. $1.3\overline{)312}$

5. $0.015\overline{)10.05}$

6. $0.048\overline{)3.36}$

7. $5.4\overline{)108}$

8. $0.67\overline{)455.6}$

9. $0.45\overline{)0.0162}$

Copy and Do

10. $630 \div 0.3$

11. $96 \div 0.6$

12. $4.8 \div 0.08$

13. $63 \div 1.4$

14. $184.8 \div 0.33$

15. $675 \div 0.9$

16. $1,909 \div 0.83$

17. $2.52 \div 0.07$

18. $12.9 \div 2.15$

Apply

Solve these problems.

19. A rope is 17.4 meters long. How many 0.03-meter pieces can be cut from the rope?

20. How long will it take to save $22.80 if you save $0.38 every other day?

EXCURSION

A special operation is called **SquareAdd.** We square the first number and add the second. For example, $3 \text{ SquA } 2 = 3^2 + 2 = 11$

1. $5 \text{ SquA } 3 = $ _____

2. $2 \text{ SquA } 7 = $ _____

3. $6 \text{ SquA } 1 = $ _____

Answer **yes** or **no.**

4. Does $2 \text{ SquA } 5 = 5 \text{ SquA } 2$? _____

5. Does $4 \text{ SquA } 3 + 5 \text{ SquA } 3 = (4 + 5) \text{ SquA } 3$? _____

6. Does $5 \text{ SquA } 2 + 3 \text{ SquA } 2 = (5 \times 3) \text{ SquA } 2$? _____

Rounding Quotients

Mrs. Heading bought supplies in bulk for the civic club's pancake breakfast. Besides flour, eggs and butter, she bought maple syrup. How much did she pay per gallon of maple syrup?

We want to know the price of one gallon of syrup.

We know that Mrs. Heading bought _____

gallons of syrup, and she paid _____.

To find the cost per gallon, we divide the total price by the number of gallons purchased. We divide

_____ by _____.

When a division continues to have a remainder, we can round the quotient. Sometimes it is necessary to write extra zeros to extend the dividend. In this problem, we carry the division to thousandths to find the cost to the nearest cent.

Multiply the divisor and dividend by 10.

$$9.6\overline{)\$12.3\,5}$$

Divide. Round the quotient to cents.

$$\begin{array}{r} 1.286 \approx \$1.29 \\ 9.6\overline{)\$12.3\,500} \\ 96 \\ \hline 27\,5 \\ 19\,2 \\ \hline 8\,3\,0 \\ 7\,6\,8 \\ \hline 6\,2\,0 \\ 5\,7\,6 \\ \hline 4\,4 \end{array}$$

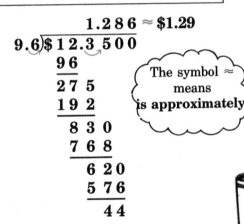

The symbol ≈ means is approximately.

✔ Remember, always carry the division one place value beyond the place to which you want to round.

Mrs. Heading paid about _____ per gallon of syrup.

Getting Started

Divide. Round to the nearest tenth.

Divide. Round to the nearest hundredth.

1. $5\overline{)9.21}$

2. $4.6\overline{)8.7}$

3. $1.6\overline{)5.69}$

4. $7.3\overline{)8.7}$

203

Practice

Divide. Round each quotient to the nearest tenth.

1. $4\overline{)6.83}$

2. $8\overline{)9.44}$

3. $0.6\overline{)5.732}$

4. $0.3\overline{)8.175}$

5. $0.9\overline{)5.736}$

6. $1.3\overline{)6.845}$

7. $4.7\overline{)9.51}$

8. $3.6\overline{)5.3}$

Divide. Round each quotient to the nearest hundredth.

9. $7\overline{)3.964}$

10. $9\overline{)12.857}$

11. $0.2\overline{)5.615}$

12. $0.8\overline{)0.0651}$

13. $1.9\overline{)5.623}$

14. $7.6\overline{)0.178}$

15. $2.6\overline{)4.96}$

16. $3.8\overline{)9.7}$

Apply

Solve these problems.

17. At the Snack Shoppe this week, you can buy 3 Super Submarine Sandwiches for $8.50. To the nearest cent, how much does 1 sandwich cost?

18. Inga weighs 0.88 as much as Nick. If Nick weighs 146 pounds, how much does Inga weigh to the nearest pound?

19. Dinah's test scores this semester are 91.6, 89.25, 94.8, 83.35 and 97.4. The class average is 95.5. To the nearest hundredth, how much does Dinah's average differ from the class average?

20. A lazy ant travels at a steady rate of 1.7 centimeters per minute. To the nearest tenth of a minute, how long does the ant take to travel 106.56 centimeters?

Renaming Fractions as Decimals

Marie is the lead-off hitter on the softball team. What is Marie's batting average to the nearest thousandths?

Lincoln Batting Averages			
Girl	At Bat	Hits	Average
Marie	15	7	?
Rita	13	6	?
Joan	16	7	?

We want to know Marie's batting average.

We know that she has been at bat _____ times, and

she has had _____ hits. Marie has hit the ball $\frac{7}{15}$ of the time.

To find her batting average, we name $\frac{7}{15}$ as a decimal.

Write the fraction as a division.	Divide the numerator by the denominator. Round the quotient to thousandths.

$$\frac{7}{15} = 1\,5\overline{)7}$$

$$\begin{array}{r} 0.4\,6\,6\,6 \approx 0.467 \\ 1\,5\overline{)7.0\,0\,0\,0} \\ \underline{6\ 0} \\ 1\ 0\ 0 \\ \underline{9\ 0} \\ 1\ 0\ 0 \\ \underline{9\ 0} \\ 1\ 0\ 0 \end{array}$$

Marie has a batting average of _____.

✔ Some fractions are renamed as decimals in tenths or hundredths. Others don't have an exact decimal equivalent. These we usually round to a particular place value.

Getting Started

Rename these fractions as decimals. Round to the nearest hundredths.

1. $\frac{2}{3}$ 2. $\frac{5}{6}$ 3. $\frac{1}{16}$ 4. $\frac{1}{12}$ 5. $\frac{3}{8}$

205

Practice

Rename these fractions as decimals. Round to the nearest hundredths.

1. $\frac{1}{6}$
2. $\frac{5}{12}$
3. $\frac{1}{2}$
4. $\frac{3}{16}$
5. $\frac{5}{8}$

6. $\frac{4}{7}$
7. $\frac{3}{13}$
8. $\frac{7}{11}$
9. $\frac{3}{4}$
10. $\frac{1}{8}$

11. $\frac{7}{16}$
12. $\frac{8}{9}$
13. $\frac{1}{7}$
14. $\frac{11}{15}$
15. $\frac{17}{20}$

16. $\frac{3}{11}$
17. $\frac{17}{25}$
18. $\frac{5}{9}$
19. $\frac{7}{8}$
20. $\frac{1}{12}$

Apply

Solve these problems. Round answers to thousandths.

21. The Eliot basketball team played 18 games and won 11 of them. What is the Eliot basketball team's winning average?

22. In the free throw contest, Ken made 9 shots and missed 5 shots. What is his shooting average?

23. Dennis was at bat 54 times and struck out only 14 times. What is his batting average?

24. Bill has 5 hits in 8 times at bat. How much will his batting average increase if he gets 2 hits in his next 2 turns at bat?

EXCURSION

When the only prime factors of the denominator are 2 or 5, the decimal will have no remainder.

$$\frac{1}{8} = 8\overline{)1.000}$$

```
       0.125
   8)1.000
       8
      ──
       20
       16
      ──
       40
       40
      ──
        0
```

When the prime factors of the denominator include factors other than 2 or 5, the decimal has a repeating remainder.

$$\frac{1}{3} = 3\overline{)1.000}$$

```
       0.333
   3)1.000
       9
      ──
       10
        9
      ──
       10
        9
      ──
       10
```

Circle the fractions that will have a repeating remainder.

$\frac{3}{4}$ $\frac{1}{7}$ $\frac{2}{3}$ $\frac{7}{8}$ $\frac{1}{12}$ $\frac{7}{9}$ $\frac{3}{5}$ $\frac{5}{11}$ $\frac{4}{15}$ $\frac{3}{10}$

Working Backwards

Marlene spent Saturday afternoon at the carnival. She spent one half of her money on tickets for the rides. She spent $3.00 on games. She then spent one half of what was left on food. When Marlene arrived home she had $2.00 left. How much money did Marlene take to the carnival?

★ SEE

We want to know how much Marlene took to the carnival. She spent one half of her money on the rides. She then

spent _____ on games. She spent one half of what was

left for food. Marlene had _____ left when she arrived home.

★ PLAN

Since we know that Marlene had $2.00 left and we know how she spent her money, we can work backwards to find out how much she had at the start.

★ DO

We double what she had at the end to find out what she had before eating.

$2.00 × 2 = _____

We add to what she had before eating. $3.00 + _____ = _____

We can double the amount she had left to find out how much she had before buying tickets.

_____ × 2 = _____   Marlene took _____ to the carnival.

★ CHECK

We can check our solution by working through the problem in the correct order.

1/2 of $14.00 = _____
amount spent on rides

$14.00 − $7.00 = _____
amount left

$7.00 − $3.00 = _____
amount after games

1/2 of $4.00 = _____
amount spent on food

$4.00 − $2.00 = _____ amount left.

207

Apply

Work backwards to solve these problems.

1. José was paid for mowing the lawn on Monday. On Tuesday he spent $1.75 and on Wednesday he earned $1.00 walking the neighbor's dog. On Thursday, José had $7.00 left. How much was José paid for mowing the lawn?

2. Three boys got on a scale together and found their combined weight to be 283 pounds. One boy stepped off the scale and it showed 188 pounds. When a second boy jumped off the scale, it showed 103 pounds. What was the weight of each of the three boys?

3. Marilyn bought some strawberries. She gave two to Todd, three to Mark and four to Brian. She then had eight left. How many strawberries did Marilyn buy?

4. Gary, Joe and Sandy came home from school and raided the cookie jar. Gary had twice as many cookies as Joe, and Joe had three more than Sandy. Sandy had four cookies. How many cookies did Gary and Joe have?

5. There were 40 boys on the football team. 18 liked chocolate ice cream and 12 liked vanilla ice cream. 16 liked neither. How many boys liked both chocolate and vanilla ice cream?

6. Adam, Bob, Charles and Don were having a contest to see who could score highest on a dart board. Adam scored 10 more than Don, and Don scored 7 more than Charles. Charles scored 9 less than Bob. Bob scored 45. What were the scores of the others?

7. What if, in Problem 1, José was paid $10.00 to mow the lawn? How much would he have left on Thursday?

8. Write a problem that can be solved by working backwards where the answer is the number in a dozen.

9. If you round an amount to the nearest whole dollar and multiply by a one-digit number, what is the greatest amount you can be from the actual answer?

10. Five students are in a race. Two of them have already crossed the finish line. How many ways can the others cross the line? Prove that you are correct.

Calculators and Repeating Decimals

Fractions can be thought of as divisions in which the numerator is divided by the denominator. Enter these fractions into a calculator and write what appears on the screen.

$$\frac{1}{11} = \underline{\hspace{2cm}} \qquad \frac{5}{9} = \underline{\hspace{2cm}} \qquad \frac{8}{15} = \underline{\hspace{2cm}}$$

These decimals are called **repeating decimals.**
One way to write repeating decimals is to place a bar over the digit or digits that repeat.

$$\frac{1}{11} = 0.\overline{09} \qquad \frac{5}{9} = 0.\overline{5} \qquad \frac{8}{15} = 0.5\overline{3}$$

Enter these fractions into a calculator and write them using bars.

$$\frac{1}{9} = \underline{\hspace{1.5cm}} \qquad \frac{7}{30} = \underline{\hspace{1.5cm}} \qquad \frac{7}{66} = \underline{\hspace{1.5cm}}$$

Follow these steps to rename repeating decimals as fractions:

$$0.41\overline{6} = \frac{\boxed{?}}{\boxed{?}}$$

- The numerator is equal to the difference between the entire decimal number and the digits that don't repeat.

$$416 - 41 = \underline{\hspace{2cm}}$$

- The denominator will always start with 9 and there will be one 9 for every repeating digit. The 9's will be followed by one 0 for every non-repeating digit.

One repeating digit
$$\downarrow$$
$$9\underline{00}$$
$$\uparrow$$
two non-repeating digits

$$0.41\overline{6} = \underline{\hspace{2cm}}$$

Use a calculator to check this.
Rename $0.4\overline{5}$ as a fraction.

The numerator will be \underline{\hspace{1.5cm}}.

The denominator will be \underline{\hspace{1.5cm}}.

The fraction will be \underline{\hspace{1.5cm}}.
We check by entering the fraction into a calculator.

$$\underline{\hspace{2cm}} = \underline{\hspace{2cm}}$$

Practice

Write each fraction as a repeating decimal. Place a bar over any repeating digits.

1. $\frac{2}{3}$ = _____

2. $\frac{3}{8}$ = _____

3. $\frac{7}{12}$ = _____

4. $\frac{7}{15}$ = _____

5. $\frac{13}{24}$ = _____

6. $\frac{8}{90}$ = _____

7. $\frac{4}{7}$ = _____

8. $\frac{5}{13}$ = _____

9. $\frac{3}{11}$ = _____

10. $\frac{12}{37}$ = _____

11. $\frac{1}{9}$ = _____

12. $\frac{15}{16}$ = _____

13. $\frac{7}{8}$ = _____

14. $\frac{1}{12}$ = _____

15. $\frac{3}{4}$ = _____

16. $\frac{6}{11}$ = _____

Write each repeating decimal as a fraction. Simplify the fraction.

17. $0.2\overline{3}$ = ____

18. $0.\overline{45}$ = ____

19. $0.08\overline{3}$ = ____

20. $0.2\overline{6}$ = ____

21. $0.3\overline{6}$ = ____

22. $0.7\overline{3}$ = ____

23. $0.91\overline{6}$ = ____

24. $0.\overline{39}$ = ____

25. $0.7\overline{5}$ = ____

26. $0.2\overline{87}$ = ____

27. $0.4\overline{12}$ = ____

28. $0.\overline{142857}$ = ____

EXCURSION

What has a part always on the go?

You can solve this riddle by decoding the answers to these nine problems.

1. 1.8×5.31 = _____

2. 2.05×1.3 = _____

3. $10.48 - 1.982$ = _____

4. 3.4×0.07 = _____

5. $8.82 \div 3.6$ = _____

6. $11.904 \div 3.72$ = _____

7. 6.4×1.21 = _____

8. $0.598 + 1.852$ = _____

9. $61.295 \div 23$ = _____

Code Table	
A	0.238
D	9.558
E	2.665
L	1.67
M	0.035
P	8.498
R	2.45
S	4.061
T	3.2
U	7.744

___ ___ ___ ___ ___ ___ ___ ___ ___
 1   2   3   4   5   6   7   8   9

Multiply.

1. $\begin{array}{r} 5.6 \\ \times\ \ 8 \\ \hline \end{array}$

2. $\begin{array}{r} 4.21 \\ \times\ \ \ 6 \\ \hline \end{array}$

3. $\begin{array}{r} 25 \\ \times\ 1.6 \\ \hline \end{array}$

4. $\begin{array}{r} 3.05 \\ \times\ \ 28 \\ \hline \end{array}$

5. $\begin{array}{r} 3.85 \\ \times\ 0.3 \\ \hline \end{array}$

6. $\begin{array}{r} 4.7 \\ \times\ 0.13 \\ \hline \end{array}$

7. $\begin{array}{r} 3.761 \\ \times\ \ \ 2.5 \\ \hline \end{array}$

8. $\begin{array}{r} 9.64 \\ \times\ 5.3 \\ \hline \end{array}$

9. $\begin{array}{r} 0.004 \\ \times\ \ \ 15 \\ \hline \end{array}$

10. $\begin{array}{r} 0.04 \\ \times\ 0.03 \\ \hline \end{array}$

11. $\begin{array}{r} 0.006 \\ \times\ \ \ 0.4 \\ \hline \end{array}$

12. $\begin{array}{r} 5.03 \\ \times\ 0.008 \\ \hline \end{array}$

Divide.

13. $4\overline{)14.4}$

14. $3\overline{)1.68}$

15. $8\overline{)2.848}$

16. $7\overline{)44.1}$

17. $0.05\overline{)3.261}$

18. $0.9\overline{)0.036}$

19. $1.6\overline{)6.08}$

20. $4.3\overline{)1.505}$

21. $2.6\overline{)208}$

22. $0.5\overline{)0.1}$

23. $0.016\overline{)3.2}$

24. $6.5\overline{)52}$

Write each fraction as a decimal rounded to the nearest thousandth.

25. $\frac{5}{7} \approx$ _____

26. $\frac{7}{16} \approx$ _____

27. $\frac{3}{7} \approx$ _____

28. $\frac{11}{15} \approx$ _____

Circle the letter of the correct answer.

1 $9 - 3 \div 3 = n$
$n = ?$

- **a** 2
- **b** 8
- **c** 9
- **d** NG

2   34,358
 + 6,582

- **a** 40,840
- **b** 40,940
- **c** 41,940
- **d** NG

3   30,465
 − 16,587

- **a** 13,872
- **b** 23,872
- **c** 26,122
- **d** NG

4   1,596
 × 9

- **a** 14,364
- **b** 14,366
- **c** 14,464
- **d** NG

5 $27\overline{)365}$

- **a** 13 R14
- **b** 14 R13
- **c** 131 R4
- **d** NG

6 $2\frac{1}{3}$
 $+ 3\frac{2}{5}$

- **a** $5\frac{3}{8}$
- **b** $5\frac{11}{15}$
- **c** $6\frac{11}{15}$
- **d** NG

7 $7\frac{1}{3}$
 $- 4\frac{3}{4}$

- **a** $2\frac{1}{2}$
- **b** $2\frac{7}{12}$
- **c** $3\frac{7}{12}$
- **d** NG

8 $4\frac{1}{2} \times 3\frac{1}{3}$

- **a** $\frac{1}{15}$
- **b** $2\frac{7}{10}$
- **c** 15
- **d** NG

9 $2\frac{1}{2} \div 3\frac{1}{4}$

- **a** $\frac{10}{13}$
- **b** $1\frac{3}{10}$
- **c** $8\frac{1}{8}$
- **d** NG

10 What is the place value of the 6 in 13.2684?

- **a** tens
- **b** ones
- **c** tenths
- **d** NG

11   7.83
 + 2.648

- **a** 10.47
- **b** 10.478
- **c** 10.578
- **d** NG

 score

10 MEASUREMENT

Working with Units of Time

Our busy world makes it necessary to use many different units of time during our daily activities.

60 seconds (sec) = 1 minute (min)	
60 minutes = 1 hour (h)	
24 hours = 1 day (d)	

365 days = 1 year (yr)
7 days = 1 week (wk)
52 weeks = 1 year
12 months (mo) = 1 year
10 years = 1 decade
100 years = 1 century

We often have to change from one unit to another. How many hours and minutes are there in 158 minutes?

158 minutes = 158 ÷ 60 = 2 R38 = ____ hr ____ min

How many years and months are there in 39 months?

39 months = 39 ÷ 12 = 3 R3 = ____ yr ____ mo

How many hours are there in 6 days and 9 hours?

6 days = 6 × 24 = 144 hours + 9 hours = ____ hours.

We can add or subtract units of time.

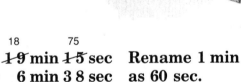

5 h 2 8 min + 2 h 5 2 min 7 h 8 0 min	Rename 80 min as 1 h 20 min.

$\overset{18}{\cancel{19}}$ min $\overset{75}{\cancel{15}}$ sec   Rename 1 min
− 6 min 3 8 sec   as 60 sec.

8 h ____ min

Getting Started

Rename the units of time.

1. 400 min = ____ h ____ min   2. 8 wk 2 d = ____ d   3. 4 yr 21 wk = ____ wk

Add or subtract.

4.   6 h 36 min
    − 2 h 29 min

5.   13 min 45 sec
    + 12 min 36 sec

6.   9 h 15 min 7 sec
    − 3 h 6 min 45 sec

Practice

Rename the units of time.

1. 6 wk 3 d = _____ d

2. 27 mo = _____ yr _____ mo

3. 57 d = _____ wk _____ d

4. 146 min = _____ h _____ min

5. 63 h = _____ d _____ h

6. 265 min 14 sec = _____ sec

7. 3 yr 12 wk = _____ wk

8. 6 d = _____ h

9. 3 wk 4 d = _____ d

10. 8 h = _____ sec

11. 810 d = _____ yr _____ d

12. 75 wk = _____ yr _____ d

13. 487 min = _____ h _____ min

14. 3 h 4 min 59 sec = _____ sec

15. 82 yr = _____ d

16. 10 yr = _____ wk

17. 107 mo = _____ yr _____ mo

18. 97 h = _____ sec

Add or subtract.

19.
```
    5 wk 4 d
  + 1 wk 8 d
```

20.
```
    3 d 14 h
  + 2 d 16 h
```

21.
```
   14 h 12 min
 −  9 h 36 min
```

22.
```
   15 min 46 sec
 + 17 min 18 sec
```

23.
```
   14 wk 3 d
 −  6 wk 5 d
```

24.
```
    6 h 25 min
  + 2 h 39 min
```

25.
```
   11 h  6 min
 −  4 h 25 min
```

26.
```
    2 yr 214 d
  + 3 yr 163 d
```

27.
```
   48 min 16 sec
 − 12 min 45 sec
```

28.
```
   38 wk 6 d
 +  6 wk 6 d
```

29.
```
   14 min 29 sec
 + 18 min 53 sec
```

30.
```
   10 h 15 min
 −  6 h 35 min
```

Apply

Solve these problems.

31. Mary worked out in the gym 2 hours and 28 minutes on Monday. Her workout lasted 1 hour and 35 minutes on Tuesday. How long did Mary work out on Monday and Tuesday?

32. Don agreed to work for 8 hours. He worked 3 hours and 32 minutes on Saturday and 2 hours and 25 minutes on Sunday. How much more time does Don need to work?

Understanding Schedules

Brigit is taking the bus from her home in Milbrea, to her grandmother's house in Saratoga. If Brigit leaves on the 10:15 bus, how long will it take to get to her grandmother's?

Peninsula Express			Valley Lines		
City	Arrive	Leave	City	Arrive	Leave
Milbrea	10:00	10:15	Sunnyvale	12:30	12:45
Redwood City	10:40	11:00	Santa Clara	1:05	1:20
Palo Alto	11:20	11:40	Saratoga	1:35	1:55
Sunnyvale	12:00	12:15	Los Gatos	2:30	
San Jose	1:00				

We want to know the total time needed for Brigit's trip. We know she will take the 10:15 Peninsula Express

bus from Milbrea to Sunnyvale, arriving at _____. She will leave Sunnyvale on the Valley Lines bus at

_____, and arrive at Saratoga at _____. To find the total time, we can add each of the times together.

Milbrea to Sunnyvale	10:15 to 12:00	____ hr ____ min	
Waiting time	12:00 to 12:45	____ hr ____ min	
Sunnyvale to Saratoga	12:45 to 1:35	+ ____ hr ____ min	
Total time		____ hr ____ min = ____ hr ____ min	

It will take Brigit ____ hours ____ minutes to make the trip.

Getting Started

Use the bus schedule to solve these problems.

1. How long does it take to travel from Redwood City to San Jose?

2. How long does it take to travel from Palo Alto to Los Gatos?

3. It takes Robert 45 minutes to walk to the bus station. What is the latest time he can leave home and catch the bus leaving Santa Clara?

4. How much longer does it take to travel from Sunnyvale to Los Gatos than from Redwood City to Sunnyvale?

Practice

Use the bus schedules to solve these problems.

ILLINI LINES		
	Arrive	Leave
Aurora	1:05 PM	1:20 PM
Naperville	1:48 PM	2:05 PM
Wheaton	2:36 PM	2:45 PM
Chicago	4:00 PM	—

PLAINS LINES		
	Arrive	Leave
Peoria	—	8:00 AM
LaSalle	9:30 AM	9:45 AM
Ottawa	10:24 AM	10:50 AM
Aurora	12:00 PM	12:20 PM
Joliet	1:40 PM	—

FOX LINES		
	Arrive	Leave
Wheaton	2:38 PM	3:00 PM
Elgin	3:52 PM	4:10 PM
DeKalb	5:16 PM	5:35 PM
Rockford	6:31 PM	—

1. What time does the Plains Line bus leave Ottawa?

2. How long does the Fox Lines bus stay in DeKalb?

3. How long does the bus take to travel from LaSalle to Ottawa?

4. How long does the Illini Lines bus stay in Naperville?

5. How long does the bus take to travel from Ottawa to Joliet?

6. How long does the bus take to travel from Naperville to Chicago?

7. How long does the bus take to travel from Peoria to Joliet?

8. How long does the bus take to travel from Wheaton to Rockford?

EXCURSION

The clock at the corner bank says 7:30. Ted's watch is 25 minutes fast, and Ned's watch is 15 minutes slow. Ted and Ned agree to meet when Ted's watch says 8:15. What time will it be on Ned's watch? What time will it be on the clock at the bank?

Using Customary Units of Length

Robert, Janis and Jonathan are being measured for band uniforms. What is Robert's height in inches?

We want to rename Robert's height in inches.

We know that he is _____ feet _____ inches tall.

To rename feet and inches as inches, we multiply the number of feet, by the number of inches in a foot, then add the extra inches.

We multiply _____ by _____ and add _____.

$$\begin{array}{r} 1\,2 \\ \times\ \ 6 \\ \hline \\ +\ \ 4 \\ \hline \end{array}$$

Robert is _____ inches tall.

To rename a mixed number like $5\frac{1}{2}$ feet as inches,

we **multiply** $5\frac{1}{2}$ by _____.

$5\frac{1}{2} \times 12 = \frac{11}{2} \times 12 =$ _____ inches

To rename smaller units as larger units like

48 inches as yards, we **divide** 48 by _____.

$\frac{48}{36} = 1\frac{12}{36} =$ _____ yards

✔ Remember, multiply to rename larger units as smaller ones. Divide to rename smaller units as larger ones.

We can add or subtract measurements of length.

$$\begin{array}{r} \textbf{5 ft 6 in.} \\ \textbf{+ 7 ft 8 in.} \\ \hline \textbf{1 2 ft 1 4 in.} \end{array}$$
(14 in. = 1 ft 2 in.)

$$\begin{array}{r} \textbf{3 yd 1 ft} \\ \textbf{- 1 yd 2 ft} \\ \hline \end{array}$$
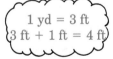
1 yd = 3 ft
3 ft + 1 ft = 4 ft

Getting Started

Rename.

1. $7\frac{1}{2}$ yd = _____ ft

2. 5 ft 4 in. = _____ in.

3. 68 in. = _____ yd

Add or subtract.

4. $\begin{array}{r} 6 \text{ ft } 9 \text{ in.} \\ - 2 \text{ ft } 11 \text{ in.} \\ \hline \end{array}$

5. $\begin{array}{r} 5 \text{ yd } 2 \text{ ft} \\ + 3 \text{ yd } 1 \text{ ft} \\ \hline \end{array}$

6. $\begin{array}{r} 7 \text{ yd } 2 \text{ ft } 3 \text{ in.} \\ - 5 \text{ yd } 1 \text{ ft } 6 \text{ in.} \\ \hline \end{array}$

217

Practice

Rename.

1. 5 ft 6 in. = _____ in.

2. 96 in. = _____ ft _____ in.

3. 7 yd 2 ft = _____ ft

4. 3 mi = _____ yd

5. 6 yd 8 in. = _____ in.

6. 5 mi = _____ ft

7. 104 in. = _____ ft _____ in.

8. $6\frac{2}{3}$ ft = _____ in.

9. 8 yd 2 ft = _____ ft

10. 54 in. = _____ ft

11. 10,560 ft = _____ mi

12. 2 yd 2 ft 6 in. = _____ in.

13. 2 mi = _____ ft

14. 18 yd 1 ft = _____ in.

15. 784 ft = _____ yd _____ ft

16. 10,000 ft = _____ mi _____ ft

17. 880 ft = _____ yd _____ ft

18. 1 mi = _____ in.

Add or subtract.

19.   5 ft 5 in.
    + 2 ft 9 in.

20.   6 ft 3 in.
    − 2 ft 7 in.

21.   4 ft 7 in.
    + 3 ft 5 in.

22.   8 yd 1 ft
    − 4 yd 2 ft

23.   6 yd 14 in.
    + 9 yd 21 in.

24.   7 mi 860 yd
    + 3 mi 925 yd

25.   17 ft 1 in.
    − 9 ft 6 in.

26.   13 yd 3 ft
    − 6 yd 2 ft

27.   12 yd 2 ft
    + 6 yd 2 ft

28.   9 yd 14 in.
    − 6 yd 18 in.

29.   6 ft 7 in.
    + 15 ft 9 in.

30.   3 yd 2 ft 9 in.
    + 5 yd 1 ft 7 in.

Apply

Solve these problems.

31. Bart long jumped 15 feet 8 inches on his first try and 16 feet 5 inches on his second try. How much longer was Bart's second try?

32. A fabric costs $5.40 per yard. A decorator bought $2\frac{1}{2}$ yards of blue fabric and $3\frac{1}{3}$ of yellow fabric. How much did the decorator pay for the fabric?

Computing Perimeters

Professor Landon is putting a fence around the archeological dig he started by the river. The distance around a flat region is called the **perimeter.** What is the perimeter of Professor Landon's dig?

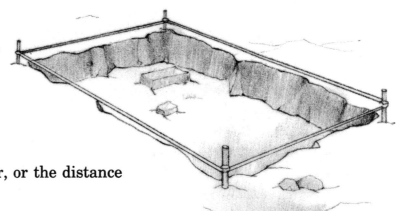

We want to know the perimeter, or the distance around the site.

We know that the length of the dig is ____ feet and

it is ____ feet wide.

To find the perimeter of a rectangle, we find the sum of the lengths of the sides.

$$
\begin{array}{r}
4\,0 \text{ ft} \\
2\,5 \text{ ft} \\
4\,0 \text{ ft} \\
+\,2\,5 \text{ ft} \\
\hline
\end{array}
$$

Or we can use the formula:

Perimeter = 2 × Length + 2 × Width or
P = 2 × (L + W)
P = 2 × (40 + 25)
P = 2 × 65

P = ____

The perimeter of the dig is ____ feet.

Getting Started

Find the perimeter.

1.
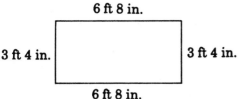

2.
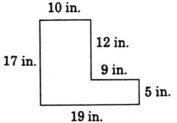

Find the perimeter of each rectangle.

3. Length: 25 in.
   Width: 16 in.

4. Length: $3\frac{1}{2}$ ft
   Width: 7 ft

5. Length: 6 yd
   Width: 6 yd

Practice

Find the perimeter.

1.

12 in.

12 in. 12 in.

12 in. 12 in.

12 in.

2.

6 ft 3 in. 12 ft 6 in.

12 ft 8 in.

3.

$6\frac{1}{2}$ in. $6\frac{1}{2}$ in.

$8\frac{3}{4}$ in.

4.

25 ft

25 ft 25 ft

25 ft

Find the perimeter of each rectangle.

5. Length: 21 ft
Width: 7 ft

6. Length: $6\frac{3}{4}$ in.
Width: $8\frac{1}{2}$ in.

7. Length: 3.5 ft
Width: 1.6 ft

8. Length: $12\frac{2}{3}$ ft
Width: $8\frac{1}{2}$ ft

9. Length: 16 in.
Width: 24 in.

10. Length: 16 in.
Width: $2\frac{1}{2}$ ft

11. Length: 27 ft
Width: 18 in.

12. Length: $2\frac{1}{4}$ in.
Width: $8\frac{1}{2}$ in.

13. Length: $17\frac{3}{8}$ ft
Width: $12\frac{2}{5}$ ft

Apply

Solve these problems. Draw a picture to help.

14. A lot in the shape of a triangle is 48 feet on each side. What is the perimeter of the lot?

15. A square has a perimeter of 64 inches. How long is each side?

16. The Martins are fencing in a rectangular yard. The cost of the fence is $8.75 per foot. If the yard is 25 feet long and 30 feet wide, what will it cost to fence the yard?

17. The width of a rectangle is twice its length. The perimeter is 48 inches. How wide is the rectangle?

18. Charmaine is buying fabric to make a dress. She needs a piece of silk $4\frac{3}{8}$ yards long by 36 inches wide. How many yards is the perimeter of Charmaine's fabric?

19. Bela is putting a border of tile around his bathroom. Each tile is 6 inches wide. How many tiles will Bela need if his bathroom is 6 feet long and 8 feet wide?

Computing Circumferences

The distance around a circle is called its **circumference.** The distance across the center of a circle is called its **diameter.** About how many times larger is the circumference of a circle than its diameter?

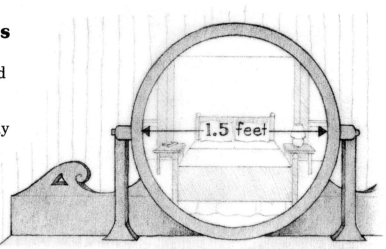

1.5 feet

The ancient Greek mathematicians found that the circumference divided by the diameter of a circle is always the same. They named this number with the Greek letter **pi, π.** We use 3.14 as the approximate value of π.

The circumference of a circle is _____ times larger than its diameter.
This comparison can be shown by the formula:

> **Circumference = pi times diameter**
> $C = \pi \times d$
> $C = 3.14 \times d$

To find the circumference of the bedroom mirror,

we multiply pi by the diameter. We multiply _____

by _____.

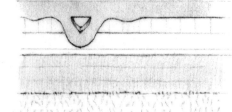

$$\begin{array}{r} 3.14 \\ \times \quad 1.5 \\ \hline \end{array}$$

The circumference of the mirror is _____.

Getting Started

Find the circumference.

1. d = 4 in.

2. d = 1.5 yd

3. d = 2.25 ft

Complete the table.

4.
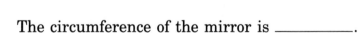

diameter	5.1 in.	7 ft	4.25 yd	8 ft
circumference				

Practice

Find the circumference.

1. d = 3 in.

2. d = 1.8 ft

3. d = 9 ft

4. d = 12 ft

5. d = 7 yd

6. $d = 2\frac{1}{2}$ in.

7. d = 3.72 in.

8. d = 4.5 yd

9. d = 7.05 ft

10. d = 86 yd

11. d = 29 ft

12. d = .06 yd

Complete the table.

13.

diameter	3.2 in.	4 ft	3.65 yd	5 ft	4.5 yd	6.65 ft	24 in.
circumference							

Apply

Solve these problems.

14. A ball has a diameter of 9 inches. How far will the ball roll in one complete turn?

15. A bicycle wheel has a diameter of 32 inches. How far will the bike travel after the wheel makes 6 full turns?

16. Martin is putting a low fence around a circular fishpond that has a diameter of 4 feet. The fence material costs $6.80 a foot. To the nearest cent, how much is the fence material?

17. Ann is running a circular track that has a 133.33 yard diameter. To the nearest yard, how far is it around the track?

EXCURSION

How much smaller is the circumference of the small circle than the circumference of the large circle?

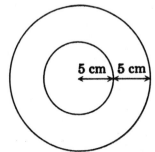

5 cm   5 cm

Using Customary Units of Capacity and Weight

Isabelle is mixing salad dressing to be put on each of the 32 tables set up for the awards banquet. Each dressing bottle holds 6 ounces. How many pints of salad dressing should Isabelle mix?

Capacity	Weight
8 ounces (oz) = 1 cup (c)	16 ounces (oz) = 1 pound (lb)
2 cups = 1 pint (pt)	2,000 pounds = 1 ton (T)
2 pints = 1 quart (qt)	
4 quarts = 1 gallon (gal)	

We want to know how many pints of salad dressing

Isabelle should prepare. We know there are ____

tables, and that each will contain a ____-ounce bottle.

To find the total ounces needed, we multiply the number of tables, by the number of ounces each will be served.

To rename ounces as pints, we divide the total ounces by the number of ounces in one pint.

We multiply ____ by ____ and divide by ____.

$$\begin{array}{r} 3\,2 \leftarrow \text{number of tables} \\ \times \quad 6 \leftarrow \text{number of ounces per table} \\ \hline \leftarrow \text{total ounces needed} \end{array}$$

number of ounces → 16)‾‾‾ ← number of pints
in 1 pint   ← number of ounces

Isabelle needs to mix ____ pints of salad dressing.

Getting Started

Rename.

1. $3\frac{1}{2}$ pt = ____ oz

2. 11 qt = ____ gal ____ qt

3. 136 oz = ____ lb

Add or subtract.

4. 4 gal 3 qt
   + 2 gal 2 qt

5. 15 lb 8 oz
   − 9 lb 12 oz

6. $3\frac{1}{2}$ lb + $2\frac{3}{4}$ lb = ____

223

Practice

Rename.

1. 5 qt = _____ gal _____ qt

2. $5\frac{1}{2}$ gal = _____ pt

3. 4 lb 6 oz = _____ oz

4. 18 qt = _____ gal

5. 5,000 lb = _____ T

6. 52 oz = _____ pt _____ oz

7. $7\frac{1}{2}$ pt = _____ c

8. 76 oz = _____ c _____ oz

9. $4\frac{3}{4}$ lb = _____ oz

10. $5\frac{3}{5}$ T = _____ lb

11. $3\frac{1}{4}$ pt = _____ c

12. 4 gal 8 pt = _____ pt

Add or subtract.

13.   2 c 4 oz
    + 3 c 15 oz
    _____

14.   9 lb 7 oz
    − 6 lb 10 oz
    _____

15.   5 qt 1 pt
    + 3 qt 5 pt
    _____

16.   6 gal 3 qt
    − 2 gal 5 qt
    _____

17. $5\frac{1}{4}$ gal + $3\frac{2}{3}$ gal = _____

18. $9\frac{1}{5}$ T + $5\frac{3}{4}$ T = _____

Apply

Solve the problems.

19. A recipe calls for $2\frac{1}{2}$ cups white flour and 6 ounces rye flour. How many ounces of flour are needed for the recipe?

20. Robert has $5\frac{1}{2}$ pounds of cashews. He is putting them in 4-ounce cups for a party. How many cups of cashews can Robert pour?

EXCURSION

There are ten pennies and a pan balance. One of the pennies is heavier than the others. How can you find the heavy penny in 3 weighings or less?

Using Metric Units of Length

The **meter** is the basic unit of length in the metric system.

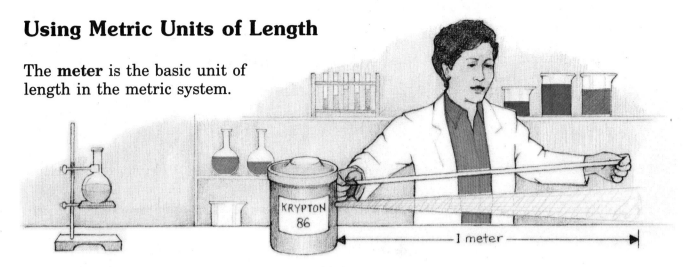

1 meter

The metric system is based on powers of 10. Each unit is 10 times greater than the next smaller unit, and 0.1 the size of the next larger unit.

kilometer (km)	hectometer (hm)	decameter (dam)	basic unit (m)	decimeter (dm)	centimeter (cm)	millimeter (mm)
1,000 m	100 m	10 m	1 m	0.1 m	0.01 m	0.001 m

How many millimeters are in 1.5 meters?
How many kilometers are in 3,500 meters?

✔ To rename a larger unit as a smaller unit, multiply by the corresponding power of 10. To rename 1.5 meters as millimeters, multiply by 1,000.

1.5 × 1,000 = _____

There are _____ millimeters in 1.5 meters.

✔ To rename a smaller unit as a larger unit, divide by the corresponding power of 10. To rename 3,500 meters as kilometers, divide by 1,000.

3,500 ÷ 1,000 = _____

There are _____ kilometers in 3,500 meters.

Getting Started

Rename.

1. 3 cm = _____ mm

2. 2 m = _____ cm

3. 25 mm = _____ m

4. 20 cm = _____ dm

5. 16.5 cm = _____ mm

6. 86,000 mm = _____ m

Write >, < or =.

7. 43 m ___ 4.3 km

8. 26 cm ___ 260 mm

9. 350 dm ___ 3.5 m

10. 8.2 m ___ 82 km

11. 760 cm ___ 7.6 dm

12. 1,200 mm ___ 1.2 m

225

Practice

Find the missing number.

1. 1 cm = _____ mm

2. 2.5 km = _____ m

3. 15 dm = _____ m

4. 6 m = _____ cm

5. 0.025 m = _____ mm

6. 525 m = _____ km

7. 146 dam = _____ km

8. 28.6 m = _____ mm

9. 0.78 dm = _____ m

10. 250 m = _____ km

11. 326 hm = _____ m

12. 4.95 m = _____ cm

13. 12 mm = _____ cm

14. 6 km = _____ m

15. 75 cm = _____ m

16. 0.38 dam = _____ m

17. 25 dm = _____ cm

18. 159.6 mm = _____ cm

Write >, < or =.

19. 45 cm ___ 4.5 mm

20. 3 m ___ 300 dm

21. 5 km ___ 500 m

22. 1.5 m ___ 150 cm

23. 560 m ___ 5.6 hm

24. 180 cm ___ 1.8 mm

25. 200 cm ___ 0.2 m

26. 0.321 km ___ 3,210 cm

27. 0.6 km ___ 60 m

28. 500 mm ___ 50 cm

29. 2.3 m ___ 230 mm

30. 3.01 cm ___ 301 mm

31. 586 mm ___ 5.86 cm

32. 0.25 km ___ 250 cm

33. 0.111 km ___ 1,110 cm

34. 8 km ___ 800 dam

35. 0.19 dm ___ 0.19 m

36. 24 m ___ 2,400 dm

Apply

Solve these problems.

37. Jackie ran in a 10,000-meter race. How many kilometers did Jackie run?

38. Nat's kite has a tail 1.5 times longer than Bill's kite. If the tail on Bill's kite is 3.6 meters long, how many centimeters long is the one on Nat's kite?

Find the perimeter.

39.

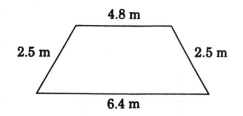

4.8 m

2.5 m   2.5 m

6.4 m

40.

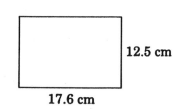

12.5 cm

17.6 cm

Using Metric Units of Capacity and Weight

The **liter** is the basic unit of capacity in the metric system. If a jar holds 2.35 liters of juice, how many milliliters does it hold?

The **gram** is the basic unit of weight. If a bar of soap weighs 400 grams, what is its weight in kilograms?

1 liter (L) = 1,000 milliliters
1 mL = 0.001 L

1 gram (g) = 1,000 milligrams (mg)
1,000 g = 1 kilogram (kg)
1,000 kg = 1 metric ton (T)

✔ To rename a larger unit as a smaller unit, multiply by the corresponding power of 10. To rename 2.35 liters as milliliters, multiply by 1,000.

✔ To rename a smaller unit as a larger unit, divide by the corresponding power of 10. To rename 400 grams as kilograms, divide by 1,000.

2.35 × 1,000 = _____

400 ÷ 1,000 = _____

The jar holds _____ milliliters.

The soap weighs _____ of a kilogram.

Getting Started

Rename.

1. 6.5 kg = _____ g

2. 536 mL = _____ L

3. 2.6 T = _____ kg

4. 56 L = _____ mL

5. 875 g = _____ kg

6. 20 kg = _____ T

Write >, < or =.

7. 6.91 kg ___ 691 g

8. 700 mL ___ 0.7 L

9. 0.21 g ___ 2,100 mg

10. 48 g ___ 4.8 mg

11. 7,800 kg ___ 78 T

12. 200 mL ___ 0.2 L

227

Practice

Rename.

1. 648 g = _____ kg   2. 5.1 kg = _____ g   3. 5.268 mL = _____ L

4. 5,860 kg = _____ T   5. 0.61 L = _____ mL   6. 4.21 T = _____ kg

7. 500 mL = _____ L   8. 3.96 kg = _____ mg   9. 5.9 kg = _____ g

10. 9,256 mg = _____ g   11. 859 kg = _____ T   12. 2.961 L = _____ mL

Write >, < or =.

13. 5.6 L ___ 5,600 mL   14. 0.215 T ___ 21.5 kg   15. 5,000 mg ___ 50 g

16. 6,249 mg ___ 6.249 g   17. 0.5 kg ___ 500 g   18. 0.82 L ___ 82 mL

Apply

Solve these problems.

19. A large truck weighs about 1.2 metric tons. How many kilograms does the truck weigh?

20. Tom weighs 82.6 kilograms, Ted weighs 76.5 kilograms and Rich weighs 80.3 kilograms. What is the average weight of the boys?

21. Ronnie is making hamburger patties that weigh 126 grams. How many kilograms of hamburger will Ronnie need to buy to serve 15 hamburgers?

22. A pitcher holds 1.5 liters of juice. Marty has poured 2 glasses of juice from the pitcher. If each glass holds 480 milliliters of juice, how many milliliters of juice are left in the pitcher?

EXCURSION

There are two buckets. One holds exactly 5 liters of water. The other holds exactly 7 liters of water. How can you use the two buckets to measure 3 liters of water?

Using a Formula, Writing an Open Sentence

A rectangular swimming pool has a
140-meter perimeter. What is the area
of the pool if it is 50 meters long?

★ SEE

We want to know the area of the swimming pool.

The perimeter of the pool is _____ meters.

The length of the pool is _____ meters.

★ PLAN

We need to know the width to find the area. We use
the formula for finding perimeter to help us write an
open sentence to find the width of the pool. Once we
know the width, we can then multiply it by the length
to find the area of the pool.

★ DO

(Length × 2) + (Width × 2) = Perimeter
(50 × 2) + (Width × 2) = 140
(100) + (Width × 2) = 140

Since we are missing an addend in this example, we will
need to subtract to find the value of the width times 2.

$$\begin{array}{r} 140 \\ -100 \\ \hline \end{array}$$

The width doubled is _____, so by dividing by 2 we find
the measure of one width.

Length × Width = Area

50 × _____ = _____
The area of the pool is _____ square meters.

★ CHECK

We can check our work by substituting the actual
length and width in the perimeter and area formulas.

(2 × Length) + (2 × Width) = Perimeter

(2 × 50) + (2 × _____) = ?

_____ + _____ = _____

Length × Width = Area

50 × _____ = _____

229

Apply

Use a formula or write an open sentence to help solve these problems.

1. A rectangular playground has a perimeter of 200 meters. Its length is 60 meters. What is its width?

2. An equilateral triangle is a triangle having all three sides the same length. Write a formula to find the perimeter of an equilateral triangle. If one side of a equilateral triangle is 18 inches, what is the perimeter?

3. The volume of a rectangular solid is found by multiplying the length, width and height. Determine the volume of a rectangular solid having a length of 5 centimeters, a width of 3 centimeters and a height of 9 centimeters.

4. The volume of a rectangular solid is 1,260 cubic inches. The length of the solid is 18 inches and the width is 7 inches. Write a formula for finding the height and use it to find the missing measurement.

5. The area of a circle can be found by the formula:
Area = 3.14 × radius × radius.
Determine the area of a circle whose radius is 8 inches.

6. A computer floppy disk cover is a square 5.25 inches on a side. The hole in the center has a radius of approximately 0.5 of an inch. Determine the area of the disk cover.

7. Suppose the length of the rectangle in Problem 1 was 50 meters instead of 60 meters. How would this make the rectangle special?

8. A picometer is a metric unit of measure. A picometer is one trillionth of a meter. How does 1 picometer compare to 1 millimeter?

9. The formula for the number of handshakes possible in a group of n people is: $H = \frac{1}{2} \times n \times (n - 1)$. How many handshakes are possible with 5 people? Explain the answer when you try the formula with 1 person.

10. Lois has a garden shaped like a rectangle. The length is a whole number of meters as is the width. The perimeter is 20 meters. What are the possible dimensions of the rectangle?

Add or subtract.

1.   5 h 18 min
   + 3 h 24 min

2.   18 min 48 sec
   + 9 min 18 sec

3.   6 h 4 min
  − 2 h 36 min

4.   8 ft 3 in.
  − 2 ft 6 in.

5.   8 yd 29 in.
  + 6 yd 16 in.

6.   9 ft 8 in.
  + 4 ft 7 in.

7.   12 min 48 sec
 − 6 min 49 sec

8.   14 h 15 min
 − 12 h 50 min

9.   8 yd 11 in.
 + 16 yd 48 in.

Find the perimeter or circumference.

10.
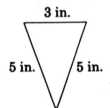

11.
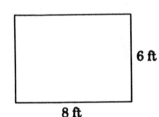

12.
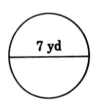

Add or subtract.

13.   9 gal 2 qt
  + 6 gal 3 qt

14.   3 pt 7 oz
  + 9 pt 5 oz

15.   15 lb 9 oz
  − 6 lb 15 oz

16.   9 lb 6 oz
  + 4 lb 15 oz

17.   2 gal 1 qt
  − 1 gal 2 qt

18.   17 pt 1 oz
  − 5 pt 7 oz

Find the missing numbers.

19. 25 cm = _____ mm

20. 6,246 m = _____ km

21. 515 mm = _____ m

22. 840 mm = _____ cm

23. 6.2 km = _____ m

24. 48 mm = _____ m

25. 720,000 mm = _____ km

26. 572 T = _____ kg

27. 0.02 g = _____ mg

28. 920 kg = _____ mg

29. 53 cm = _____ dm

30. 747 T = _____ kg

31. 2.92 km = _____ m

32. 0.003 T = _____ g

33. 0.0006 g = _____ mg

231

Circle the letter of the correct answer.

1
$$\begin{array}{r} 53 \\ \times\ 36 \end{array}$$

a 577
b 1,898
c 1,908
d NG

2 $9\overline{)348}$

a 3 R86
b 38
c 38 R6
d NG

3
$$\begin{array}{r} 2\frac{1}{8} \\ +\ 5\frac{1}{3} \\ \hline \end{array}$$

a $7\frac{2}{11}$
b $7\frac{11}{24}$
c $8\frac{11}{24}$
d NG

4
$$\begin{array}{r} 9\frac{1}{5} \\ -\ 2\frac{2}{3} \\ \hline \end{array}$$

a $6\frac{8}{15}$
b $7\frac{1}{2}$
c $7\frac{8}{15}$
d NG

5 $2\frac{1}{4} \times 5\frac{1}{3}$

a $\frac{27}{64}$
b $\frac{1}{12}$
c 12
d NG

6 $6\frac{2}{3} \div 1\frac{1}{4}$

a $\frac{3}{16}$
b $5\frac{1}{3}$
c $8\frac{1}{3}$
d NG

7 What is the place value of the 9 in 5.2974?

a tenths
b hundredths
c thousandths
d NG

8
$$\begin{array}{r} 2.3 \\ 4.68 \\ +\ 1.925 \\ \hline \end{array}$$

a 7.805
b 8.905
c 8.005
d NG

9
$$\begin{array}{r} 25.06 \\ -\ 9.875 \\ \hline \end{array}$$

a 15.195
b 15.285
c 16.285
d NG

10
$$\begin{array}{r} 3.4 \\ \times\ 0.08 \\ \hline \end{array}$$

a 0.072
b 0.272
c 2.72
d NG

11 $0.008\overline{)4.624}$

a 5.78
b 57.8
c 578
d NG

12 Write $\frac{1}{8}$ as a decimal rounded to tenths.

a 0.1
b 0.13
c 0.125
d NG

 score

232

GEOMETRY

Understanding Basic Geometric Ideas

A **plane** is a flat surface that extends forever in all directions. A **point** is any position on the plane. A plane is named by any three of its points. Other basic geometric figures are also named by points they contain.

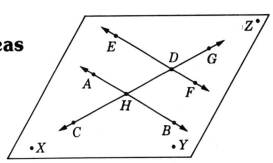

Plane *XYZ*

A **line segment** connects two points that are called **endpoints.** If two line segments are the same length, they are **congruent.**

line segment *EF* ($\overline{EF}$)
line segment *FE* ($\overline{FE}$)

A **line** has no endpoints. It extends forever in opposite directions.

line *AB* ($\overleftrightarrow{AB}$)
line *BA* ($\overleftrightarrow{BA}$)

A **ray** is part of a line, with only one endpoint.

ray *DF* ($\overrightarrow{DF}$)

Some lines intersect or meet. The point of intersection for $\overleftrightarrow{EF}$ and $\overleftrightarrow{CG}$ is point *D*. If there is no point of intersection, the lines are **parallel.**

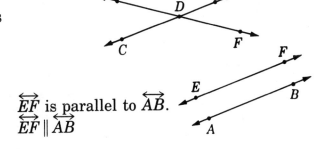

$\overleftrightarrow{EF}$ is parallel to $\overleftrightarrow{AB}$.
$\overleftrightarrow{EF} \parallel \overleftrightarrow{AB}$

Getting Started

Name the figure.

1.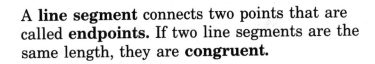
   X   *Y*

   _____

2.
   M   *N*

   _____

3.
   R   *S*

   _____

Draw and label.

4. Line segment $\overline{ST}$

5. $\overleftrightarrow{AB} \parallel \overrightarrow{VW}$

Practice

Name the figure.

1.

_____

2.

_____

3.

_____

4.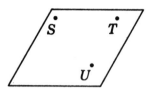

_____

5.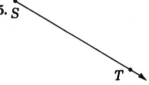

_____

6.

_____

Draw and label.

7. line XY

8. line segment PQ

9. point P in a plane

10. $\overleftrightarrow{RT}$ intersecting $\overleftrightarrow{XY}$

11. ray $\overrightarrow{ST}$

12. $\overleftrightarrow{RS} \parallel \overleftrightarrow{MN}$

EXCURSION

Complete the chart.

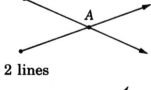

2 lines

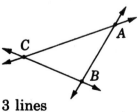

3 lines

4 lines

Number of Lines	Number of Points of Intersection
2	___
3	___
4	___
5	___
6	___

234

Classifying Angles

An **angle** is formed by two rays with a common endpoint. The rays intersect at the **vertex.** An angle is named with the vertex in the middle. What type of an angle is angle *ABC*?

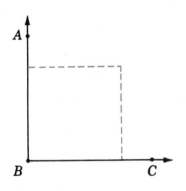

The angle formed can be named:
angle *ABC*(∠*ABC*)
angle *CBA*(∠*CBA*)
angle *B*(∠*B*)

We can use the corner of this page to classify angles.

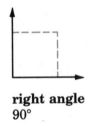

right angle
90°

acute angle
less than a
right angle

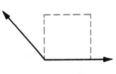

obtuse angle
greater than
a right angle

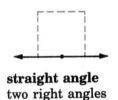

straight angle
two right angles

Angle *ABC* is a _____ angle.

Getting Started

Name each angle three different ways. Name the rays and vertex. Classify each angle.

1.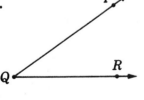

2.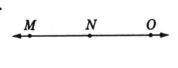

3.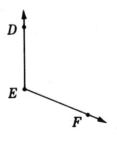

_____

_____

_____

Practice

Name each angle three different ways. Name the rays and vertex.
Classify each angle.

1.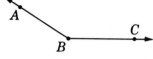

_____

_____

_____

2.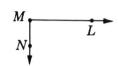

_____

_____

_____

3.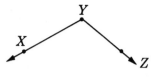

_____

_____

_____

4.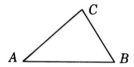

_____

_____

_____

5.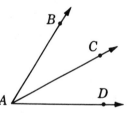

_____

_____

_____

6.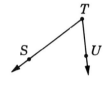

_____

_____

_____

Apply

Name three angles in each figure.

7.

8.

EXCURSION

Use the pattern to complete the table.

Rows	Dots
1	___
2	___
3	___
4	___
5	___
6	___
10	___

How does the table compare to the one on page 234? _____

Measuring Angles

The basic unit of angle measure is the **degree** (°). A **protractor** is used to measure angles. What is the measure of angle ABC?

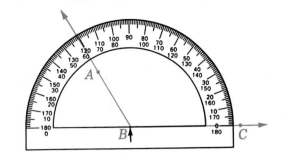

To read a protractor, place the arrow on the vertex, and the zero angle on one ray of the angle. The measure of the angle is read on the outside scale. The measure of angle ABC is 120°. We write:

m∠ABC = 120°.

m∠COA = _____

∠COA is a _____ angle.

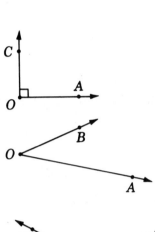

m∠BOA = _____

∠BOA is an _____ angle.

m∠DOA = _____

∠DOA is an _____ angle.

m∠EOA = _____

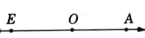

∠EOA is a _____ angle.

Angles with the same measure are called **congruent angles.**

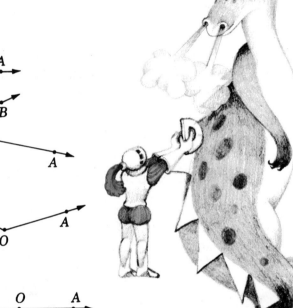

Getting Started

Give the measure and classify each angle.

1. m∠RKL = _____

_____

2. m∠QKL = _____

_____

3. m∠PKL = _____

_____

4. m∠JKL = _____

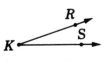

_____

5. m∠RKS = _____

_____

6. m∠JKQ = _____

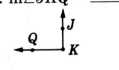

_____

237

Practice

Give the measure and classify each angle.

1. m∠*XOZ* = _____

   _____

2. m∠*VOY* = _____

   _____

3. m∠*VOZ* = _____

   _____

4. m∠*XOU* = _____

   _____

5. m∠*UOZ* = _____

   _____

6. m∠*WOY* = _____

   _____

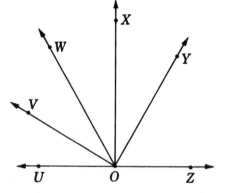

Apply

Give the measure of each angle. Use your protractor to draw an angle congruent to each angle.

7.

8.

9.

10.

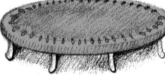

11. Draw $\overrightarrow{AB}$. Draw an angle of 45° with ray *AB* as one side.

12. Draw $\overleftrightarrow{XY}$ with point *T*. Draw ∠*XTA* with measure 135°.

Understanding Lines and Angles

In a plane, two lines either intersect or are parallel. What can we say about the angles formed by intersecting lines? We will use letters to represent lines and numbers to represent angles.

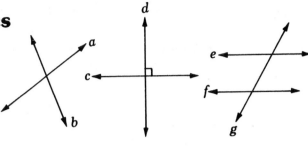

When two lines intersect, _____ angles are formed. The angles opposite each other are called **vertical angles.**

Angle 1 and _____ are vertical angles. Use your protractor to measure angles 2 and 4.
What do you think is true of vertical

angles? _____

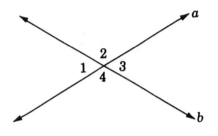

If two lines intersect and form a right angle, the lines are **perpendicular.** We write: $c \perp d$. All the angles formed by perpendicular lines are right angles. If $m\angle 5 = 90°$, then $m\angle 5 = m\angle 6 = m\angle 7 = m\angle 8$.

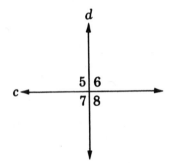

If two lines do not intersect, they are parallel. We write: $e \parallel f$. A line that intersects two other lines is called a **transversal.** Use your protractor to find each of the following.

$m\angle 7 =$ _____ $m\angle 11 =$ _____

$m\angle 10 + m\angle 12 =$ _____

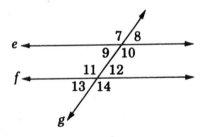

Getting Started

1. Name the perpendicular segments.

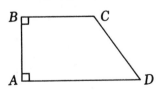

_____

2. Name the parallel segments.

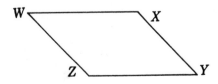

_____

239

Practice

Name the perpendicular segments.

1.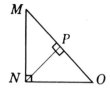

2.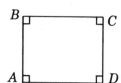

3.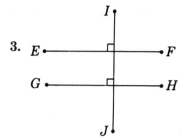

Name the parallel segments.

4.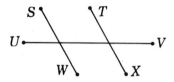

5.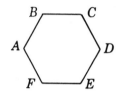

6.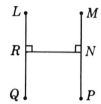

Apply

Use your protractor to measure the angles.

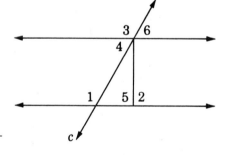

7. m∠1 = _____

8. m∠2 = _____

9. m∠3 = _____

10. m∠4 = _____

11. m∠5 = _____

12. m∠6 = _____

13. m∠2 + m∠5 = _____

14. m∠3 + m∠6 = _____

15. m∠1 + m∠4 = _____

16. m∠3 + m∠4 = _____

EXCURSION

Study this pattern for finding the total number of squares.

1 square

1 square
+ 4 new squares
----
5 squares

1 square
4 squares
+ 9 new squares
----
14 squares

1 square
4 squares
9 squares
+ 16 new squares
----
30 squares

How many squares will be in the next figure?

Working with Circles

A **circle** is the set of all points the same distance from a point called the **center.** The circular line around a circle is called the **circumference.** We use a compass to construct the circumference of a circle.

A line segment from the center to the circle is called a **radius.** Line segment *AO* is a radius in circle *O.*

A line segment with its endpoints on the circle is called a **chord.** Line segment *DE* is a chord.

A **diameter** is a chord that passes through the center. Its length is twice the length of the radius. Line segment *BC* is a diameter.

An angle with its vertex at the center is called a **central angle.** Angle *AOC* is a central angle.

An **arc** is part of the circumference that is formed by a central angle. The curved line from *A* to *C* is an arc.
We write: $\overset{\frown}{AC}$.

The measure of an arc is the same as the measure of the central angle.
We write: $m\overset{\frown}{AC} = m\angle AOC$

A circle contains 360 degrees.

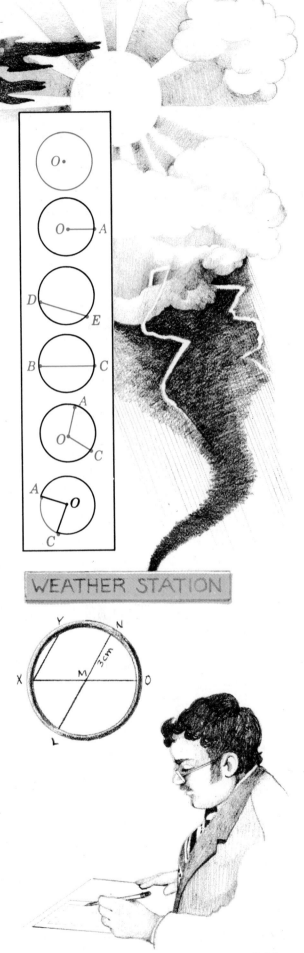

Getting Started

Complete the following.

1. $\overline{MN}$ is a(n) _____.

2. $m\angle NMO =$ _____; $m\angle LMO =$ _____

3. $\overline{XY}$ is a(n) _____.

4. $\overset{\frown}{ON}$ is a(n) _____.

5. The length of the diameter is _____.

241

Practice

Complete the following.

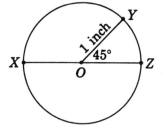

1. $\overline{YO}$ is a(n) _____.   2. $\overset{\frown}{YZ}$ is a(n) _____.

3. $\overline{XZ}$ is a(n) _____.   4. $m\overset{\frown}{YX}$ = _____.

5. The length of the diameter is _____.

Draw and label these parts of a circle.

6. arc BE 7. central angle EOD

8. diameter BC 9. chord FG

10. radius OD

Apply

Complete the table. Remember $C = \pi \times d$.

11.	radius	2 in.			6.5 in.		4.38 in.	7.05 in.
	diameter		10 in.	8 in.		8.4 in.		
	circumference							

EXCURSION

Use your compass and ruler to copy the figure. Then draw other figures with your compass and ruler.

Bisecting Line Segments and Angles

To **bisect** means to divide into two
congruent parts. We bisect line
segments and angles with a compass
and straightedge.

To bisect a line segment, follow these steps:

- Draw a line segment and label the endpoints
  A and B. With your compass, select a radius
  which is larger than half the length of $\overline{AB}$.
  With point A as center, construct an
  arc above and an arc below $\overline{AB}$.

- Keep your compass setting
  unchanged. With point B as center,
  construct two arcs which intersect
  the arcs constructed in the first step.
  Label the intersections C and D.

- Draw $\overleftrightarrow{CD}$. $\overleftrightarrow{CD}$ bisects $\overline{AB}$. $\overline{AM}$ is congruent
  to $\overline{MB}$. M is the midpoint of $\overline{AB}$.
  We write: $\overleftrightarrow{CD} \perp \overline{AB}$.

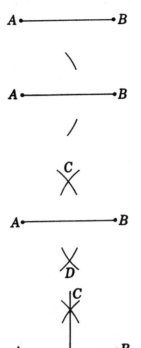

To bisect an angle, follow these steps:

- Draw $\angle ABC$.
  With B as center, construct an arc
  intersecting $\angle ABC$ at points M
  and N.

- Keep your compass setting unchanged.
  With M and N as centers, construct
  two arcs intersecting in the interior
  of $\angle ABC$. Label the intersection D.

- Draw $\overrightarrow{BD}$. $\overrightarrow{BD}$ bisects $\angle ABC$.
  $\angle ABD$ is congruent $\angle DBC$.

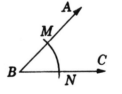

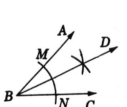

Getting Started

Bisect each segment or angle.

1.

2.

Practice

Bisect each segment or angle.

1.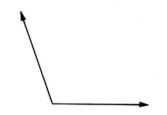

2.

3.

4.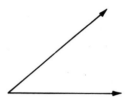

Apply

Draw the figure with your ruler or protractor. Bisect the figure. Check the result.

5. segment, 6 centimeters

6. angle, 120°

7. angle, 48°

8. segment, 5 centimeters

244

Copying Line Segments and Angles

We use a compass and a straightedge
to copy geometric figures.

To copy $\overline{AB}$, follow these steps:

A •————————• B

Draw ray EF.

Set the points of the
compass on A and B.
Mark an arc on $\overrightarrow{EF}$.

Label the intersection G.
$\overline{EG}$ is congruent to $\overline{AB}$.

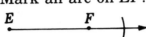

To copy $\angle PQR$, follow these steps:

- Set the compass point at Q and
  draw an arc through both rays.
  Label the intersections X and Y.

- Keep your compass setting
  unchanged. Draw the same arc at
  point S intersecting $\overrightarrow{ST}$ at U.

- Using your compass, measure the
  distance from Y to X. Measure the
  same distance on the arc made
  through point U. Label this point V.

- Draw $\overrightarrow{SV}$. $\angle VSU$ is congruent to
  $\angle PQR$.

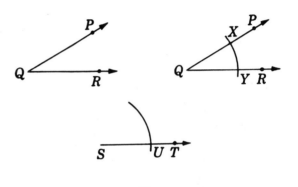

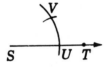

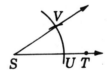

Getting Started

Copy each figure on the given ray.

1. $\overline{AB}$

A •————• B

•————————————▶

2. $\angle MON$

M
│
│
│
O └————▶ N

•————▶

245

Practice

Copy each figure on the given ray.

1. $\overline{AB}$

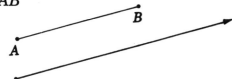

2. $\overline{LM}$

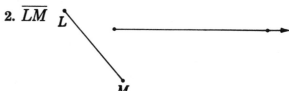

3. $\angle A$

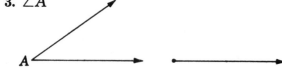

4. $\angle J$

5. $\angle T$

6. $\angle X$

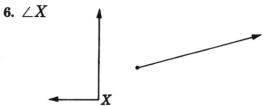

Apply

7. Draw an acute angle with your protractor. Use a compass and straightedge to copy the angle. Check the new angle with your protractor.

8. Draw an obtuse angle with your protractor. Use a compass and straightedge to copy the angle. Check the new angle with your protractor.

Understanding Polygons

A **polygon** is a closed plane figure formed by line segments. The line segments are called **sides**. The point where the segments meet is called a **vertex**.

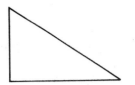

Triangle
3 sides

Quadrilateral
4 sides

A **diagonal** of a polygon joins any two vertices that are not endpoints of the same segment.

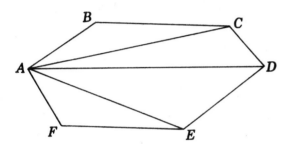

Pentagon
5 sides

Hexagon
6 sides

$\overline{AC}$, $\overline{AD}$ and $\overline{AE}$ are the diagonals drawn from vertex A of hexagon $ABCDEF$. Diagonals that could be drawn from vertex B would be

_____.

Heptagon
7 sides

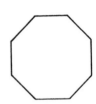

Octagon
8 sides

In a **regular polygon**, all sides are congruent, and all angles are congruent. The only irregular polygons shown on the right are the _____,

and the _____.

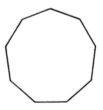

Nonagon
9 sides

Decagon
10 sides

Getting Started

Identify the polygon. Write **regular** or **irregular**.

1.

_____

_____

2.

_____

_____

3.
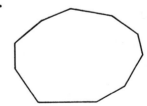

_____

_____

247

Practice

Identify the polygon. Write **regular** or **irregular**.

1.

_____

_____

2.

_____

_____

3.

_____

_____

4.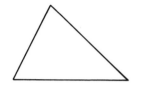

_____

_____

5.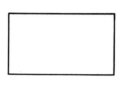

_____

_____

6.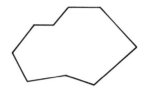

_____

_____

7.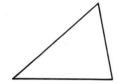

_____

_____

8.

_____

_____

9.

_____

_____

Apply

Complete the chart.

10.

Polygon	Triangle	Quadrilateral	Pentagon	Hexagon	Heptagon	Octagon	Nonagon	Decagon
Number of sides	3							
Number of vertices	3							
Number of diagonals from one vertex	0							
Total number of diagonals	0							

248

Working with Triangles

A **triangle** is a polygon with 3 sides and 3 angles. We name a triangle by its vertices.

We call this triangle ABC. We write: $\triangle ABC$.
What kind of triangle is $\triangle ABC$?
We classify a triangle by sides.

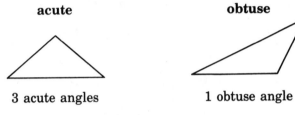

equilateral	isosceles	scalene
3 sides congruent	2 sides congruent	0 sides congruent

We also classify a triangle by its largest angle.

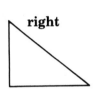

acute	obtuse	right
3 acute angles	1 obtuse angle	1 right angle

Classified by sides, $\triangle ABC$ is a _____ triangle.

Classified by angles, $\triangle ABC$ is a _____ triangle.

✔ The sum of the angle measures of any triangle is 180°.

$$m\angle A + m\angle B + m\angle C = 180°$$

If we know the measures of two of the angles of a triangle, we can determine the measure of the third by adding the measures of the two known angles, and subtracting the sum from 180°.
In triangle ABC, $m\angle C = 30°$ and $m\angle B = 90°$.

$30° + 90° =$ _____ $180° -$ _____ $=$ _____

The measure of angle A is _____.

Getting Started

Classify the triangle and find the missing angle measure.

1.
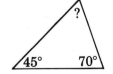

45°   70°   ?

_____

_____

2.
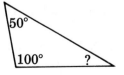

50°
100°   ?

_____

_____

3.
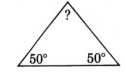

50°   50°   ?

_____

_____

Practice

Classify the triangle and find the missing angle measure.

1.

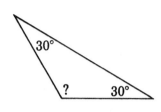

_____

_____

2.

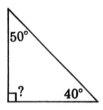

_____

_____

3.

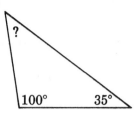

_____

_____

4.

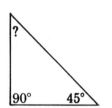

_____

_____

5.

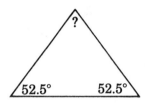

_____

_____

6

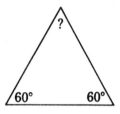

_____

_____

7.

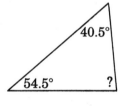

_____

_____

8.

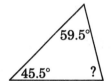

_____

_____

9.

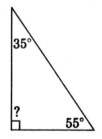

_____

_____

EXCURSION

Connect the nine dots without lifting your pencil or retracing your steps.

Working with Quadrilaterals

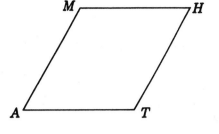

A **quadrilateral** is a polygon with 4 sides and 4 angles. We name a quadrilateral by its vertices. What kind of quadrilateral is figure MATH?

 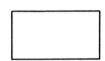 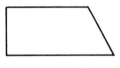 

square **rectangle** **rhombus** **trapezoid** **parallelogram**

We classify quadrilaterals by sides or by angles. A **parallelogram** has opposite sides parallel and congruent.

A **rectangle** is a parallelogram with four right angles.

A **rhombus** is a parallelogram with all sides congruent.

A **square** is a rectangle with all sides congruent.

A **trapezoid** is a quadrilateral with exactly one pair of parallel sides.

Figure MATH is a _____.

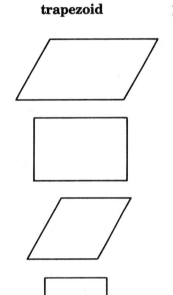

Getting Started

Name each figure. Name any sides that are congruent or parallel.

1.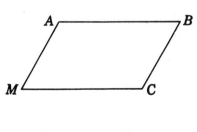

_____

_____

_____

2.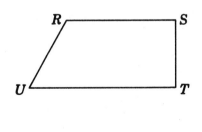

_____

_____

251

Practice

Name each figure. Name any sides that are congruent or parallel.

1.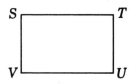

_____

_____

_____

2.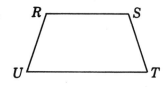

_____

_____

3.

_____

_____

_____

4.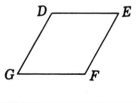

_____

_____

_____

5.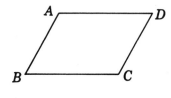

_____

_____

_____

6.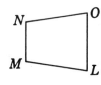

_____

_____

_____

7.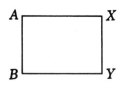

_____

_____

_____

8.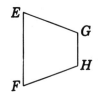

_____

_____

_____

9.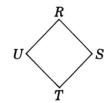

_____

_____

_____

EXCURSION

This is a set of four squares: ☐ ☐ ☐ ☐
Four squares can form 12 networks.
Here are 4. Draw 8 more.

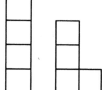

Identifying Congruent Figures

Figures that are the same size and shape are called **congruent figures.** The parts of each figure that match are called **corresponding parts.**
$\triangle ABC$ is congruent to $\triangle PQR$.
We write: $\triangle ABC \cong \triangle PQR$.

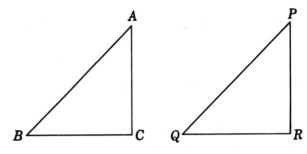

Corresponding Sides	Corresponding Angles
$\overline{AB} \longleftrightarrow \overline{PQ}$	$\angle A \longleftrightarrow \angle P$
$\overline{BC} \longleftrightarrow$ ___	$\angle B \longleftrightarrow$ ___
$\overline{AC} \longleftrightarrow$ ___	$\angle C \longleftrightarrow$ ___

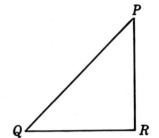

The corresponding parts of congruent figures are themselves congruent.

$\overline{AB} \cong \overline{PQ}$ $\angle A \cong \angle P$ We can conclude:

$\overline{BC} \cong$ ___ $\angle B \cong$ ___ $\triangle ABC \cong$ _____

$\overline{AC} \cong$ ___ $\angle C \cong$ ___.

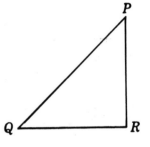

Getting Started

Are the figures congruent? Write **yes** or **no.**

1.

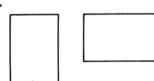

_____

2.

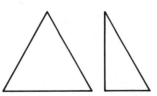

_____

3.

_____

These figures are congruent.

4. Name the congruent sides.

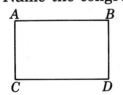

_____

_____

5. Name the congruent angles.

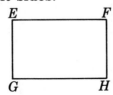

_____

253

Practice

Are the figures congruent? Write **yes** or **no.**

1.

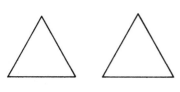

_____

2.

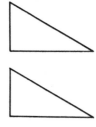

_____

3.

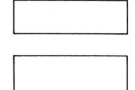

_____

4.

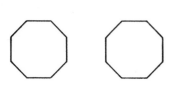

_____

5.

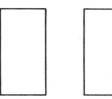

_____

6.

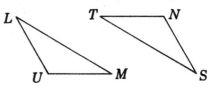

_____

These figures are congruent.

7. Name the congruent sides.

_____

_____

8. Name the congruent angles.

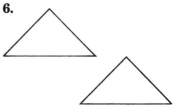

_____

9. Name the congruent sides in △AOB and △DOC.

_____

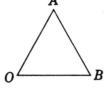

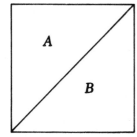
254

Identifying Symmetrical Figures

If you can fold a figure so that both
halves are congruent, the figure is
symmetrical. The fold line is called
a **line of symmetry.** How many lines
of symmetry does the square have?

We can fold the square along each dotted line.

The square has _____ lines of symmetry.

If you hold a mirror along a line
of symmetry, the mirror image
or **reflection** is shown.

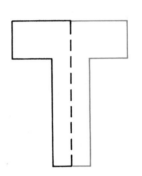 

Getting Started

Draw lines of symmetry. Write **none** if there is no
line of symmetry.

1.

2.

3.

Draw the reflection of each figure.

4.

5.

6.

255

Practice

Draw lines of symmetry. Write **none** if there is no line of symmetry.

1.

2.

3.

4.

5.

6.

7.

8.

9.

Draw the reflection of each figure.

10.

11.

12.

13.

14.

15.

16.

17.

18.

256

Restating the Problem in Your Own Words

Jonathan bought a ball, a book and a drum for $26.25. The cost of the book was $\frac{1}{6}$ the cost of the drum; the cost of the ball was $\frac{1}{2}$ the cost of the book. What did each article cost?

★ **SEE**

We want to know the cost of each item.

He spent _____ altogether. The cost of the

book was _____ the cost of the drum and

the ball was _____ the cost of the book.

★ **PLAN**

We can restate the problem in our own words. The guess and check strategy and making a table will then be helpful in reaching a solution.

★ **DO**

The drum costs _____ times as much as the book. The book cost

_____ times as much as the ball. We can use a table to help organize our guessing and checking.

Cost of Ball	Cost of Book	Cost of Drum	Total Cost ($26.25)
$1.00	$2.00	$12.00	$15.00
$1.50			
$2.00			

The ball cost _____. The book cost

_____. The drum cost _____.

★ **CHECK**

We can check our solution by using the numbers in the original problem.

1. $\frac{1}{6} \times$ _____ = _____

2. $\frac{1}{2} \times$ _____ = _____

3. _____ + _____ + _____ = _____

257

Apply

Restate these problems in your own words to help solve them.

1. While at the supermarket, I noticed that three apples cost as much as one melon. A melon costs as much as 18 strawberries. How many strawberries cost as much as one apple?

2. In ten years Bob will be three times as old as he is now. How old is Bob now?

3. At the amusement park you can buy a cold drink in a souvenir glass for $2.00. The glass cost $0.70 more than the drink. How much does the drink cost?

4. What day is tomorrow if four days after the day before yesterday is Saturday?

5. A large block weighs as much as 4 small blocks. Two large blocks and three small blocks weigh 88 pounds. How much does a small block weigh? How much does a large block weigh?

6. A ruler, a pencil and a pen cost $2.70. The pencil was $1.00 more than the ruler. The pen was $0.30 more than the total cost of the pencil and ruler. How much did the pen cost?

7. What if, in Problem 3, the glass cost $\frac{1}{4}$ as much as the glass and drink combined? How much would the drink cost then?

8. Fernando's Flower Shop is having a sale on mixed bouquets of fresh flowers. Small bouquets are $3.88 and large bouquets are $5.88. Use this information to write a problem where the answer is $0.24.

9. Use mental computation to find the number that is twice the number that is one half of the number that is 10 less than 100.

10. Use mental computation to find the number that is double one half of 99 added to the difference between 99 and itself.

Name each figure.

1.

_____

2.

_____

3.

_____

Use a protractor to measure each angle. Classify each angle according to its size.

4.

_____

_____

5.
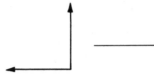

_____

_____

6.

_____

_____

Complete the statements.

7.
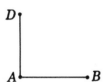

$\overline{AD}$ is perpendicular to ____.

8.

The radius is ____.

9. Copy angle P on $\overrightarrow{AB}$.
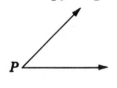

10. Bisect $\overline{MN}$.

11. Identify the polygon. Draw a diagonal.

_____

12. Find m∠XZY.
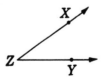

_____

13. The triangles are congruent. Name the angle congruent to ∠BCA.
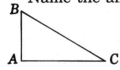

_____

14. Draw all possible diagonals.

CUMULATIVE REVIEW

Circle the letter of the correct answer.

1 $4\frac{3}{5}$

   $+ \quad \frac{2}{3}$

a $1\frac{1}{15}$

b $4\frac{1}{15}$

c $5\frac{1}{15}$

d NG

2 $6\frac{1}{8}$

   $- 2\frac{5}{6}$

a $3\frac{7}{24}$

b $4\frac{7}{24}$

c $8\frac{3}{7}$

d NG

3 $1\frac{1}{2} \times 5\frac{1}{3}$

a $5\frac{1}{6}$

b 8

c $8\frac{1}{6}$

d NG

4 $2\frac{1}{3} \div 3\frac{1}{2}$

a $\frac{2}{3}$

b $\frac{3}{7}$

c $8\frac{1}{6}$

d NG

5 What is the place value
  of the 7 in 23.0178?

a tenths

b hundredths

c thousandths

d NG

6   2.61
      0.48
   $+ 5.9$

a 8.89

b 8.99

c 9.00

d NG

7 $16.5 - 9.36$

a 6.71

b 7.14

c 7.26

d NG

8   3.61
   $\times \quad 2.5$

a 9.05

b 9.025

c 90.25

d NG

9 $0.03\overline{)0.762}$

a 25.4

b 254

c 2,540

d NG

10   10 min 38 sec
   $+ \quad$ 6 min 25 sec

a 15 min
      3 sec

b 16 min
      3 sec

c 21 min
      3 sec

d NG

11 Find the perimeter.

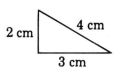

2 cm   4 cm

3 cm

a 8 cm

b 9 cm

c 12 cm

d NG

12 5 km = ___?___ m

a 50

b 500

c 5,000

d NG

 score

12
AREA AND VOLUME

Computing the Area of Rectangles and Squares

The **area** of a region is the number of square units needed to cover the region. What is the area of Paul's patio in square meters?

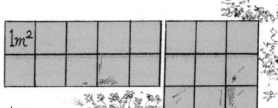

We need to know how many square meters are needed to cover the patio region. To find the area, we follow a formula for each shape.

To find the area of a rectangle, multiply the length by the width.

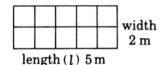

width
2 m

length (*l*) 5 m

$$A = l \times w$$
$$A = 5 \times 2$$

$$A = \underline{\quad}$$

Area = ___ m²

To find the area of a square, multiply the length of one side by itself.

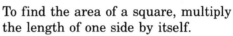

side
3 m

$$A = s^2$$
$$A = 3 \times 3$$

$$A = \underline{\quad}$$

Area = ___ m²

The area of the patio is ___ square meters added to

___ square meters.

The total area is _____.

Getting Started

Find the area.

1.

32 cm

48 cm

$A = $ _____

2.

18 cm

$A = $ _____

3.

2.5 mm

6.2 mm

$A = $ _____

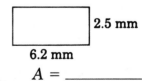

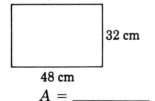

Find the area.

4. $l = 4.5$ m
$w = 9.8$ m

5. $l = 123$ mm
$w = 214$ mm

6. $s = 8.25$ km

261

Practice

Find the area.

1.

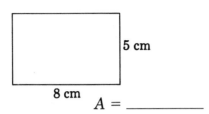

A = _____

2.

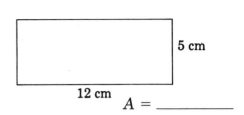

A = _____

3.

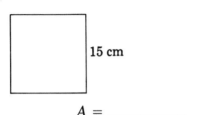

A = _____

4.

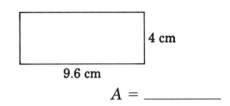

A = _____

5.

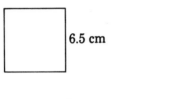

A = _____

6.

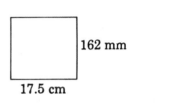

A = _____

Copy and Do

7. $l = 9$ m
   $w = 6$ m

8. $l = 16$ km
   $w = 5$ km

9. $l = 4.3$ cm
   $w = 6$ cm

10. $s = 12.1$ mm

11. $l = 116$ mm
    $w = 45$ mm

12. $l = 8.6$ m
    $w = 5.3$ m

13. $l = 14$ m
    $w = 9.5$ m

14. $s = 45$ mm

15. $l = 215$ mm
    $w = 35$ mm

16. $s = 9.3$ km

17. $l = 126$ cm
    $w = 7.8$ cm

18. $l = 4.25$ m
    $w = 123$ cm

Apply

Solve these problems. Draw a picture to help.

19. Joe is buying cork to cover a bulletin board. The bulletin board is 0.85 meters long and 53 centimeters wide. What is the area of the bulletin board?

20. Jeanette is painting a rectangular wall. The wall is 6 meters long and 3.2 meters high. A window in the wall is 1.5 meters long and 1 meter high. What is the area of the wall that must be painted?

Computing the Area of Parallelograms

Justin is making a mosaic from tiles that are one square centimeter in area. How many tiles will he need for the parallelogram design at the right?

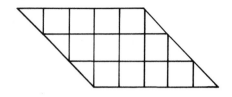

We can use what we know about finding the area of a rectangle to find the formula for the area of a parallelogram.

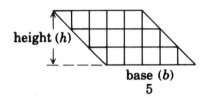

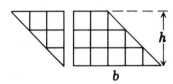

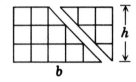

Measure the base and the height of the parallelogram. The **height** is a perpendicular line segment between any pair of parallel sides.

Cut one end off the parallelogram and slide it to the other end.

You should have a rectangle with the same base and height as the parallelogram.

To find the area of a parallelogram, we multiply the length of the base by the length of the height.

$$A = b \times h$$
$$A = 5 \times 3$$

$$A = \underline{}$$

$$\text{Area} = \underline{} \text{ cm}^2$$

Justin needs _____ tiles.

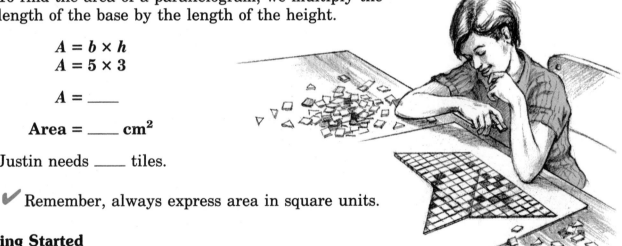

✔ Remember, always express area in square units.

Getting Started

Find the area.

1.

18 mm

25 mm

$A = $ _____

2.

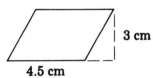

3 cm

4.5 cm

$A = $ _____

3.

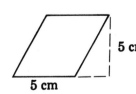

5 cm

5 cm

$A = $ _____

Find the area.

4. $b = 5.2$ km
$h = 3.7$ km

5. $b = 85$ cm
$h = 24$ cm

6. $b = 0.32$ m
$h = 2{,}415$ mm

Practice

Find the area.

1.

5 cm

6 cm

$A =$ _____

2.

3.1 cm

7 cm

$A =$ _____

3.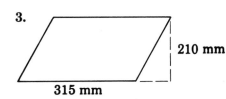

210 mm

315 mm

$A =$ _____

Copy and Do

4. $b = 2$ km
$h = 5.6$ km

5. $b = 112$ mm
$h = 36$ mm

6. $b = 4.3$ cm
$h = 5.8$ cm

7. $b = 22.4$ cm
$h = 8.7$ cm

8. $b = 6.7$ mm
$h = 0.09$ cm

9. $b = 3.02$ m
$h = 85$ cm

Apply

Solve these problems.

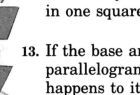

10. How many square centimeters are in one square meter?

11. How many square millimeters are in one square meter?

12. The area of a parallelogram is 625 m². If the height is 25 m, how long is the base?

13. If the base and height of a parallelogram are doubled, what happens to its area?

EXCURSION

Given a string 16 centimeters long, make as many rectangles as possible whose length and width are whole numbers. Complete the table. Write the dimensions of the rectangle with the greatest area.

l	1	2	3	4	5	6	7
w							
A							

_____

Computing the Area of Triangles

Tuwayne is seeding his triangular front lawn. He bought enough grass seed to cover 25 square meters. Can Tuwayne seed the yard without buying more seed?

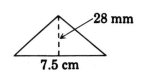

We can use what we know about finding the area of a parallelogram to find the formula for the area of a triangle.

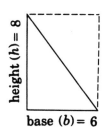

Draw a congruent triangle to form a parallelogram.

The area of each triangle is $\frac{1}{2}$ the area of the parallelogram.

To find the area of a triangle, multiply the product of the base and the height by $\frac{1}{2}$.

$A = \frac{1}{2} \times b \times h$

$A = \frac{1}{2} \times 6 \times 8$

$A = \underline{\hspace{1cm}}$

Area = $\underline{\hspace{1cm}}$ m^2

Tuwayne $\underline{\hspace{1cm}}$ enough seed to plant his yard.

Getting Started

Find the area.

1.

15 cm

9 cm

$A = \underline{\hspace{2cm}}$

2.

32 mm

26 mm

$A = \underline{\hspace{2cm}}$

3.

28 mm

7.5 cm

$A = \underline{\hspace{2cm}}$

$\underline{\hspace{2cm}}$

Find the area.

4. $b = 5.3$ km
   $h = 6$ km

5. $b = 45$ mm
   $h = 76$ mm

6. $b = 0.035$ m
   $h = 2.7$ cm

Practice

Find the area.

1.

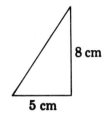

8 cm

5 cm

A = _____

2.

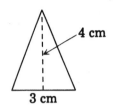

4 cm

3 cm

A = _____

3.

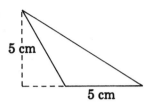

5 cm

5 cm

A = _____

4.

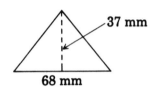

37 mm

68 mm

A = _____

5.

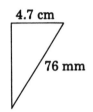

4.7 cm

76 mm

A = _____

_____

6.

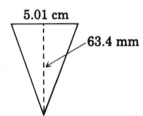

5.01 cm

63.4 mm

A = _____

_____

Copy and Do

7. $b = 7$ m
   $h = 8$ m

8. $b = 15$ km
   $h = 4$ km

9. $b = 11$ mm
   $h = 46$ mm

10. $b = 6.3$ km
    $h = 8$ km

11. $b = 8$ m
    $h = 4.5$ m

12. $b = 16$ cm
    $h = 16$ cm

13. $b = 4.1$ mm
    $h = 3.4$ mm

14. $b = 0.96$ m
    $h = 0.08$ m

15. $b = 5.15$ km
    $h = 2.6$ km

16. $b = 24$ mm
    $h = 4.5$ cm

17. $b = 0.05$ m
    $h = 21.6$ cm

18. $b = 4.1$ m
    $h = 117$ mm

Apply

Solve these problems. Draw a picture to help.

19. The 3 sides of a tent are congruent. Each base is 3 meters and each height is 3.6 meters. What is the area of the three sides of the tent?

20. An equilateral triangle has a base of 12 centimeters and a height of 10.3 centimeters. Find the perimeter and the area of the triangle.

21. Find the area of the isosceles trapezoid. (Hint: Find the area of 2 congruent triangles and a rectangle.)

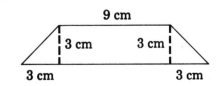

9 cm

3 cm   3 cm

3 cm   3 cm

Computing the Area of Circles

Air controllers use radar to track the flight of airplanes. What is the area of this radar screen?

The radius of the circle is the same length as one side of the smaller square.

The area of the smaller square is found by multiplying a side by itself or in this case a radius by itself.

The area of the larger square is _____ times the area of the smaller square. The area of the circle is less than 4 times this smaller square. Ancient Greek mathematicians figured it was approximately 3.14 times as large. They named this factor by the Greek letter pi, which is written as π. We say that the area of any circle is pi times the radius squared.

$A = \pi \times r^2$
$A = 3.14 \times 40 \times 40$

$A = $ _____

Area = _____ cm^2

The area of the radar screen is _____.

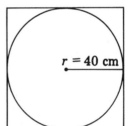

$r = 40$ cm

Getting Started

Find the area.

1.
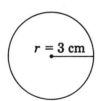

$r = 3$ cm

$A = $ _____

2.
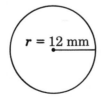

$r = 12$ mm

$A = $ _____

3.
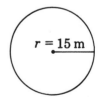

$r = 15$ m

$A = $ _____

Find the area.

4. $r = 4$ cm

5. $d = 12$ m

6. $r = 6.1$ km

Practice

Find the area.

1.

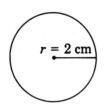

A = _____

2.

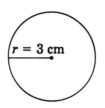

A = _____

3.

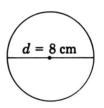

A = _____

4.

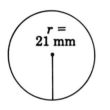

A = _____

5.

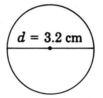

A = _____

6.

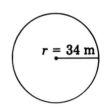

A = _____

Copy and Do

7. $r = 4$ cm

8. $r = 1$ m

9. $d = 10$ km

10. $r = 9$ m

11. $d = 14$ km

12. $r = 1.8$ m

13. $r = 36$ mm

14. $r = 9.5$ cm

15. $r = 0.01$ km

16. $r = 2.5$ cm

17. $d = 100$ mm

18. $r = 10$ cm

EXCURSION

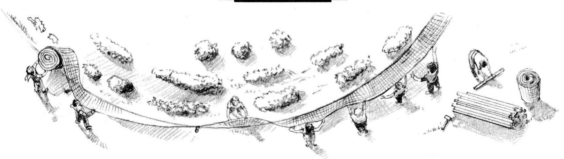

The area of a circular garden is 7,850 ft². About how much fencing is needed to enclose the garden?

Identifying Solid Figures

Solid figures formed from polygons
are called **polyhedrons**. Polyhedrons
have faces, edges and vertices. How
many vertices, edges and faces does
a rectangular pyramid have?

square prism
or cube

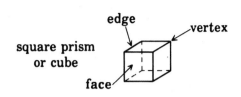

rectangular
prism

A rectangular pyramid has ____ vertices,

____ edges and ____ faces.

triangular
prism

triangular
pyramid

Some solid figures have curved surfaces.

square
pyramid

cone   cylinder   sphere

hexagonal
pyramid

Getting Started

What solid figure does each object suggest?

1.

2.

3.

_____   _____   _____

Write the number of faces, edges and vertices for each polyhedron.

4.

____ faces

____ edges

____ vertices

5.

____ faces

____ edges

____ vertices

269

Practice

What solid figure does each object suggest?

1.

_____

2.

_____

3.

_____

4.

_____

5.

_____

6.

_____

Write the number of faces, edges and vertices for each polyhedron.

7.

____ faces

____ edges

____ vertices

8.

____ faces

____ edges

____ vertices

9.

____ faces

____ edges

____ vertices

EXCURSION

This solid figure is made by folding this pattern.

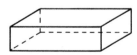 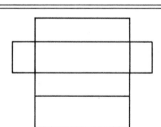

Draw the pattern for each solid figure.

270

Computing the Volume of Solid Figures

A **cubic unit** has 3 dimensions: length, width and height. We use cubic units to measure volume. The number of cubic units needed to make or fill a solid figure is called the **volume** of the figure. We write cubic units: **unit³**. What is the volume of the rectangular prism in cubic centimeters?

1 cm³

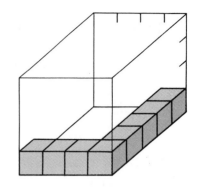

We need to know the number of cubes in the whole figure.
We know that the bottom of the prism

is ____ centimeter cubes long and ____ cubes

wide, and that it is also ____ cubes high.
To find the total number of centimeter cubes, we multiply to find the number of cubes on the bottom layer, and then multiply by the number of layers.

We multiply ____ by ____ by ____.

$$\underset{\substack{\text{length} \\ \text{number of cubes} \\ \text{on bottom layer}}}{\underline{5}} \times \underset{\substack{\text{width} \\}}{\underline{4}} \times \underset{\substack{\text{height} \\ \text{number} \\ \text{of layers}}}{\underline{4}} = \underline{\quad} \text{ centimeter cubes}$$

The volume of the box is ____ cm³.
The formula for finding the volume of a rectangular prism is: $V = l \times w \times h.$

✔ Reminder: always express volume in cubic units.

Getting Started

Find the volume.

1.

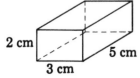

2 cm
5 cm
3 cm

$V =$ _____

2.

22 mm
40 mm
36 mm

$V =$ _____

Find the volume.

3. $l = 6$ cm
$w = 9$ cm
$h = 7$ cm

4. $l = 3$ km
$w = 1.3$ km
$h = 2.1$ km

5. $l = 4.2$ m
$w = 1.3$ m
$h = 2.6$ m

271

Practice

Find the volume.

1.

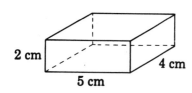

V = _____

2.

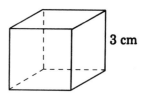

V = _____

3.

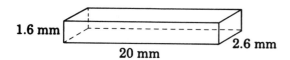

V = _____

4.

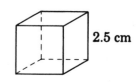

V = _____

Copy and Do

5. $l = 4$ cm
  $w = 9$ cm
  $h = 12$ cm

6. $l = 7$ m
  $w = 3.2$ m
  $h = 5$ m

7. $l = 0.063$ km
  $w = 0.128$ km
  $h = 0.009$ km

8. $l = 5.8$ m
  $w = 3.2$ m
  $h = 5.7$ m

Apply

Solve these problems.

9. A warehouse the shape of a rectangular prism has a length of 30 meters, a width of 25 meters and a height of 12 meters. How many cubic meters of goods will the warehouse hold?

10. If each side of a cube is doubled, what happens to the volume?

EXCURSION

Each cube is 1 centimeter on each edge.

 = =

1 cubic centimeter of water   1 milliliter of water   1 gram of water

How many liters will it take to fill an aquarium 50 by 30 by 20 centimeters?

Computing Surface Area of Solid Figures

The total area on the outside of
a solid figure is called the figure's
surface area. Tina put a gift in a
box the shape of a cube. How much
paper is needed to cover the gift box?

We want to know the total area on the
outside of the box.

We know that the shape of each face is a _____,

and that each edge is ____ inches long. To find the
surface area, we find the area of one side and
multiply by the number of congruent sides.

Area of 1 face = ____ × ____ = ____ in.²

Area of 6 faces = 6 × ____ = ____ in.²

Tina will need ____ square inches of paper.

A rectangular prism has 3 pairs of
congruent faces: top and bottom; side
and side; front and back. To find the
surface area of a rectangular prism,
follow these steps:

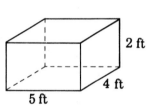

Multiply to find the area of the front. Double the product.	Multiply to find the area of one side. Double the product.	Multiply to find the area of the top. Double the product.	Add the products.
5 × 2 = ____ ft²	4 × 2 = ____ ft²	5 × 4 = ____ ft²	____ + ____ +
____ × 2 = ____ ft²	____ × 2 = ____ ft²	____ × 2 = ____ ft²	____ = ____ ft²

The surface area of the rectangular prism is ____ square feet.

Getting Started

Find the surface area.

1.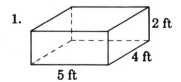

surface area = _____

2.

surface area = _____

3.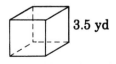

surface area = _____

273

Practice

Find the surface area.

1.

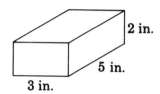

2 in.
5 in.
3 in.

surface area = _____

2.

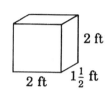

2 ft
2 ft
$1\frac{1}{2}$ ft

surface area = _____

3.

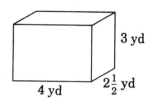

3 yd
4 yd
$2\frac{1}{2}$ yd

surface area = _____

4.

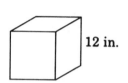

12 in.

surface area = _____

5.

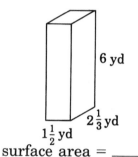

6 yd
$2\frac{1}{3}$ yd
$1\frac{1}{2}$ yd

surface area = _____

6.

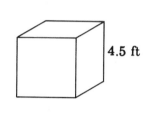

4.5 ft

surface area = _____

Apply

Solve these problems.

7. A box measures 6 inches wide, 9 inches long and 5 inches deep. How many square inches of paper are needed to cover the box?

8. The length and width of a rectangular prism are each doubled. What happens to the surface area?

9. 1 square foot = _____ square inches

1 square yard = _____ square feet

1 square yard = _____ square inches

10. 1 cubic foot = _____ cubic inches

1 cubic yard = _____ cubic feet

1 cubic yard = _____ cubic inches

EXCURSION

The surface area of a sphere = $4 \times \pi \times r \times r$
The volume of a sphere = $\frac{4}{3} \times \pi \times r \times r \times r$ $\left(\text{use 1.3 for } \frac{4}{3}\right)$
Complete the table.

radius	1 in.	2 in.	3 in.	4 in.	5 in.
surface area					
volume					

Identifying a Subgoal

Four friends are planning a class party. Andy bought $5.00 worth of cold drinks. Shawn spent $2.50 on decorations. Beth bought a cake that cost $9.50. Rod spent $4.00 on snacks and bought paper products that cost $3.00. If they plan to share the cost of the party equally, who owes money to whom?

★ **SEE**

We want to share the cost equally among the four friends.

Andy spent _____.

Shawn spent _____.

Beth spent _____.

Rod spent a total of _____.

★ **PLAN**

Before we can determine which persons owe money and to whom, we need to find each one's equal share. We can do this by finding the average of all the expenses. Then we can determine how much above or below the average each person spent.

★ **DO**

```
   $5.00
    2.50     4)‾‾‾‾‾
    9.50
 +  7.00     Each person's share is _____.
 _____
```

	Andy		Shawn
	− 5.00		− 2.50
Beth	$9.50	Rod	$7.00
	−		−

_____ owes _____ _____.

_____ owes _____ _____.

★ **CHECK**

We can check by adding what one owes to what one spent, or subtracting what is owed from what was spent, whichever the case may be.

Apply

Identify subgoals to help you solve these problems.

1. A gallon of paint costing $11.50 covers 270 square feet with one coat. Find the cost of painting a fence with one coat on each side if the fence is 4 feet 6 inches high and encloses a rectangular lot 50 feet long and 25 feet wide.

2. An acre contains 43,560 square feet. Approximately how many acres are in a lot 400 feet by 600 feet?

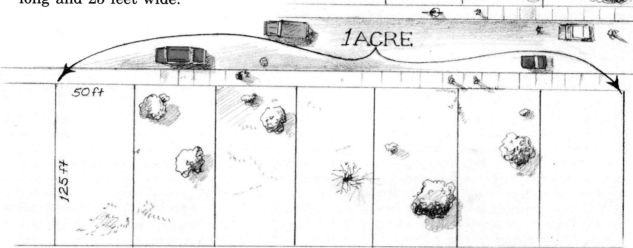

3. How many bricks 8 inches long by 4 inches wide will be required to lay a walk 6 feet 8 inches wide by 64 feet long?

4. The sun is approximately 93 million miles from the earth. The light from the sun travels at 186,000 miles per second. How long will it take the light to reach the earth?

5. One board is 18 feet 2 inches long while the other is 7 feet 10 inches long. What is the difference in these two lengths?

6. A clock takes 5 seconds to chime 6 times. How long will it take to chime 12 times?

7. Angelo is planting a rectangular garden 15 feet long by 8 feet wide. Angelica wants to plant a garden that has twice the area. Should she double both the length and width or just the length? Explain why.

8. Archie is making a circular garden. So is Luanne, but the radius of her garden is twice as long as the radius of Archie's garden. Tell how the area of Luanne's garden will compare to that of Archie's garden, and prove it.

9. If the number of linear units in the circumference of a circle is the same as the number of square units in the area, how long is the radius?

10. Guess and then verify your guess. If all three dimensions of a shoe box are doubled, how does this affect the volume?

276

Find the area of these rectangles.

1. 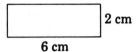 2 cm

6 cm

$A =$ _____

2. 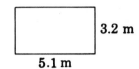 3.2 m

5.1 m

$A =$ _____

3. $l = 0.09$ km
   $w = 18$ cm

$A =$ _____

Find the area of these squares.

4. 9 m

$A =$ _____

5. 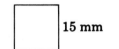 15 mm

$A =$ _____

6. $s = 3.2$ cm

$A =$ _____

Find the area of these parallelograms.

7. 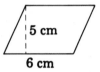 5 cm

6 cm

$A =$ _____

8. 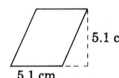 5.1 cm

5.1 cm

$A =$ _____

9. $b = 0.031$ km
   $h = 45$ m

$A =$ _____

Find the area of these triangles.

10.  30 mm

40 mm

$A =$ _____

11. 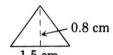 0.8 cm

1.5 cm

$A =$ _____

12. $b = 0.4$ m
    $h = 25$ cm

$A =$ _____

Find the area of these circles.

13. 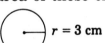 $r = 3$ cm

$A =$ _____

14. 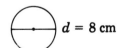 $d = 8$ cm

$A =$ _____

15. $r = 2.1$ m

$A =$ _____

Find the surface area of each box.

16. 3 ft

2 ft 2 ft

surface area = _____

17. 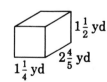 $1\frac{1}{2}$ yd

$2\frac{4}{5}$ yd

$1\frac{1}{4}$ yd

surface area = _____

Find the volume.

18. 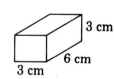 3 cm

6 cm

3 cm

$V =$ _____

CUMULATIVE REVIEW

Circle the letter of the correct answer.

1. $3\frac{3}{4}$
   $+ 2\frac{3}{8}$

   a $5\frac{1}{8}$
   b $5\frac{1}{2}$
   c $6\frac{1}{8}$
   d NG

2. $4\frac{1}{3}$
   $- 1\frac{3}{4}$

   a $2\frac{7}{12}$
   b $3\frac{5}{12}$
   c $3\frac{7}{12}$
   d NG

3. $2\frac{1}{3} \times 1\frac{5}{7}$

   a $3\frac{3}{5}$
   b $5\frac{3}{5}$
   c 28
   d NG

4. $5\frac{1}{3} \div \frac{5}{6}$

   a $6\frac{2}{5}$
   b $3\frac{7}{12}$
   c $4\frac{4}{9}$
   d NG

5. What is the place value of the 0 in 9.0321?

   a tenths
   b hundredths
   c thousandths
   d NG

6. 16.96
   $+ 2.853$

   a 18.813
   b 19.113
   c 19.813
   d NG

7. $8.06 - 4.392$

   a 3.672
   b 3.678
   c 3.668
   d NG

8. 6.3×0.09

   a 0.547
   b 5.47
   c 54.7
   d NG

9. $0.02\overline{)19.64}$

   a 9.82
   b 98.2
   c 982
   d NG

10. 6 lb 9 oz
    $+ 3$ lb 8 oz

    a 9 lb 1 oz
    b 10 lb 1 oz
    c 10 lb 7 oz
    d NG

11. Find the perimeter.

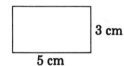

    a 15 cm
    b 15 cm^2
    c 16 cm
    d NG

12. Find the missing angle measure.

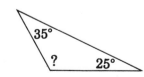

    a 60°
    b 110°
    c 120°
    d NG

 score

278

Writing Ratios

We use ratios to compare two quantities. The ratio of black pins to red pins is 2 to 3. We write this as **2:3,** or as the fraction $\frac{2}{3}$. We say: **the ratio 2 to 3.** What is the ratio of red pins to all the pins?

We want to write the ratio that compares two quantities. We know that there are _____ red pins, and there are _____ pins altogether.

The ratio of red pins to total pins is _____ to _____, or $\frac{\square}{\square}$.

Getting Started

Write each ratio as a fraction. Do not simplify.

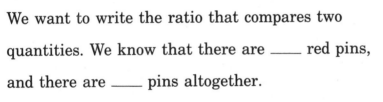

1. black marbles to red marbles _____

2. red marbles to black marbles _____

3. black marbles to total marbles _____

4. red marbles to total marbles _____

Write each ratio as a fraction. Do not simplify.

5.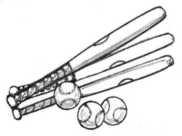

_____

6.

_____

7.

_____

Practice

Write each ratio as a fraction. Do not simplify.

1. cats to birds ____

2. dogs to guinea pigs ____

3. guinea pigs to total pets ____

4. dogs and cats to guinea pigs ____

5. pencils to rulers

6. length to width

7. dimes to dollars

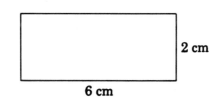

2 cm

6 cm

____

____

____

Apply

Solve these problems.

8. Raisins cost 87¢ for 3 boxes. What is the ratio of boxes to cost?

9. Jim ran 5 kilometers in 25 minutes. What is the ratio of time to distance?

10. There are 7 boys and 8 girls playing softball. What is the ratio of girls to players?

11. On Monday, Nancy got 2 hits in 4 tries. On Tuesday, she got 1 hit in 3 tries. What is the ratio of total hits to total tries?

12. Jeff has 18 Tiger's Eye marbles and Sharon has 15 agate marbles. What is the ratio of Sharon's marbles to Jeff's?

13. Troubles, Silvia's dog, had 9 puppies. Seven were black and 2 were white. What is the ratio of white to black puppies?

Identifying Equal Ratios

Donald is the quarterback for his junior high football team. He completed 10 out of 15 passes in Saturday's game. His cousin, Dick, played on the rival team. Compare the ratios of their completed passes.

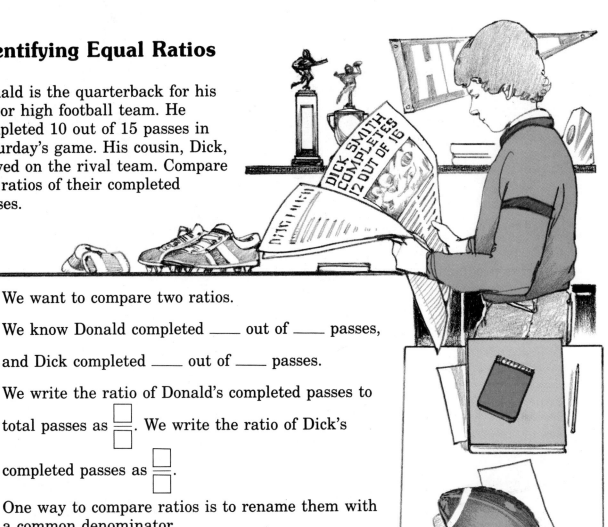

We want to compare two ratios.

We know Donald completed _____ out of _____ passes,

and Dick completed _____ out of _____ passes.

We write the ratio of Donald's completed passes to total passes as $\frac{\square}{\square}$. We write the ratio of Dick's

completed passes as $\frac{\square}{\square}$.

One way to compare ratios is to rename them with a common denominator.

$\frac{10}{15} = \frac{2}{3} = \frac{\square}{12}$

$\frac{12}{16} = \frac{3}{4} = \frac{\square}{12}$

$\frac{8}{12} \neq \frac{9}{12}$

not equal

Another way to compare ratios is to use the cross-products test.

$\frac{10}{15} \bowtie \frac{12}{16}$

$10 \times 16 = 160$
$15 \times 12 = 180$
$160 \neq 180$

The boys' ratios of completed passes are _____.

Getting Started

Use equivalent fractions. Write = or $\neq$.

1. $\frac{5}{8}$ ___ $\frac{15}{24}$

2. $\frac{3}{9}$ ___ $\frac{4}{15}$

3. $\frac{6}{24}$ ___ $\frac{4}{16}$

Use the cross products test. Write = or $\neq$.

4. $\frac{9}{2}$ ___ $\frac{50}{12}$

5. $\frac{8}{48}$ ___ $\frac{20}{120}$

6. $\frac{16}{40}$ ___ $\frac{18}{45}$

Practice

Use equivalent fractions. Write = or ≠.

1. $\frac{5}{6}$ —— $\frac{40}{54}$

2. $\frac{3}{7}$ —— $\frac{15}{35}$

3. $\frac{9}{24}$ —— $\frac{12}{32}$

4. $\frac{5}{6}$ —— $\frac{9}{21}$

5. $\frac{30}{36}$ —— $\frac{5}{6}$

6. $\frac{8}{3}$ —— $\frac{40}{15}$

7. $\frac{18}{27}$ —— $\frac{5}{45}$

8. $\frac{5}{7}$ —— $\frac{3}{5}$

9. $\frac{5}{16}$ —— $\frac{4}{9}$

10. $\frac{4}{17}$ —— $\frac{16}{54}$

11. $\frac{12}{15}$ —— $\frac{48}{60}$

12. $\frac{14}{28}$ —— $\frac{16}{37}$

Use the cross products test. Write = or ≠.

13. $\frac{3}{4}$ —— $\frac{5}{6}$

14. $\frac{5}{6}$ —— $\frac{7}{9}$

15. $\frac{25}{35}$ —— $\frac{6}{14}$

16. $\frac{7}{12}$ —— $\frac{1}{2}$

17. $\frac{7}{24}$ —— $\frac{5}{9}$

18. $\frac{1}{8}$ —— $\frac{5}{40}$

19. $\frac{14}{3}$ —— $\frac{42}{9}$

20. $\frac{6}{9}$ —— $\frac{8}{12}$

21. $\frac{5}{2}$ —— $\frac{21}{9}$

22. $\frac{8}{7}$ —— $\frac{12}{15}$

23. $\frac{2}{3}$ —— $\frac{7}{8}$

24. $\frac{7}{15}$ —— $\frac{14}{30}$

Apply

Solve these problems.

25. Pat drew a rectangle 6 inches wide and 5 inches long. Tom drew a rectangle 18 inches wide and 15 inches long. Was the ratio of width to length the same for both rectangles?

26. Sal mixed 4 cans of juice with 6 cans of water. Ben mixed 6 cans of juice with 8 cans of water. Was the concentration of juice to water the same?

EXCURSION

Use an arrow to show the direction the third wheel will move.
Write the number of times it will turn.

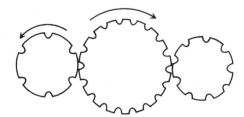

The first wheel makes $\frac{1}{2}$ of a turn. _____

The first wheel makes 2 turns. _____

282

Solving Proportions

Bob and his uncle mixed cream paint and tan paint in a ratio of 3 to 5. They used 4.5 liters of tan paint. How many liters of cream paint did they use?

We want to know how much cream paint was used.

We know they used _____ of tan paint.

The ratio of cream paint to tan paint is $\dfrac{\square}{\square}$.

If we let **n** equal the liters of cream paint, we can write an equal ratio, $\dfrac{n}{4.5}$, to use in an equation.

✔ A **proportion** is an expression of two equal ratios.

$$\begin{array}{l}\text{cream paint} \rightarrow \\ \text{tan paint} \rightarrow\end{array} \quad \frac{3}{5} = \frac{n}{4.5}$$

To write a proportion as an equation we use the cross-products test.

$$5 \times n = 3 \times 4.5$$
$$5 \times n = 13.5$$

To solve for n, we divide by the number that n is multiplied by.

$$n = 13.5 \div 5$$
$$n = 2.7$$

Bob and his uncle used ____ liters of cream paint.

Getting Started

Solve.

1. $\dfrac{2}{3} = \dfrac{n}{9}$

2. $\dfrac{n}{10} = \dfrac{4}{8}$

3. $\dfrac{4}{n} = \dfrac{2}{2.5}$

4. $\dfrac{n}{2.4} = \dfrac{9}{1.6}$

Practice

Solve.

1. $\dfrac{3}{4} = \dfrac{n}{16}$

2. $\dfrac{n}{8} = \dfrac{21}{24}$

3. $\dfrac{5}{6} = \dfrac{15}{n}$

4. $\dfrac{n}{9} = \dfrac{12}{27}$

5. $\dfrac{1}{n} = \dfrac{5}{25}$

6. $\dfrac{10}{7} = \dfrac{n}{70}$

7. $\dfrac{3}{n} = \dfrac{15}{40}$

8. $\dfrac{4}{6} = \dfrac{n}{12}$

9. $\dfrac{6}{n} = \dfrac{9}{12}$

10. $\dfrac{4}{16} = \dfrac{5}{n}$

11. $\dfrac{n}{2.5} = \dfrac{3}{5}$

12. $\dfrac{1.5}{6} = \dfrac{n}{12}$

13. $\dfrac{12}{n} = \dfrac{8}{3}$

14. $\dfrac{5.6}{2} = \dfrac{n}{4}$

15. $\dfrac{n}{3.5} = \dfrac{1}{7}$

16. $\dfrac{3.6}{15} = \dfrac{1.2}{n}$

17. $\dfrac{2.8}{7} = \dfrac{n}{4}$

18. $\dfrac{18}{25} = \dfrac{n}{7}$

19. $\dfrac{n}{3.7} = \dfrac{4}{29.6}$

20. $\dfrac{15}{n} = \dfrac{1.2}{7}$

Apply

Solve these problems.

21. To make punch, Tom uses 3 cups of lemonade for every 2 cups of grape juice. Tom used 12 cups of lemonade. How many cups of grape juice did he use?

22. Mary ran 2 kilometers in 15 minutes. At the same rate, how far can she run in 25 minutes?

23. Glasses are on sale at 6 for $6.90. How much will Mrs. Cavell pay for 4 glasses?

24. A tree grows 3 inches every 5 months. How many inches will the tree grow in 9 months?

EXCURSION

Complete the table to find the ratio of the area to the perimeter of the squares.

Length of Side of Square	Area of Square	Perimeter of Square	$\dfrac{A}{P}$
1	1	4	$\dfrac{1}{4}$
2	4	8	
3	9		
4			
5			

Working with Similar Polygons

Similar polygons are the same shape, but not always the same size. The angles or sides that are in the same relative positions are called **corresponding.** The corresponding angles of similar polygons are congruent.

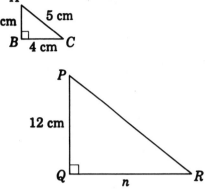

The corresponding sides of similar polygons are proportional. If triangle *ABC* is similar to triangle *PQR*, what is the measurement of line segment *QR*?

We need to know the length of one side of triangle *PQR*. We know triangles *PQR* and *ABC* are similar.

In the triangles, side *AB* corresponds to side ____,

and the ratio of $\overline{AB}$ to $\overline{PQ}$ is $\dfrac{\square}{\square}$.

Side *BC* corresponds to side ____, and the ratio of $\overline{BC}$ to $\overline{QR}$ is $\dfrac{\square}{\square}$.

To find the length of $\overline{QR}$, write and solve a proportion.

$$\frac{m(\overline{AB})}{m(\overline{PQ})} = \frac{m(\overline{BC})}{m(\overline{QR})} \qquad \frac{3}{12} = \frac{4}{n}$$

$$3 \times n = 12 \times 4$$
$$3 \times n = 48$$
$$n = 48 \div 3$$
$$n = 16$$

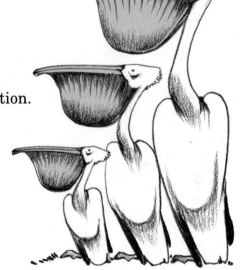

The length of $\overline{QR}$ is ____ centimeters.

Getting Started

The figures are similar. Name the corresponding sides.

1.
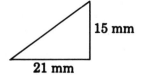

_____

2.
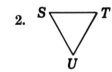

_____

The figures are similar. Solve for *n*.

3.
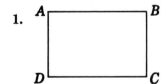

_____

4.

_____

Practice

The figures are similar. Name the corresponding sides.

1.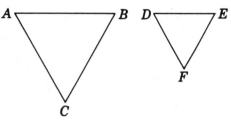

_____

2.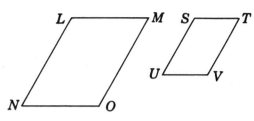

_____

3.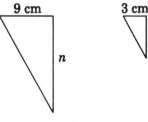

_____

4.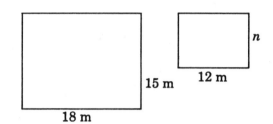

_____

These figures are similar. Solve for _n_.

5.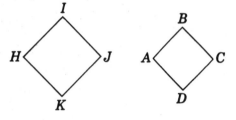

_____

6.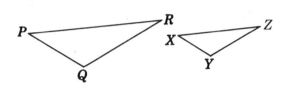

_____

7.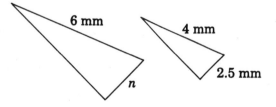

_____

8.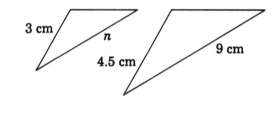

_____

Apply

Solve these problems.

9. Theo is mixing paint. The ratio of blue paint to white paint is 5 to 11. How many quarts of blue paint does he need if he uses 2.75 quarts of white paint?

10. Shana is buying picture frames. One of her pictures is 10 centimeters wide and 12 centimeters long. She has an enlargement that is 18 centimeters wide. How long should the frame be for the larger picture?

Working with Scale Drawings

This map scale shows what every centimeter on the map represents in actual kilometers. Using proportion, we can find the actual distance between any two points on the map. How far is it from Lakeville to East City?

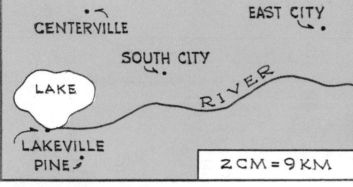

We want to know the actual distance between two places on the map.

We know that the ratio in the scale drawing is $\dfrac{\square}{\square}$.

By measuring, we find that the map distance from

Lakeville to East City is ____ centimeters. To find the actual distance from Lakeville to East City, we write a proportion and solve for n.

$\dfrac{2}{9} = \dfrac{8}{n}$ ← map distance in centimeters
← actual distance in kilometers

$2 \times n = 9 \times 8$
$2 \times n = 72$

$n = 72 \div$ ____

$n =$ ____

It is ____ kilometers from Lakeville to East City.

Getting Started

Measure the map distance and find the actual distance.

1. From South City to Centerville

2. From Pine to South City

3. From Centerville to East City

4. From Lakeville to Centerville

287

Practice

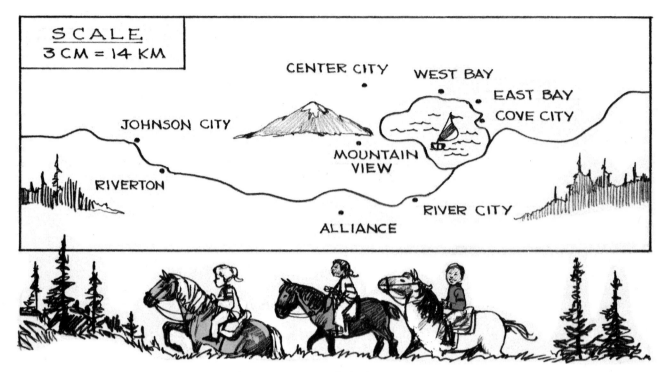

Measure the map distance and find the actual distance.

1. From Riverton to Center City

2. From Johnson City to River City

3. From Center City to West Bay

4. From East Bay to West Bay

5. From Mountain View to Center City

6. From River City to Riverton

7. From Alliance to Riverton

8. From East Bay to Cove City

Apply

Solve these problems.

9. On a scale drawing of a kitchen, 3 cm = 4 meters. If one side of the kitchen wall is 5 cm long in the drawing, what is its actual length?

10. The dinosaur model in the museum is built to a scale of 5 cm = 8 m. If the dinosaur was actually 42 meters in length, what is the length of the model?

11. On a scale drawing of his house, Mr. Edwards uses a scale of 2 cm = 7 meters. The outside dimensions of Mr. Edwards' house are 10 meters by 15 meters. What will be the dimensions of the scale drawing?

12. The statue of George Washington in the park is built to a scale of 9 in. = 1.75 ft. If the statue is 14 feet tall, what was George Washington's height in feet?

Understanding Percents

There are 16 trumpet players and 25 drummers in the Allentown marching band. There are 100 members in the band altogether. We can write the ratio, $\frac{16}{100}$, to compare the number of trumpet players to all the band members. Another way to express the same comparison is to use a percent. **Percent** means that amount per 100 and is shown by a % sign. We say 16% of the players are trumpeters. What percent of the band members are drummers?

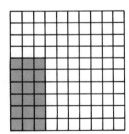

We want to use a percent to compare the number of drummers to the total band.

We know that there are _____ drummers,

and that there are _____ musicians in all.

The ratio of drummers to total membership is $\frac{\square}{\square}$.

We say _____% of the musicians are drummers. We can write a percent as a decimal by dividing by 100.

$$16\% = 0.16$$

$$25\% = \underline{\hspace{1cm}}$$

We can write a decimal as a percent by multiplying by 100.

$$0.09 = 9\%$$

$$0.45 = \underline{\hspace{1cm}}$$

Getting Started

Write the percent.

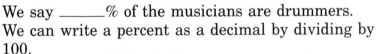

1. shaded squares _____

2. unshaded squares _____

Write as a percent.

3. $0.65 =$ _____   4. $0.01 =$ _____   5. $0.25 =$ _____

Write as a decimal.

6. $16\% =$ _____   7. $89\% =$ _____   8. $75\% =$ _____

Practice

Write the percent.

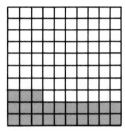

1. shaded squares _____

2. unshaded squares _____

Write as a percent.

3. 0.39   4. 0.17   5. 0.02   6. 0.98   7. 0.37   8. 0.16

_____   _____   _____   _____   _____   _____

9. 0.05   10. 0.40   11. 0.51   12. 0.65   13. 0.39   14. 0.87

_____   _____   _____   _____   _____   _____

15. 1.87   16. 0.01   17. 0.57   18. 0.19   19. 2.87   20. 0.99

_____   _____   _____   _____   _____   _____

Write as a decimal.

21. 50%   22. 36%   23. 12%   24. 85%   25. 7%   26. 19%

_____   _____   _____   _____   _____   _____

27. 16%   28. 1%   29. 70%   30. 10%   31. 99%   32. 12%

_____   _____   _____   _____   _____   _____

33. 75%   34. 200%   35. 4%   36. 53%   37. 107%   38. 12%

_____   _____   _____   _____   _____   _____

Apply

Solve these problems.

39. In a telephone poll, 4 out of 100 people had pets. What percent of the people called had pets?

40. Student Council members want to raise $100 to buy new books for the library. So far, they have raised $83. What percent of their goal must they still raise?

41. Robert bought a suit for $100. He paid $7 in sales tax. What percent was the sales tax?

42. Leon wants to jog 100 miles this month. So far, he has jogged 45 miles. What percent of his goal does Leon have left?

Renaming Fractions, Decimals and Percents

We can use what we have learned about ratios to rename equivalent fractions, decimals and percents. What percent of the geometric figures are triangles?

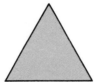

We want to name a ratio as a percent. We know that the ratio of triangles to geometric figures is $\dfrac{\square}{\square}$.

To rename $\dfrac{2}{3}$ as a decimal and a percent, follow these steps:

Divide the numerator by the denominator. Carry the division to hundredths. Write the remainder as a fraction.	Write the decimal as a percent by multiplying by 100.

$$0.66\tfrac{2}{3} = \underline{\qquad}$$

$$
\begin{array}{r}
0.66\tfrac{2}{3} \\
3\overline{)2.00} \\
\underline{1\,8} \\
2\,0 \\
\underline{1\,8} \\
2
\end{array}
$$

_____% of the geometric figures are triangles.

To rename a percent as a decimal and a fraction, follow these steps:

Write the percent as a decimal by dividing by 100.	Write the decimal as a fraction by writing the value over 100.	Rename the fraction in simplest form.

$$75\% = 0.75 \qquad 0.75 = \dfrac{}{100} \qquad \dfrac{75}{100} = \underline{}$$

Getting Started

Write as a percent.

1. $\dfrac{3}{5} =$ _____

2. $\dfrac{7}{25} =$ _____

3. $\dfrac{1}{2} =$ _____

4. $\dfrac{1}{3} =$ _____

5. $\dfrac{1}{8} =$ _____

Write as a fraction.

6. $82\% =$ ____

7. $16\% =$ ____

8. $25\% =$ ____

9. $48\% =$ ____

10. $15\% =$ ____

291

Practice

Write as a percent.

1. $\frac{3}{5}$ = _____
2. $\frac{1}{8}$ = _____
3. $\frac{1}{6}$ = _____
4. $\frac{3}{7}$ = _____
5. $\frac{5}{8}$ = _____

6. $\frac{3}{4}$ = _____
7. $\frac{1}{3}$ = _____
8. $\frac{7}{8}$ = _____
9. $\frac{9}{20}$ = _____
10. $\frac{16}{25}$ = _____

11. $\frac{17}{50}$ = _____
12. $\frac{5}{9}$ = _____
13. $\frac{3}{11}$ = _____
14. $\frac{17}{20}$ = _____
15. $\frac{1}{9}$ = _____

Write as a fraction.

16. 35% = ____
17. 40% = ____
18. 75% = ____
19. 16% = ____

20. 6% = ____
21. 10% = ____
22. 21% = ____
23. 58% = ____

24. 65% = ____
25. 70% = ____
26. 35% = ____
27. 88% = ____

28. 90% = ____
29. 79% = ____
30. 8% = ____

Apply

Solve these problems.

31. Kuni tried to kick 10 goals. He scored 6 times. What is Kuni's scoring percent?

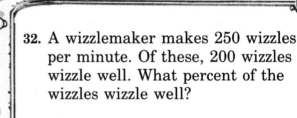

32. A wizzlemaker makes 250 wizzles per minute. Of these, 200 wizzles wizzle well. What percent of the wizzles wizzle well?

33. Todd scored 90% on a test. Peggy received 8 out of 9 correct. Who has the higher score?

34. Audrey planted $\frac{3}{25}$ of her garden with carrots, $\frac{1}{10}$ with beans and $\frac{7}{20}$ with tomatoes. What percent of her garden is still unplanted?

EXCURSION

Complete the pattern.

$0.99 = \frac{99}{100}$ = _____ %

$1.00 = \frac{}{100}$ = _____ %

$1.01 = \frac{}{100}$ = _____ %

Solve the equations.

1.25 = _____ %

1.09 = _____ %

1.8 = _____ %

1.06 = _____ %

150 = _____ %

2.00 = _____ %

Finding Percents of Numbers

Dawn bought her father a shirt for Father's Day. The sales tax on clothing is 6%. How much tax did Dawn pay? What was the total cost of the shirt?

We need to know how much Dawn paid for her father's gift.

We know that the shirt cost _____, and that the sales tax rate is _____%.

To find the amount of tax, we need to find 6% of $18.50.

To find the percent of a number, follow these steps:

Rename the percent as a decimal.

$$6\% = 0.06$$

Multiply the cost of the shirt by the rate.

$$\begin{array}{r} \$18.50 \\ \times\ \ 0.06 \\ \hline \$1.1100 \end{array}$$

The amount of sales tax was _____.

To find the total cost of the shirt, we add _____ and _____.

$$\begin{array}{r} \$18.50 \\ +\ \ \ 1.11 \\ \hline \end{array}$$

Dawn paid a total of _____ for her father's gift.

Getting Started

Write the percent of each number.

1. 25% of 28 = _____   2. 30% of 30 = _____   3. 75% of 48 = _____

Write the percent of each number. Use a decimal.

4. 12% of 70 = _____   5. 15% of 116 = _____   6. 8% of 36 = _____

293

Practice

Write the percent of each number.

1. 20% of 35 = _____

2. 50% of 94 = _____

3. 40% of 18 = _____

4. 75% of 64 = _____

5. 30% of 16 = _____

6. 10% of 120 = _____

7. 60% of 420 = _____

8. 25% of 248 = _____

9. 90% of 1,400 = _____

10. 86% of 230 = _____

11. 25% of 32 = _____

12. 6% of 30 = _____

Write the percent of each number.

13. 21% of 70 = _____

14. 37% of 19 = _____

15. 68% of 215 = _____

16. 6% of 315 = _____

17. 29% of 116 = _____

18. 48% of 39 = _____

19. 67% of 87 = _____

20. 1% of 750 = _____

21. 96% of 600 = _____

22. 200% of 10 = _____

23. 28% of 82 = _____

24. 32% of 98 = _____

Apply

Solve these problems.

25. The Lincoln School has 460 students. 45% of the students are boys. How many boys are in Lincoln School?

26. The Swim Club needs to raise $800. So far, they have raised 70% of what they need. How much more money does the Swim Club need?

27. Jerome bought a $25 item and paid a 4% sales tax. His friend bought the same item in another state for $25, but paid a 5% sales tax. How much less tax than his friend did Jerome pay?

28. At the restaurant, Mr. Wilson's chicken dinner cost $7.25. Mrs. Wilson's dinner cost $6.95. The check included a 5% tax. How much did the Wilsons pay for dinner?

29. Chris and Terry own and operate the Myers Inn. Chris owns 56% of the hotel. What percent of the Myers Inn belongs to Terry?

Computing Interest

Miss King deposits $850 in a money market account. How much interest will her account earn in one year?

Interest Rates	
Money Market	8%
Pass Book	5%
Certificates	$12\frac{1}{2}\%$

We want to know the amount of interest Miss King's deposit will earn in one year.

We know that she deposits _____ in a money market account.

The rate of interest is _____.

To find the interest for one year, we multiply the amount of the deposit by the rate of interest.

We multiply _____ by _____.

To compute interest for one year, follow these steps:

Name the rate of interest as a decimal.

$$8\% = \underline{\hspace{1cm}}$$

Multiply the amount of the deposit by the rate of interest.

$$\begin{array}{r} \$850 \\ \times \underline{\hspace{1.5cm}} \end{array}$$

Miss King will earn _____ in interest for one year.

To find the total balance in Miss King's account, we add the deposit and the interest.

$$\begin{array}{r} \$850 \leftarrow \text{amount deposited} \\ + \quad 68 \leftarrow \text{interest} \\ \hline \$918 \end{array}$$

Miss King will have a balance of _____ in her account after one year.

Getting Started

Write the interest for one year.

1. 3% on $250 = _____ 2. 8% on $980 = _____ 3. 12% on $35,600 = _____

Write the total amount after one year.

4. $1,256 at 5% = _____   5. $5,000 at 6% = _____   6. $725 at 7% = _____

295

Practice

Write the interest for one year.

1. 5% on $360 = _____
2. 6% on $580 = _____
3. 4% on $175 = _____

4. 10% on $750 = _____
5. 7% on $700 = _____
6. 7% on $800 = _____

7. 8% on $6,000 = _____
8. 12% on $1,960 = _____
9. 9% on $800 = _____

10. 16% on $2,000 = _____
11. 3% on $786 = _____
12. 11% on $72 = _____

Write the total amount after one year.

13. $825 at 8% = _____
14. $1,200 at 9% = _____

15. $2,500 at 7% = _____
16. $1,860 at 6% = _____

17. $1,325 at 5% = _____
18. $2,290 at 7% = _____

19. $1,450 at 5% = _____
20. $3,050 at 11% = _____

21. $975 at 12% = _____
22. $3,000 at 12% = _____

23. $629 at 8% = _____
24. $330 at 4% = _____

Apply

Solve these problems.

25. Scott put $450 in a bank for one year. The bank paid 6% interest. Margie put $440 in a different bank, also for one year. This bank paid 9% interest. At the end of the year, who will have the greater amount? How much greater?

26. Nancy put $500 in a one-year certificate at 8% interest. After the first year, she put the total back in the same account. How much will Nancy have after the second year?

27. The Morgans bought a new car for $9,500. They paid $\frac{2}{5}$ of the price in cash, and borrowed the rest at 8% for one year. If they repaid their loan at the end of the year, how much did they have to pay for the car?

28. Mr. Chen plans to borrow $2,500 for one year. One bank charges 7% interest and another bank charges 8% interest. How much can Mr. Chen save if he borrows the money from the bank that charges the lower interest rate?

Determining Missing Data, Collecting Data

Elaine is writing reports on each planet and the sun for her science class. When she finishes the reports, she would like to put them in order beginning with the sun and then arranging the other planets in order according to their distance from the sun. The planet furthest from the sun will be the last chapter. In what order should Elaine arrange the chapters?

★ **SEE**

We want to arrange the planets in order according to their distance from the sun. We need to know the name of each planet and its distance from the sun.

★ **PLAN**

Since the data we need to solve the problem is not given, we will need to look in a reference book to find the name of each planet and its distance from the sun. Once we have obtained this data, we can put the planets in order.

★ **DO**

Planet	Earth	Jupiter	Mars	Mercury					
Distance from the Sun*									

*in millions of miles

Elaine should put the reports in the following order:

—————, —————, —————, —————, —————,

—————, —————, —————, —————.

✔ Reference books are just one type of the many resources from which we can collect data.

★ **CHECK**

We can check our work to be sure we have correctly copied the information and that we have put the planets in the correct order. When we are collecting data, we can use more than one reference book to verify its correctness.

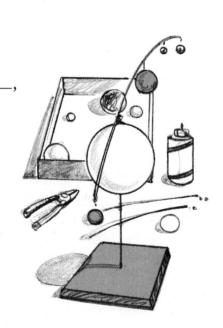

Apply

Determine what data you need to know to solve these problems. You will need to collect this data from outside sources.

1. What is the average height of the sixth graders in your class?

2. What is the favorite pet among the second graders in your school?

3. List the five Great Lakes in order from largest to smallest.

4. What are the five longest rivers in the United States?

5. What is the perimeter of the cover of your math book to the nearest centimeter?

6. List the seven continents in order from the most populated to the least populated.

7. Eight states have an area of over 100,000 square miles. In order from largest to smallest, they are Alaska, Texas, California, Montana, New Mexico, Arizona, Nevada and Colorado. List these eight states in order beginning with the state that has the greatest population and ending with the state that has the least population.

8. The school wants to buy carpeting for your classroom. Find the area of the room to the nearest square meter.

9. How many letters are in the first name of each student in your class? What is the most and least common number of letters?

10. There were 800 students in school in September. By January, enrollment increased 10%. Then, by June, enrollment decreased 10%. Were there more, fewer, or the same number of students in June as in September? Explain how you know.

11. A suit in a clothing store is on sale at 20% off. An employee of the store gets a discount of 10% on any item for sale in the store. If the employee buys the suit, is the price less than, equal to, or more than the original price less 30%? Verify your answer.

12. Tyrone and Luis were hiking across Horace Heights to the camp store. Tyrone walked 80% of the distance and then stopped to rest. Luis walked 50% of the distance, stopped to rest, and then walked another 30% of the distance before stopping to rest again. At this point along the trail, who is ahead?

13. Two friends want Alex to help them mow lawns. Cindy says that she gets $80 for the lawns she wants Alex to cut and will give him 60% of this if he works for her. Banto says that he gets $60 for the lawns he wants Alex to cut and will give Alex 80% of this. Which friend should Alex work for and why?

Calculators and Discount

When merchants have sales on their merchandise, they sometimes advertise a certain percent off the original price. This percent is called the **rate of discount.** When the original price is multiplied by the rate of discount, we can find the amount of the discount. What is the amount of discount on the radio that is on sale?

We want to know the amount we save by buying the radio on sale.

The original price is _____ and the rate of discount

is _____. To find the discount, we find _____

of _____.

48 [×] 25 [%] (_____)

The discount on the radio is _____.

To find the **sale price,** or the cost after discount, we subtract the discount from the original price.

48 [−] _____ [=] (_____)

There is another method for finding the sale price.

We know that the sale price is "25% off" so the sale price must be 75% of the original price.

48 [×] 75 [%] (_____)

This is called the **complement method.** 75% is the complement of 25%.

The complement of 60% must be _____.

The complements together should equal 100%.

Originally the radio cost 100%.

If I don't have to pay 25% of this cost, I will have to pay 75% of it.

Practice

Complete these codes.

1. 65 $\boxed{\times}$ 12 $\boxed{\%}$ $\bigcirc$

2. 12 $\boxed{\times}$ 65 $\boxed{\%}$ $\bigcirc$

3. 16 $\boxed{\times}$ 225 $\boxed{\%}$ $\bigcirc$

4. 9,000 $\boxed{\times}$ 0.5 $\boxed{\%}$ $\bigcirc$

5. 800 $\boxed{\times}$ 6.25 $\boxed{\%}$ $\bigcirc$

6. 265 $\boxed{\times}$ 9.4 $\boxed{\%}$ $\bigcirc$

Use a calculator to complete these equations.

7. 80% of $25 = _____

8. 6.25% of $80 = _____

9. 6.4% of $950 = _____

10. 236% of $75 = _____

11. 62.5% of $16 = _____

12. 500% of $6 = _____

Apply

Use a calculator to find these discounts.

BIG ED'S DISCOUNTS
★ ★ ★ ★ ★ ★
SAVE!
SAVE!
SAVE!

13.

Original Price	$75	$68	$49.50	$648
Rate of Discount	5%	4%	10%	3%
Discount				

14.

Original Price	$240	$125	$488	$960
Rate of Discount	15%	40%	12.5%	62.5%
Sale Price				

EXCURSION

When Pat saved $5,000 for one year at 8% interest, she ended with $5,400 in her account. Shelby saved her money at 8% compound interest. Each quarter (3 months), the bank figured Shelby's interest on the money in her account plus the interest made in the quarter. Complete the following to see how much Pat would have ended with at 8% compounded interest.

8% compounded quarterly is 2% each 3 months.

Quarter 1

$5,000
×   2%
———
$ 100
+ 5,000
———
$5,100

Quarter 2

$5,100
×   2%
———
$ 102
+ 5,100
———

Quarter 3

×   2%
———

Quarter 4

×   2%
———

Write each ratio as a fraction.

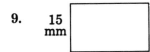

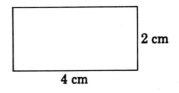

1. forks to spoons ____

2. width to length ____

3. spoons to silverware ____

4. length to perimeter ____

Solve each proportion.

5. $\frac{3}{4} = \frac{n}{16}$

6. $\frac{n}{9} = \frac{10}{30}$

7. $\frac{7}{14} = \frac{5}{n}$

8. $\frac{8}{n} = \frac{5}{9}$

$n =$ ____

$n =$ ____

$n =$ ____

$n =$ ____

The figures are similar. Solve for n.

9.

10.

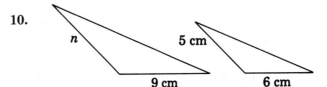

$n =$ _____

$n =$ _____

Use the scale to find the actual distance.

11.

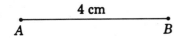

Scale: 1 cm = 8 m _____

12.

Scale: 2 cm = 8 m _____

Write each fraction as a percent.

13. $\frac{4}{5} =$ _____

14. $\frac{7}{20} =$ _____

Write each percent as a fraction.

15. 30% = _____

16. 48% = _____

Find the percent of each number.

17. 70% of 43 = _____

18. 15% of 84 = _____

19. $5\frac{1}{2}$% of \$96 = _____

20. 9.6% of \$650 = _____

21. $7\frac{3}{4}$% of \$100 = _____

22. $8\frac{1}{2}$% of 120 = _____

CUMULATIVE REVIEW

Circle the letter of the correct answer.

1 $2\frac{4}{5}$
   $+ 3\frac{2}{3}$

   a $1\frac{7}{15}$
   b $5\frac{7}{15}$
   c $6\frac{7}{15}$
   d NG

2 $5\frac{1}{8}$
   $- 3\frac{2}{3}$

   a $1\frac{11}{24}$
   b $2\frac{11}{24}$
   c $3\frac{11}{24}$
   d NG

3 $3\frac{1}{3} \times 1\frac{1}{5}$

   a $\frac{1}{4}$
   b 2
   c 4
   d NG

4 $2\frac{1}{3} \div 1\frac{1}{6}$

   a $\frac{1}{2}$
   b 2
   c $2\frac{13}{18}$
   d NG

5 What is the place value of the 7 in 2.1076?

   a tenths
   b hundredths
   c thousandths
   d NG

6 3.46 + 2.7

   a 5.16
   b 6.10
   c 6.16
   d NG

7 16.1
   $-$ 8.304

   a 7.804
   b 7.806
   c 12.204
   d NG

8 4.1 × 0.03

   a 0.123
   b 1.23
   c 12.3
   d NG

9 16 ÷ 0.01

   a 0.16
   b 1.6
   c 16
   d NG

10 16 ft 6 in.
    $-$ 6 ft 9 in.

    a 9 ft 7 in.
    b 9 ft 9 in.
    c 10 ft 3 in.
    d NG

11 Find the area.

    a 24 cm²
    b 48 cm²
    c 56 cm²
    d NG

12 Find the volume.

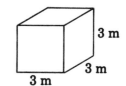

    a 9 m³
    b 18 m³
    c 27 m³
    d NG

 score

GRAPHS AND PROBABILITY

Working with Pictographs

A **pictograph** uses pictures to show data. In this pictograph, each 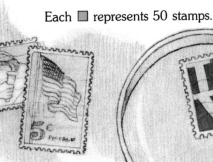 represents 50 stamps. How many stamps from England are in the collection?

Stamp Collection	
United States	▢ ▢ ▢ ▢ ▢
Canada	▢ ▢ ▯
Mexico	▢ ▢ ▢ ▢
England	▢ ▢ ▢ ▯

Each ▢ represents 50 stamps.

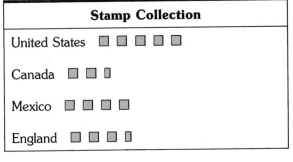

We want to know the number of English stamps in the collection.

We know that each ▢ stands for ____ stamps, and

that there are ____ ▢'s. To find the number of stamps, we multiply the number of stamps by the number of ▢'s.

We multiply ____ by ____.

$$3\frac{1}{2} \times 50 = \frac{7}{2} \times 50 = \underline{\quad}$$

There are ____ stamps from England in the collection.

Getting Started

Use the graph above to solve these problems.

1. How many stamps from the United States are in the collection?

2. How many more stamps are from Mexico than Canada?

3. What percent of the collection is United States stamps?

4. What is the ratio of Canadian stamps to the total collection?

Practice

Use the pictograph to solve problems 1–4.

1. How many biographies are in the library?

_____

2. What is the ratio of the biographies to the history books?

_____

3. Of the fiction books, 20% are new. How many fiction books are not new?

_____

Library Books	
Fiction	☐ ☐ ☐ ☐ ☐ ◨
Biography	☐ ☐ ☐
History	☐ ☐ ☐
Reference	☐ ☐ ☐ ◨

Each ☐ represents 100 books.

4. How many more fiction books are there than reference books?

_____

Use the pictograph to solve problems 5–8.

5. How many votes did Roberta receive?

_____

6. How many more votes did the winner receive than the person who got the fewest votes?

_____

7. How many students voted? _____

Bill	△ △ △ △ △ ◿
Nancy	△ △ △ △ △
Tom	△ △ △ △ ◿
Miguel	△ △ △ △ △ △
Roberta	△ △ △ ◿

Each △ represents 6 votes.

8. What is the ratio of Nancy's votes to Miguel's votes?

_____

Apply

9. Students at Hardy Middle School collected paper for one month. Some students weighed the paper and recorded the weights in the chart. Use ☐ to represent each 100 pounds.

Use the chart to complete the pictograph. Let ☐ = 100 pounds.

Grade	Pounds
1	350
2	600
3	500
4	725
5	600
6	950

1	
2	
3	
4	
5	
6	

Working with Bar Graphs

A bar graph is another way to report numerical information. For example, this bar graph shows how a group of TV viewers in two different cities rate a certain television program. Use the data in the chart to complete the bar graph.

Television Ratings		
	City A	City B
Very Good	60%	55%
Good	20%	20%
Fair	15%	10%
Poor	5%	15%

Getting Started

For this bar graph, 800 viewers in City A and 600 viewers in City B were polled. Use the graph to solve the problems.

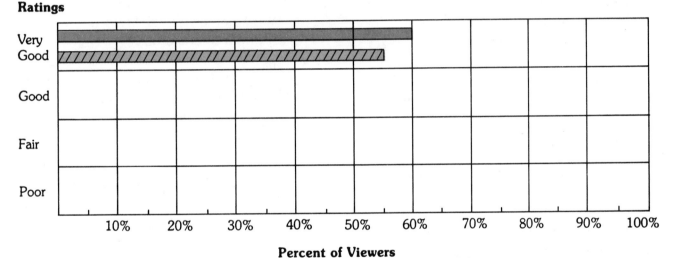

Television Ratings

- City A Viewers
- City B Viewers

Percent of Viewers

1. What percent of City A viewers rated the program **fair**?

   _____

2. What percent of City B viewers rated the program **poor**?

   _____

3. How many City A viewers rated the program **very good**?

   _____

4. How many City B viewers rated the program **good**?

   _____

5. How many viewers rated the program **fair**?

   _____

6. How many viewers did not rate the program **very good**?

   _____

Practice

For this bar graph, 180 boys and 160 girls were polled.
Use the graph to answer the questions.

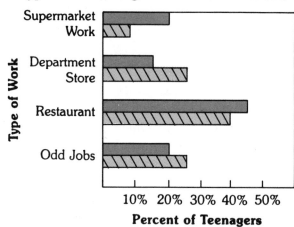

Types of Teenagers' Part-time Work

Boys
Girls

1. What percent of boys work at restaurants? _____

2. What percent of the girls work in supermarkets? _____

3. How many teenagers work at odd jobs? _____

4. How many boys work in restaurants? _____

5. How many of the boys work in department stores? _____

6. How many boys do not work in department stores? _____

7. What percent of girls do not work in department stores? _____

8. What kind of part-time work do most girls do? _____

9. How many girls work in restaurants or at odd jobs? _____

10. What percent of boys do not work in supermarkets or at odd jobs? _____

Apply

11. Use the data to construct a bar graph.

	Boys	Girls
Dogs	8	6
Cats	6	5
Birds	3	5
Other	4	3

Types of Pets

Boys
Girls

Dogs Cats Birds Others

Working with Double-line Graphs

This double-line graph shows the high values of 2 stocks for one week.

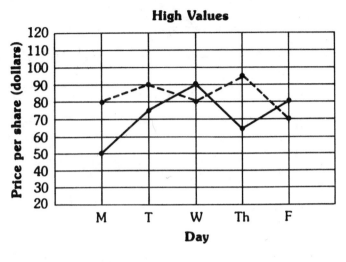

High Values

stock X ---
stock Y ———

The high value for stock Y on Monday was _____.

The weekly low for stock X was on _____.

Its value on that day was _____.

Getting Started

Use the graph above to solve these problems.

1. What is the difference between the high values of stocks X and Y on Thursday?

   _____

2. On what day of the week did Stock Y reach its highest value?

   _____

Use the chart to complete the double-line graph.

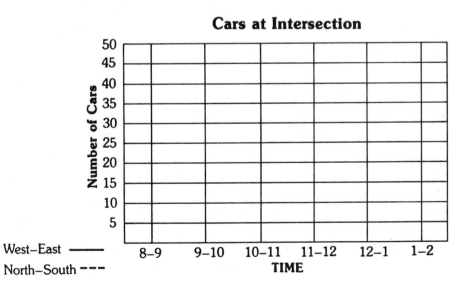

Number of Cars at Intersection		
Time Interval	Number of Cars W–E	N–S
8–9 AM	44	35
9–10 AM	20	25
10–11 AM	29	20
11–12 AM	14	24
12–1 PM	24	15
1–2 PM	40	38

Cars at Intersection

West–East ———
North–South ---

Practice

Use the graph to solve these problems.

1. What is Tom's best test score? _____

2. What is Mary's best test score? _____

3. How many more points did Tom receive than Mary on Test 3?

    _____

4. How many more points did Mary receive than Tom on Test 2?

    _____

5. What is Tom's average test score?

    _____

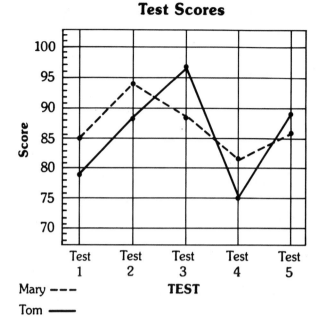

Test Scores

Mary - - -
Tom ———

6. What is Mary's average test score? _____

7. Use the data to complete the double-line graph.

Dan's and Ann's Temperatures		
Time	Ann	Dan
8 AM	101°	98°
10 AM	100°	98°
12 Noon	101°	99°
2 PM	102°	100°
4 PM	101°	99°
6 PM	99°	98°
8 PM	99°	98°

Dan's and Ann's Temperatures

Ann ———
Dan - - -

8. Use the chart to construct a double-line graph.

Monthly Rainfall		
Month	Iona	Racine
March	20 cm	25 cm
April	30 cm	35 cm
May	35 cm	30 cm
June	30 cm	40 cm
July	25 cm	25 cm
August	15 cm	20 cm

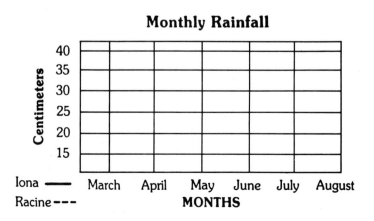

Monthly Rainfall

Iona ———
Racine - - -

Working with Circle Graphs

Todd made a circle graph to show how he usually spends a 24-hour day. About how many hours does Todd usually spend in school?

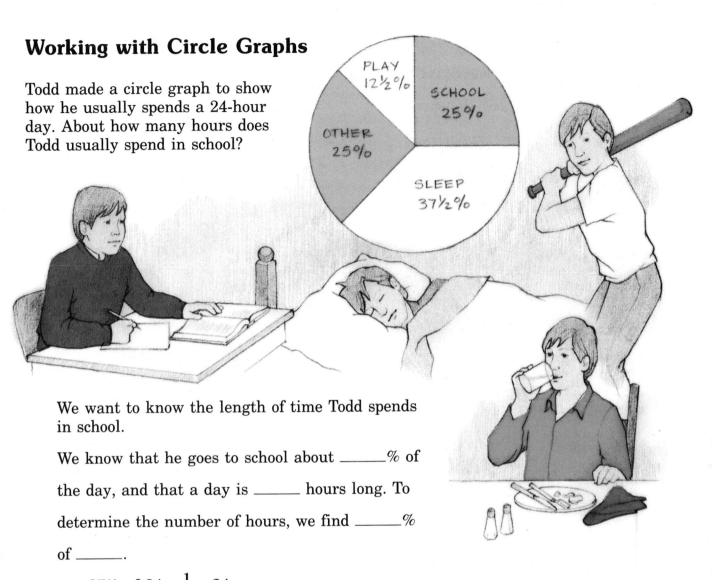

We want to know the length of time Todd spends in school.

We know that he goes to school about _____% of the day, and that a day is _____ hours long. To determine the number of hours, we find _____% of _____.

$$25\% \text{ of } 24 = \frac{1}{4} \times 24 = \text{_____}$$

Todd usually goes to school about _____ hours each day.

Getting Started

Use the circle graph above to solve these problems.

1. How many hours did Todd spend sleeping?

   _____

2. How many hours does Todd spend playing?

   _____

3. Todd spends 10% of his time eating. How many hours is this?

   _____

4. How many hours is Todd either in school or sleeping?

   _____

5. How many hours is Todd not sleeping?

   _____

6. What is the sum of the percents in the graph?

   _____

Practice

Use the circle graph to solve problems 1–5.

1. How many people took the survey?

   _____

2. How many people rated the show good?

   _____

3. How many people rated the show fair or poor?

   _____

**Movie Survey
1,200 People**

4. How many people rated the show very good?

   _____

Use the circle graph to solve problems 5–8.

5. How much is spent for housing?

   _____

6. How much is spent for food?

   _____

7. How much is spent for the car and utilities?

   _____

$3,600 Monthly Budget

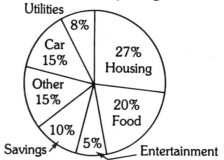

8. How much more is spent for utilities than entertainment?

   _____

EXCURSION

Use your protractor to construct a circle graph with the following data:

Favorite Shows Survey	
Show	**Percent**
Comedy	$37\frac{1}{2}$
Mystery	25
Drama	20
Talk	$12\frac{1}{2}$
News	5

Understanding Ordered Pairs and Graphs

We can use an ordered pair of numbers to locate points on a plane. The ordered pair (2, 3) locates point P. The ordered pair (0, 0) is called the **origin.** Points P, A and B are on the same straight line or **graph.** What ordered pairs locate points A and B?

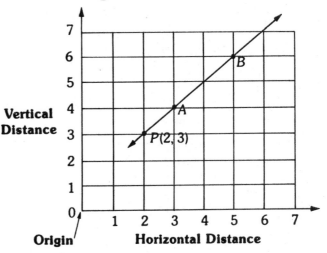

To locate points on a plane, follow these steps.

Find the horizontal distance from the origin.	Find the vertical distance from the origin.

Point A is 3 units from the origin.

Point A is 4 units from the origin.

Point A is located at _____.

Point B is located at _____.

We can graph a table of ordered pairs by joining points on the same line. Complete the table and the graph.

	A	B	C	D
n	1	2	3	4
$n + 2$	3	4		

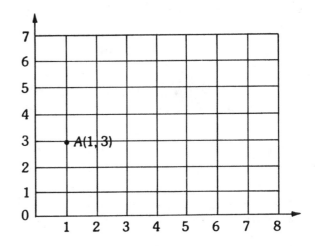

Getting Started

Name each point.

1. $A(\_\_, \_\_)$

2. $B(\_\_, \_\_)$

3. $C(\_\_, \_\_)$

4. $D(\_\_, \_\_)$

Locate and label each point.

5. $W(5, 6)$

6. $X(0, 4)$

7. $Y(3, 3)$

8. $Z(5, 1)$

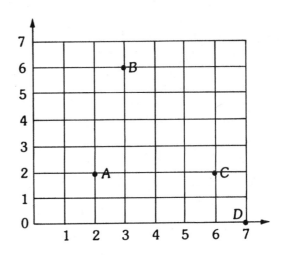

311

Practice

Name each point.

1. $A(\underline{\quad}, \underline{\quad})$
2. $B(\underline{\quad}, \underline{\quad})$
3. $C(\underline{\quad}, \underline{\quad})$
4. $D(\underline{\quad}, \underline{\quad})$
5. $E(\underline{\quad}, \underline{\quad})$
6. $F(\underline{\quad}, \underline{\quad})$
7. $G(\underline{\quad}, \underline{\quad})$
8. $H(\underline{\quad}, \underline{\quad})$
9. $I(\underline{\quad}, \underline{\quad})$
10. $J(\underline{\quad}, \underline{\quad})$

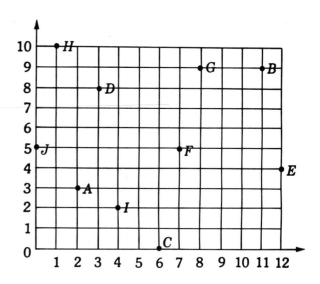

Locate and label each point.

11. $P(3, 5)$
12. $Q(6, 2)$
13. $R(0, 4)$
14. $S(5, 5)$
15. $T(11, 2)$
16. $U(5, 0)$
17. $V(3, 10)$
18. $W(9, 6)$
19. $X(7, 1)$
20. $Y(12, 10)$

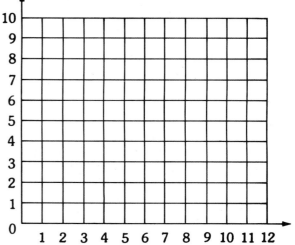

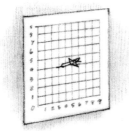

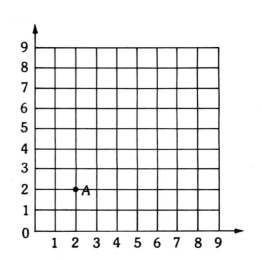

Apply

21. Complete the table and graph each ordered pair.

	A	B	C	D
n	2	4	6	8
$1 \times n$	2	___	___	___

Understanding Probability

The spinner has 9 equal parts. On each spin, it is equally possible that the pointer will stop on any of the 9 parts. Because 5 parts are labeled A, there are 5 possible outcomes where the pointer will land on A. The chance of stopping on A for any spin is 5 out of 9. The **probability** of stopping on A on any spin is $\frac{5}{9}$. What is the probability of the pointer stopping on a B?

The probability of an **event** occurring is expressed as a ratio.

$$\frac{\text{number of chances to get an outcome}}{\text{number of possible outcomes}} = \frac{\text{number of parts marked } B}{\text{number of possible stops}} = \frac{\square}{\square}$$

The probability of stopping on B is $\frac{\square}{\square}$.

Probability is measured on a scale from 0 (impossible) to 1 (certain).

✔ When a weather forecaster says the probability for rain is 70%, there is a pretty good chance (7 out of 10) that it will rain. What does it mean when a friend says, "the probability I will get a phone call today is only about 20%"?

Getting Started

Write the probability of each event.

1. You will see a comet tonight. ____

2. The sun will set tonight. ____

Find the probability if you draw one card without looking.

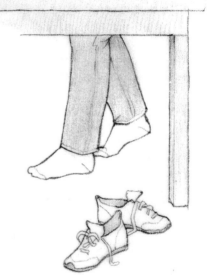

3. It will be a 3. ____

4. It will be a 2. ____

5. It will be an even number.

6. It will be greater than 1.

____

____

Practice

Write the probability of each event.

1. You will get wet when you jump in
   the pool. ____
2. Your best friend has a March
   birthday. ____
3. The sun will rise in the west.

   ____
4. Your birthday is on Friday in any

   year. ____
5. You will catch the next ball that is

   thrown to you. ____
6. You will go skating this weekend.

   _____
7. A newborn baby will be a boy.

   ____
8. You will go right home after
   school.

   _____

Find the probability if you draw one marble without looking.

9. It will be black. ____

10. It will be white. ____

11. It will be red. ____

12. It will not be red. ____

Find the probability if you draw one card without looking.

13. It will be a 5. ____

14. It will be a 10. ____

15. It will be greater than 3. ____

16. It will be less than 5. ____

17. It is divisible by 2. ____

18. It is prime. ____

19. It has 3 for a factor. ____

20. It is a multiple of 4. ____

21. It is greater than 12. ____

22. It is less than 0. ____

23. It is an odd number. ____

24. It is a factor of 30. ____

314

Listing Outcomes

Martina is going to fix a double dip frozen yogurt cone. How many possible outcomes can Martina choose?

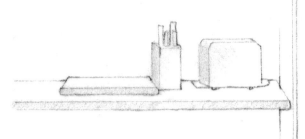

We can use a tree diagram to list the possible outcomes.

vanilla
— vanilla   (vanilla   vanilla)
— strawberry   (vanilla   strawberry)

strawberry
— vanilla   (strawberry   vanilla)
— strawberry   (strawberry   strawberry)

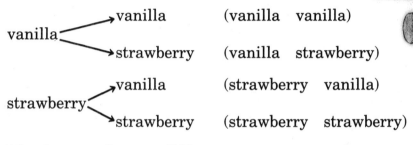

Martina can fix ____ different cones.
The possible outcomes can be written as a set of ordered pairs.
This set is sometimes called a **sample space.**
The possible outcomes listed as a sample space are (V, V), (V, S), (S, V), (S, S) where V stands for vanilla and S stands for strawberry.

Getting Started

Use a tree diagram to list the possible outcomes. Write the possible outcomes as a sample space.

1. Nat is spinning two spinners. The first has the letters *A*, *B* and *C*. The second has the letters *Y* and *Z*.

   _____

2. Tad, John, Martha, Alice and Patti are forming a committee of two. The committee will have one boy and one girl.

   _____

Practice

Use a tree diagram to list the possible outcomes. Write the possible outcomes as a sample space.

1. Emile is spinning two spinners. The first has the numbers 1, 2 and 3. The second has the numbers 1 and 2.

   _____

2. Amy has a spinner with the numbers 1, 2, 3, 4 and a nickel. She spins the spinner and tosses the nickel.

   _____

3. Ben has a blue coat, a green coat and a brown coat. He can wear his coat with brown slacks or blue slacks.

   _____

   _____

4. Juan is spinning two spinners. The first has the letters M, N and O. The second has the numbers 1, 2 and 3.

   _____

   _____

5. Michelle is tossing a penny and a dime. She is recording the heads and tails.

   _____

6. Willie is making a sandwich. He has wheat bread and rye bread. He can use ham or beef.

   _____

Working with Compound Probability

The sixth-grade class is conducting
a probability experiment with spinners.
What is the probability that in one
spin of both spinners,

FIRST
SPINNER

SECOND
SPINNER

- the first spinner is even and
  the second spinner is odd?
  P(even,odd)
- the sum of the digits is 2 or 5?
  P(sum is 2 or 5)

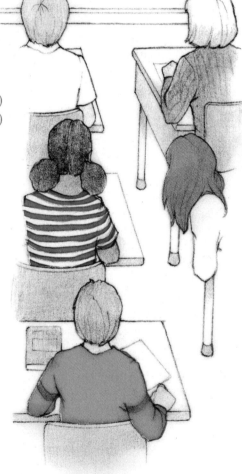

To answer these questions, follow these steps:
List the possible outcomes.

First Spinner	Second Spinner	Sample Space
1	1	(1,1), (1,2), (1,3)
1	2	(2,1), (2,2), (2,3)
1	3	
2	1	
2	2	
2	3	

List the ordered pairs from the sample space that
have the first number even and the second number
odd: (2,1), (2,3)

List the ordered pairs that have a sum of 2 or
5: (1,1), (2,3)

The probability that the first spinner is even and

the second is odd is $\dfrac{\square}{\square}$.

The probability that the sum of the digits is 2 or 5

is $\dfrac{\square}{\square}$.

Getting Started

Use the spinners above to find the probability.

1. P(both digits are the same) _____

2. P(sum = 4) _____

3. P(sum > than 1) _____

4. P(odd, odd) _____

5. P(quotient = 1) _____

6. P(product = 5) _____

Practice

Use the spinners to find the probability.

1. P(product = 10) ____

3. P(4 and 3) ____

5. P(quotient = 2) ____

7. P(sum < 8) ____

2. P(sum is odd) ____

4. P(4 and 5) ____

6. P(even, odd) ____

8. P(product is a multiple of 3) ____

Use the spinners to find the probability.

9. P(2 or 3) ____

11. P(even, even) ____

13. P(sum = 6) ____

15. P(product = 6) ____

10. P(2 and 3) ____

12. P(prime, odd) ____

14. P(sum < than 6) ____

16. P(quotient = 2) ____

Three coins are tossed. Find each probability.

17. All coins are heads. ____

18. All coins are the same. ____

19. Exactly one head. ____

20. Exactly two tails. ____

21. At least two tails. ____

22. At least one head and one tail. ____

Nickel	Penny	Dime
H	H	H
H	H	T
H	T	H
H	T	T
T	H	H
T	H	T
T	T	H
T	T	T

Making a Flow Chart

A palindrome is a word or number that is the same when read from right to left as when read from left to right. Here are some examples of palindromes:

BOB   MADAM   33   151   2332

It is possible to make any number become a palindrome by following a set of directions. How many additions will it take to make the number 59 become a palindrome?

★ SEE

We want to know the number of additions it will take to make the number 59 become a palindrome. A palindrome is a number that reads the same forward as backward.

★ PLAN

Because the directions for making a palindrome are complicated, we can simplify them by making a flow chart. Use the directions in the flow chart to make the number 59 become a palindrome.

✔ The shapes in a flow chart depend on what is happening in the steps. Ovals are for starting and finishing. Parallelograms are for action steps and diamonds are for decision steps.

It takes ____ additions to make the number 59 a palindrome.

★ DO

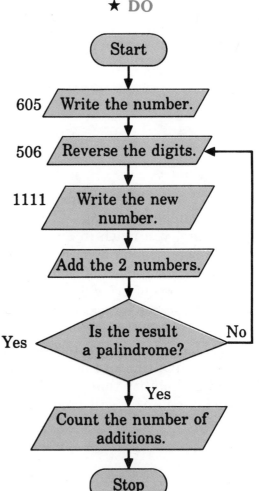

59	154	605	Write the number.
95	451	506	Reverse the digits.
154	605	1111	Write the new number.
			Add the 2 numbers.
No	No	Yes	Is the result a palindrome?

★ CHECK

Check your addition to see if you added correctly on each step. Count the number of additions to be sure you have included each one.

Apply

Make flow charts to help solve these problems.

1. Larry is doing extra credit work to raise his grade to an A+. Write a flow chart, using the unordered statements below, that will guide Larry along.
   A. DO EXTRA WORK
   B. STOP
   C. IS GRADE A+?
   D. START

2. Julie must write a story containing more than 500 words and it must be at least two pages in length. Write a flow chart to help Julie do this. Use the statements below.
   A. IS IT 500 WORDS OR GREATER YET?
   B. START
   C. END
   D. IS IT 2 PAGES OR MORE YET?
   E. WRITE

3. An ice cube tray contains 16 cubes. Use the following statements in a flow chart to guide you in determining when to fill the trays.
   A. END
   B. IS THE TRAY EMPTY?
   C. REMOVE CUBES AS NEEDED
   D. START
   E. FILL TRAY WITH WATER
   F. REMOVE TRAY FROM FREEZER

4. Use the following statements to create a flow chart that shows the steps in adding two fractions.
   A. REWRITE FRACTIONS TO HAVE THE SAME DENOMINATOR
   B. CHOOSE 2 FRACTIONS
   C. ADD NUMERATORS AND WRITE AS A SINGLE FRACTION
   D. START
   E. REDUCE FRACTION IF POSSIBLE
   F. END
   G. ARE DENOMINATORS IDENTICAL?

5. There are 3 even numbers and 1 odd number in a bag. Without looking, you reach in and draw a number. It is an even number. If you do not replace it, will the probability of drawing a second even number increase or decrease?

6. Malvin uses the 2 letters A and B to make a spinner. Mick examines the spinner and notes that spinning an A is twice as likely as spinning a B. If Mick spins, what is the probability that he will spin an A?

7. Mr. Lamont tosses a nickel. It lands heads five times in a row. What is the probability that, if he tosses the nickel again, it will land tails this time?

8. List 5 desserts that you like. Design a spinner so that 4 of the desserts will have the same probability but the fifth, your favorite, will have a probability of $\frac{1}{2}$.

Calculators and Statistics

The table of data represents the temperatures of 20 cities taken at the same time of the day. The study of **statistics** is used to collect, organize and interpret sets of data.

30	48	46	25
20	25	50	30
48	34	22	35
25	40	49	26
50	24	28	35

One way to describe the temperatures is to look at the center or middle readings.

The **mean** temperature is the average temperature. To find the mean temperature, we add the temperatures and divide by the number of readings. We divide _____ by _____.

The mean temperature is _____.

The **median** is the midway temperature. We list the temperatures in order.

20, 22, 24, 25, 25, 25, 26, 28, 30, <u>30</u>, <u>34</u>, 35, 35, 40, 46, 48, 48, 49, 50, 50

There is an even number of scores. So the median is the mean of the two midway scores. The median temperature is _____.

Another way to describe the temperature is to look at the way the data is spread out.

The **range** is the difference between the largest and smallest numbers. The range of the temperatures is _____.

A **histogram** is a bar graph that shows how the temperatures are spread out. We can make a table and draw the histogram.

Tens Digit	Ones Digit	Number of Readings
5	0, 0	2
4	0, 6, 8, 8, 9	5
3	0, 0, 4, 5, 5	5
2	0, 2, 4, 5, 5, 5, 6, 8	8

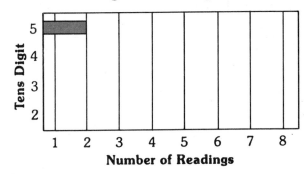

Histogram of Temperatures

How many temperatures were in the 30's? _____

321

Practice

Find the mean, the median and the range for each set of data.
Complete the table and histogram.

1. In eleven games, Marcia scored the
following number of points:
14, 14, 15, 17, 17, 14, 16, 14, 16, 17,
11,

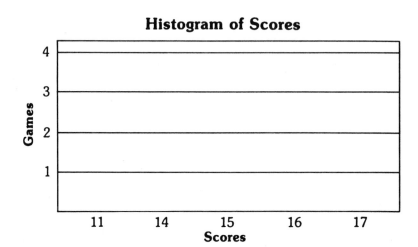

Mean ____   Median ____   Range ____

Table	
Score	Games
11	1
14	
15	
16	
17	

Histogram of Scores

(Games vs Scores: 11, 14, 15, 16, 17)

How many scores were over 15? ____

2. The heights of the sixth-grade
children are given in centimeters.

138	135	143	137	145
147	149	143	139	149
158	149	147	152	150
163	161	158	153	151
164	162	158	160	164

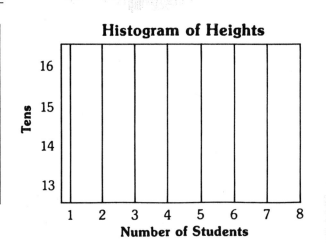

Mean ____   Median ____   Range ____

Tens	Ones	Number of Students
16		
15		
14		
13		

Histogram of Heights

(Tens vs Number of Students: 1–8)

How many students were in the 140

to 160 centimeter range? ____

Use the double-bar graph to solve these problems.

Monthly Rainfall

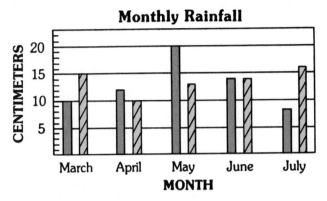

1. In which months is there more than average rainfall?

   _____

2. How much over the average did it rain in March?

   _____

3. Use the following data to draw a line graph.

Grade	Students
1	26
2	29
3	21
4	25
5	23
6	31

Lincoln Students

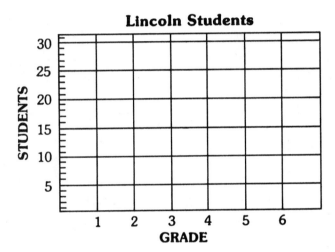

Use the circle graph to solve these problems.

Bill's Monthly Budget

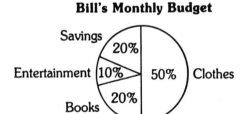

4. If Bill's monthly expenses are $350, how much is spent on entertainment?

   _____

Use the graph to solve these problems.

5. Name point C. _____

6. Locate $R(2, 4)$.

7. Graph points R, A and C.

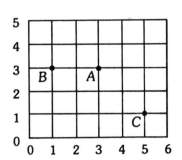

323

Circle the letter of the correct answer.

1 $5\frac{2}{3}$
$+ 6\frac{5}{8}$

a $11\frac{7}{24}$

b $11\frac{7}{11}$

c $12\frac{7}{24}$

d NG

2 $9\frac{1}{4}$
$- 4\frac{2}{3}$

a $3\frac{1}{2}$

b $4\frac{1}{2}$

c $4\frac{7}{2}$

d NG

3 $6\frac{1}{4} \times 3\frac{1}{5}$

a $\frac{1}{20}$

b $1\frac{25}{64}$

c 20

d NG

4 $4\frac{1}{2} \div 2\frac{1}{4}$

a $\frac{1}{2}$

b 2

c $2\frac{1}{4}$

d NG

5 $6.96 + 4.3$

a 7.39

b 11.2

c 11.26

d NG

6 $12.5 - 7.82$

a 4.68

b 5.38

c 5.68

d NG

7 5.6
$\times 0.004$

a 0.0224

b 0.224

c 2.24

d NG

8 $12 \div 0.04$

a 3

b 30

c 300

d NG

9 Find the area.

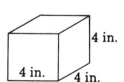

a 15 cm^2

b 18 cm^2

c 30 cm^2

d NG

10 Find the volume.

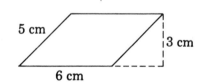

a 16 in.^{3}

b 24 in.^{3}

c 64 in.^{3}

d NG

11 $\frac{7}{20} = \underline{\quad?\quad}$

a 7%

b 35%

c 70%

d NG

 score

Understanding Integers

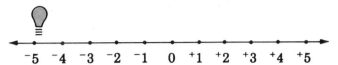

The electrical power was interrupted
5 seconds before radio station WXYZ
was to announce the winner of the
Fantasy Vacation contest. What number
describes the time the electricity went off?

Before is the opposite of **after,** just as a **negative
number** is the opposite of a **positive number.**
If we say that positive 5 (⁺5) is 5 seconds after the
announcement, and 0 is the exact time of the
announcement, then negative 5 (⁻5) is 5 seconds
before the station lost power.

We use _____ to describe the time the electricity
went out.

Positive numbers, negative numbers and zero make
up the set of **integers.** We can graph integers on a
number line. Positive integers are to the right of
zero. Negative integers are to the left of zero. Locate
the opposite of ⁻3 on the number line.

The opposite of ⁻3 is ____.

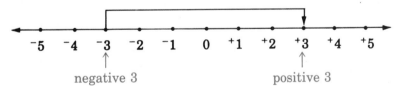

negative 3   positive 3

Getting Started

Write the opposite.

1. up _____   2. left _____   3. increase _____

4. win 5 _____   5. 4 above zero _____   6. find a dollar _____

7. ⁺5 ___   8. ⁻3 ___   9. ⁺15 ___   10. ⁺26 ___   11. 0 ___   12. ⁻16 ___

13. Locate each point on the number line.
    Write the corresponding letter.
    A. ⁺2   B. ⁻3   C. opposite of ⁻4

325

Practice

Write the opposite.

1. east _____   2. profit _____   3. right _____

4. saving $5 _____   5. losing 8 yards _____

6. plus 7 seconds _____   7. 5 meters right _____

8. left 15 miles _____   9. 10 kilometers south _____

10. 25 minutes before _____   11. climbing up 500 feet _____

12. 20 degrees below zero _____

13. $^+6$ _____   14. $^-17$ _____   15. $^+15$ _____   16. $^+19$ _____

17. $^-3$ _____   18. 0 _____   19. $^+8$ _____   20. $^+25$ _____

21. $^-1$ _____   22. $^-50$ _____   23. $^+75$ _____   24. $^-6$ _____

25. Locate each point on the number line. Write the corresponding letter.

A. $^+2$ B. $^-2$ C. 0   D. $^-6$
E. $^-3$ F. $^+7$ G. opposite of $^+3$ H. $^-7$
I. opposite of $^-9$

$$\overset{\longleftrightarrow}{\underset{^-10\ ^-9\ ^-8\ ^-7\ ^-6\ ^-5\ ^-4\ ^-3\ ^-2\ ^-1\ \ 0\ \ ^+1\ ^+2\ ^+3\ ^+4\ ^+5\ ^+6\ ^+7\ ^+8\ ^+9\ ^+10}{}}$$

Apply

Write an integer to describe these situations.

26. Burt got to the station 15 minutes before the train left.

_____

27. Angie earned $15.

_____

28. Tonya grew 6 centimeters in height.   _____

29. Dennis gained 17 yards on the third down.   _____

Solve these problems.

30. An elevator stopped at the 85th floor. Going 85 floors up, the elevator is $^+85$. What integer shows going down 85 floors?

31. The temperature dropped to 6 degrees below zero. Below zero is shown by a negative integer. What integer is used to show the temperature rising back to zero?

Adding Integers with Like Signs

Sherry withdrew $9 from her account on May 1. She withdrew some more money on May 6. How much has Sherry withdrawn from her account so far in May?

Account Holder	Account Number
Sherry Smith	555-00-555

Date ___May 6, 1988___

Amount withdrawn: _____ $6.00 _____

We need to know the total amount Sherry has withdrawn so far in May.

We know she withdrew _____ on May 1, and _____ on May 6.
We can represent the amounts Sherry withdrew with negative numbers. The $9 withdrawal is ⁻9.

The $6 withdrawal is _____.
To find the total, we add the integers on the number line. Start at zero. Move 9 units to the left. Then move 6 more units to the left.

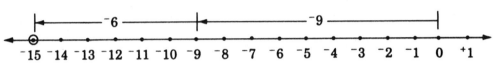

⁻9 + ⁻6 = _____

Sherry withdrew _____.
We can also add positive integers on the number line.

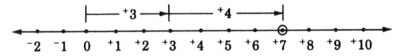

✔ The sum of two positive integers is a _____ integer.

✔ The sum of two negative integers is a _____ integer.

Getting Started

Show the addition on the number line. Complete the equation.

1.

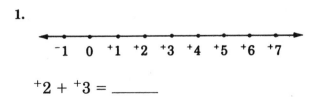

⁺2 + ⁺3 = _____

2.

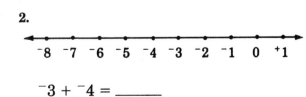

⁻3 + ⁻4 = _____

Add.

3. ⁺8 + ⁺9 = _____   4. ⁻6 + ⁻8 = _____   5. ⁻9 + ⁻3 = _____   6. ⁺8 + 0 = _____

Practice

Show the addition on the number line. Complete the equation.

1.

$^+2 + {}^+7 = $ _____

2.

$^-4 + {}^-3 = $ _____

3.

$^-4 + {}^-5 = $ _____

4.

$^+1 + {}^+7 = $ _____

Add.

5. $^-7 + {}^-8 = $ _____

6. $^+6 + {}^+4 = $ _____

7. $^+8 + {}^+5 = $ _____

8. $^-3 + {}^-4 = $ _____

9. $^+7 + {}^+3 = $ _____

10. $^+3 + {}^+8 = $ _____

11. $0 + {}^-5 = $ _____

12. $^-8 + {}^-4 = $ _____

13. $^+6 + 0 = $ _____

14. $^-4 + {}^-6 = $ _____

15. $^-2 + {}^-10 = $ _____

16. $^+14 + {}^+8 = $ _____

17. $^+3 + {}^+5 + {}^+4 = $ _____

18. $^-2 + {}^-5 + {}^-8 = $ _____

19. $^+8 + 0 + {}^+6 = $ _____

20. $^-6 + {}^-1 + {}^-3 = $ _____

Apply

Solve these problems. Write an equation to show the addition.

21. On the first play, Bill lost 9 yards. On the second play, he lost 7 more yards. How many yards did Bill lose?

22. The temperature dropped 12 degrees the first hour and 6 more degrees the second hour. How many degrees did the temperature drop?

EXCURSION

Use the integers
$^-2$, $^-4$, $^-6$, $^-8$, $^-10$, $^-12$, $^-14$, $^-16$ and $^-18$
to build a magic square
with the magic number $^-30$.

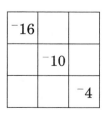

Adding Integers with Unlike Signs

Day	Point Change
Monday	⁻2
Tuesday	⁺5
Wednesday	⁻1
Thursday	⁻2
Friday	⁺3

Mr. Allmon kept track of the price of United Computer stock for several months. This record shows how the price changed during one week. By how many points had the stock price changed after the market closed on Tuesday?

We want to find one number that describes the point change after Monday's and Tuesday's trading. We know that on Monday the stock price went down

_____ points ($^-2$), and on Tuesday the price went up

_____ points ($^+5$).
To find the total point change, we add these two integers.

We add _____ and _____.
We start at zero on the number line. We move 2 units to the left and then 5 units to the right. $^-2 + {}^+5 =$ _____

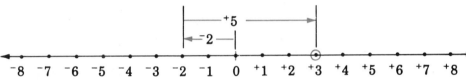

When the market closed on Tuesday, the stock had

changed _____ points.
We can add any positive and negative integers on the number line.

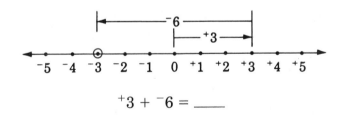

$$^+3 + {}^-6 = \underline{}$$

✔ To add a positive and a negative integer, find the difference between the two numbers and keep the sign of the larger number.

Getting Started

Show the addition on the number line. Complete the equation.

1.

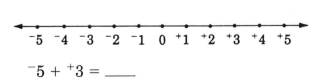

$$^-5 + {}^+3 = \underline{}$$

Add.

2. $^+2 + {}^-5 =$ _____ 3. $^-4 + {}^+3 =$ _____

4. $^-2 + {}^+7 =$ _____ 5. $^+6 + {}^-6 =$ _____

329

Practice

Show the addition on the number line. Complete the equations.

1.

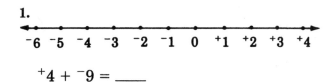

$$^-6 \quad ^-5 \quad ^-4 \quad ^-3 \quad ^-2 \quad ^-1 \quad 0 \quad ^+1 \quad ^+2 \quad ^+3 \quad ^+4$$

$$^+4 + ^-9 = \underline{\quad}$$

2.

$$^-9 \quad ^-8 \quad ^-7 \quad ^-6 \quad ^-5 \quad ^-4 \quad ^-3 \quad ^-2 \quad ^-1 \quad 0 \quad ^+1 \quad ^+2 \quad ^+3$$

$$^-9 + ^+3 = \underline{\quad}$$

Add.

3. $^+3 + ^-5 = \underline{\quad}$ **4.** $^-9 + ^+5 = \underline{\quad}$ **5.** $^-8 + ^+3 = \underline{\quad}$

6. $^+5 + ^-3 = \underline{\quad}$ **7.** $^-4 + ^+5 = \underline{\quad}$ **8.** $^+9 + ^-9 = \underline{\quad}$

9. $^-3 + ^+8 = \underline{\quad}$ **10.** $^-1 + ^+6 = \underline{\quad}$ **11.** $^-6 + 0 = \underline{\quad}$

12. $^-5 + ^+5 = \underline{\quad}$ **13.** $^+4 + ^-7 = \underline{\quad}$ **14.** $^-6 + ^+2 = \underline{\quad}$

15. $^+8 + ^-10 = \underline{\quad}$ **16.** $^-10 + ^+10 = \underline{\quad}$ **17.** $^+9 + ^-15 = \underline{\quad}$

18. $^-7 + 0 = \underline{\quad}$

Apply

Solve these problems.

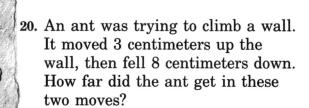

19. By Tuesday afternoon, the temperature had dropped 3 degrees. Wednesday, the sun came out, and the temperature rose 7 degrees. How much did the temperature change?

20. An ant was trying to climb a wall. It moved 3 centimeters up the wall, then fell 8 centimeters down. How far did the ant get in these two moves?

EXCURSION

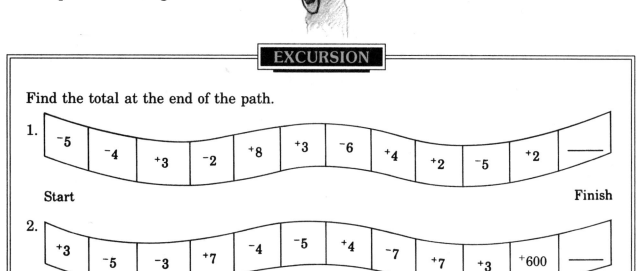

Find the total at the end of the path.

1.
Start $^-5$ $^-4$ $^+3$ $^-2$ $^+8$ $^+3$ $^-6$ $^+4$ $^+2$ $^-5$ $^+2$ $\underline{\quad}$ Finish

2.
$^+3$ $^-5$ $^-3$ $^+7$ $^-4$ $^-5$ $^+4$ $^-7$ $^+7$ $^+3$ $^+600$ $\underline{\quad}$

Subtracting Integers

The Weather Bureau predicts a cold snap in the next 24 hours. The temperature at 9 PM is ⁻4°. At 6 PM, it was ⁺8°. What is the change in the temperature since 6 PM?

We want to know how many degrees the temperature changed between 6 PM and 9 PM.

We know that the temperature at 9 PM is ____,

and it was ____ at 6 PM.

To find the change or difference in the temperature, we subtract the 9 PM temperature from the 6 PM temperature.

We subtract ____ from ____.

To subtract, think of the subtraction equation $^-4 - {}^+8 = n$, as the addition equation $n + {}^+8 = {}^-4$. The only number added to ⁺8 that would equal ⁻4 is ⁻12.

We can also find the missing addend on the number line.

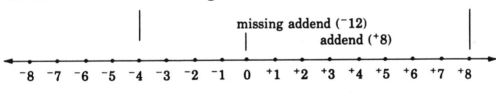

missing addend (⁻12)
addend (⁺8)

The temperature changed ____ degrees since 6 PM.

✔ To subtract an integer, rewrite the subtraction problem as an addition problem by adding the opposite of the subtrahend.

$$^-4 - \boxed{^+8} = {}^-12$$
$$^-4 + \boxed{^-8} = {}^-12$$

⁺8 and ⁻8 are opposites.

Getting Started

Write the missing addend.

1. ____ + ⁺6 = ⁻3

2. ⁻2 + ____ = ⁻6

3. ____ + ⁻7 = ⁺3

Subtract.

4. ⁺5 − ⁻6 = ____

5. ⁻7 − ⁺3 = ____

6. ⁻4 − ⁻2 = ____

331

Practice

Write the missing addend.

1. $^{+}5 +$ ____ $= {}^{-}3$

2. $^{-}4 +$ ____ $= {}^{-}5$

3. ____ $+ {}^{-}2 = {}^{-}6$

4. ____ $+ {}^{+}4 = {}^{+}2$

5. $^{+}7 +$ ____ $= {}^{+}9$

6. $^{-}3 +$ ____ $= {}^{-}5$

7. ____ $+ {}^{-}5 = 0$

8. $^{-}8 +$ ____ $= {}^{+}7$

9. ____ $+ {}^{-}1 = {}^{-}4$

Subtract.

10. $^{+}4 - {}^{-}3 =$ ____

11. $^{-}6 - {}^{+}4 =$ ____

12. $^{-}7 - {}^{-}3 =$ ____

13. $^{+}6 - {}^{+}5 =$ ____

14. $^{-}2 - {}^{-}8 =$ ____

15. $^{-}9 - {}^{+}5 =$ ____

16. $^{-}1 - {}^{-}6 =$ ____

17. $^{+}3 - {}^{-}9 =$ ____

18. $^{-}7 - 0 =$ ____

Compute.

19. $^{+}7 + {}^{-}4 + {}^{+}5 =$ ____

20. $^{-}6 - {}^{-}3 - {}^{-}1 =$ ____

21. $^{-}4 + {}^{-}6 - {}^{+}3 =$ ____

22. $^{-}9 - {}^{+}4 - {}^{-}3 =$ ____

23. $^{+}6 - {}^{+}3 + {}^{-}2 =$ ____

24. $^{+}3 - {}^{-}3 + {}^{-}2 =$ ____

Apply

Solve the problems. Write an equation to show the operation.

25. Sonia dove from the 10 meter board. She dove 6 meters under the water. How far did Sonia dive?

26. The average January temperature was $^{+}2°$. The average February temperature was $^{-}3°$. What was the difference between the two average temperatures?

EXCURSION

Find the number at the end of the path.

Start	add	subtract	add	subtract	add	subtract	add	Finish
$^{+}4$	$^{-}3$	$^{-}2$	$^{+}3$	$^{-}4$	$^{+}3$	$^{+}2$	$^{-}3$	____

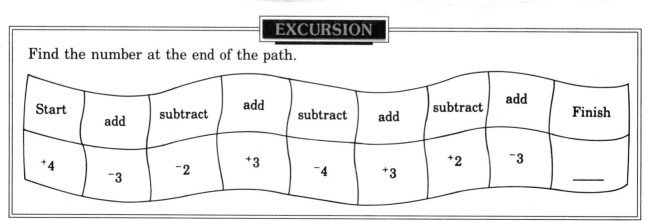

Multiplying Integers

Alex and Sidra are making a poster for math class. They want to show how to multiply with integers. What integers are Alex and Sidra missing as products on their poster?

You can show how to find the products for the first three examples on the number line. Remember, multiplication is repeated addition.

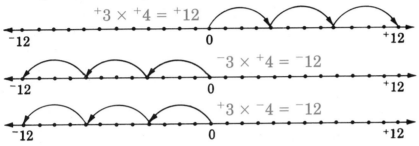

$^+3 \times {}^+4 = {}^+12$

$^-3 \times {}^+4 = {}^-12$

$^+3 \times {}^-4 = {}^-12$

✔ Just as two negatives in a sentence mean positive, so a negative times a negative equals a positive.

$^-3 \times {}^-4 = {}^+12$

For the poster, the complete equations are:

$^+3 \times {}^+4 = $ _____ $^+3 \times {}^-4 = $ _____

$^-3 \times {}^+4 = $ _____ $^-3 \times {}^-4 = $ _____

✔ The product of two positive integers is a _____ integer.

✔ The product of two negative integers is a _____ integer.

✔ The product of a positive and a negative integer

is a _____ integer.

Getting Started

Multiply.

1. $^+5 \times {}^-3 = $ _____   2. $^-2 \times {}^-5 = $ _____   3. $^+6 \times {}^+6 = $ _____

4. $^-8 \times {}^+2 = $ _____   5. $^-7 \times {}^-7 = $ _____   6. $^+7 \times {}^+7 = $ _____

Complete each pattern.

7. $^+7 \times {}^+2 = $ _____ $^+7 \times {}^+1 = $ _____ $^+7 \times 0 = $ _____ $^+7 \times {}^-1 = $ _____

333

Practice

Multiply.

1. $^-3 \times {}^+4 =$ _____

2. $^-7 \times {}^-8 =$ _____

3. $^+4 \times {}^-6 =$ _____

4. $^+7 \times {}^+6 =$ _____

5. $^-2 \times 0 =$ _____

6. $^-9 \times {}^+3 =$ _____

7. $^-1 \times {}^-1 =$ _____

8. $^+4 \times {}^-5 =$ _____

9. $^-4 \times {}^-6 =$ _____

10. $^+8 \times {}^-2 =$ _____

11. $^+7 \times {}^+4 =$ _____

12. $^-9 \times {}^-9 =$ _____

Complete each pattern.

13. $^+4 \times {}^+3 = {}^+12$
$^+4 \times {}^+2 = {}^+8$

$^+4 \times {}^+1 =$ _____

$^+4 \times 0 =$ _____

$^+4 \times {}^-1 =$ _____

14. $^+3 \times {}^+2 = {}^+6$
$^+2 \times {}^+2 = {}^+4$

$^+1 \times {}^+2 =$ _____

$0 \times {}^+2 =$ _____

$^-1 \times {}^+2 =$ _____

15. $^-5 \times {}^+3 = {}^-15$
$^-5 \times {}^+2 = {}^-10$

$^-5 \times {}^+1 =$ _____

$^-5 \times 0 =$ _____

$^-5 \times {}^-1 =$ _____

16. $^-3 \times {}^+3 =$ _____

$^-3 \times {}^+2 =$ _____

$^-3 \times {}^+1 =$ _____

$^-3 \times 0 =$ _____

$^-3 \times {}^-1 =$ _____

17. $^+5 \times {}^+2 =$ _____

$^+5 \times {}^+1 =$ _____

$^+5 \times 0 =$ _____

$^+5 \times {}^-1 =$ _____

$^+5 \times {}^-2 =$ _____

18. $^-3 \times {}^-6 =$ _____

$^-2 \times {}^-6 =$ _____

$^-1 \times {}^-6 =$ _____

$0 \times {}^-6 =$ _____

$^+1 \times {}^-6 =$ _____

EXCURSION

Write the missing factors.

1. $^+3 \times n = {}^+18$

$n =$ _____

2. $^+2 \times n = {}^-8$

$n =$ _____

3. $n \times {}^-5 = {}^-10$

$n =$ _____

4. $n \times {}^+6 = {}^-30$

$n =$ _____

5. $^-4 \times n = {}^+16$

$n =$ _____

6. $^-7 \times n = {}^-49$

$n =$ _____

Find the quotients.

7. $^-54 \div {}^-9 =$ _____

8. $^+24 \div {}^-6 =$ _____

9. $^+40 \div {}^+5 =$ _____

10. $^-36 \div {}^+6 =$ _____

11. $^-56 \div {}^-8 =$ _____

12. $0 \div {}^-6 =$ _____

Graphing Ordered Pairs of Integers

We use ordered pairs of integers to locate points on a number grid. Point A is located by the **coordinates** of the ordered pair ($^+3$, $^-2$). The graph of point A is 3 units to the right and 2 units below the origin. Where is the graph of B located?

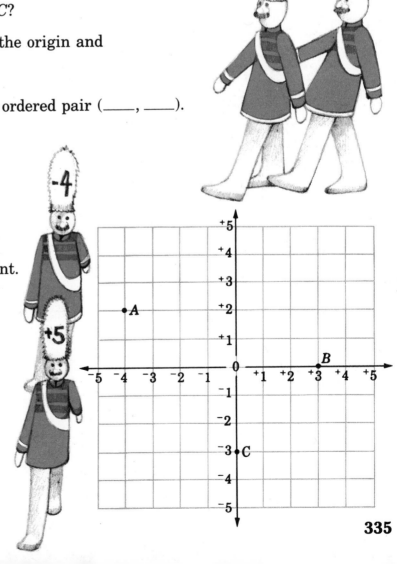

Point B is _____ units to the left of

the origin and _____ units above the line. The graph of point B is located

by the ordered pair (_____, _____). We say: the **coordinates** of B are the ordered pair ($^-3$, $^+4$)

$$(^-3, {}^+4)$$

first coordinate ↑   ↑ second coordinate

What are the coordinates of C?

C is _____ units to the left of the origin and

_____ units below the origin.

The coordinates of C are the ordered pair (_____, _____).

Getting Started

Write the coordinates of each point.

1. A(_____, _____)

2. B(_____, _____)

3. C(_____, _____)

Graph each point.

4. P($^-3$, 0)

5. Q($^+2$, $^-5$)

6. R($^-2$, $^-3$)

335

Practice

Write the coordinates of each point.

1. A(____, ____)   2. B(____, ____)

3. C(____, ____)   4. D(____, ____)

5. E(____, ____)   6. F(____, ____)

7. G(____, ____)   8. H(____, ____)

9. I(____, ____)

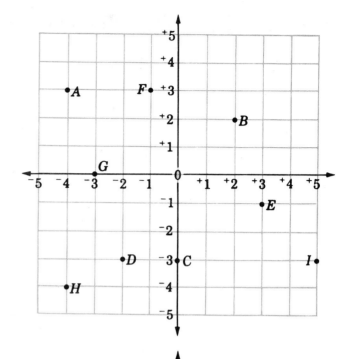

Graph each point.

10. R($^+$3, $^+$4)   11. S($^-$3, $^-$4)

12. T($^+$3, $^-$4)   13. U($^-$3, $^+$4)

14. V($^-$4, $^-$3)   15. W($^-$2, $^+$2)

16. X($^+$3, $^-$2)   17. Y($^-$5, $^-$5)

18. Z($^-$4, 0)

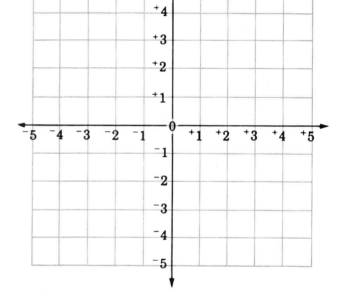

Apply

For each problem, make a grid, graph the points and connect them in order with line segments. Name the figure.

19. A($^-$3, $^+$3), B($^+$2, $^+$2), C($^+$2, $^-$2),
    D($^-$3, $^-$3), A($^-$3, $^+$3)

20. L($^-$3, 0), M($^+$4, $^+$3), N($^+$4, $^-$3),
    L($^-$3, 0)

21. P($^+$4, $^+$5), Q($^+$4, $^+$1), R($^-$4, $^-$5),
    S($^-$4, $^+$7), P($^+$4, $^+$5)

22. W($^-$2, $^-$1), X($^+$2, $^-$1), Y($^+$2, $^-$4),
    Z($^-$2, $^-$4), W($^-$2, $^-$1)

Using the Coordinate Plane

Two perpendicular number lines that intersect at the origin form the **coordinate plane.** The horizontal number line is called the **x-axis.** The vertical number line is called the **y-axis.** The x-coordinate of A is $^-2$, and the y-coordinate is $^-1$. Graph this table on the coordinate plane.

	B	C	D
x	$^-1$	$^+2$	$^+4$
y	0	$^+3$	$^+5$

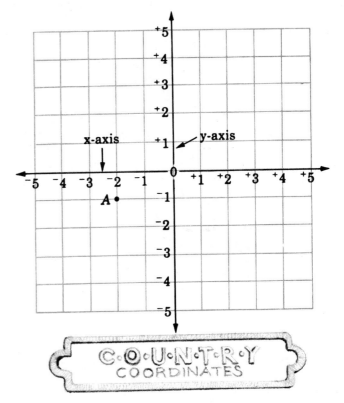

We graph the coordinates

$B(^-1, 0)$, $C(^+2, {}^+3)$, $D(^+4, {}^+5)$.

Draw a line connecting the coordinates. Complete this table by adding $^+2$ to the x-coordinate to identify the y-coordinate.

	E	F	G
x	$^-3$	0	$^+3$
y	$^-1$		

Since $0 + {}^+2 = {}^+2$, the coordinates of the second point are (0, ____). The coordinates of the third point are ($^+3$, ____).

Getting Started

Complete the table and graph the ordered pairs on the coordinate plane. Draw lines connecting each set of coordinates.

1.

Multiply by $^+2$		
x	$^-2$	0	$^+2$
y	$^-4$		

2.

Subtract $^+1$		
x	$^-2$	$^+1$	$^+3$
y	$^-3$		

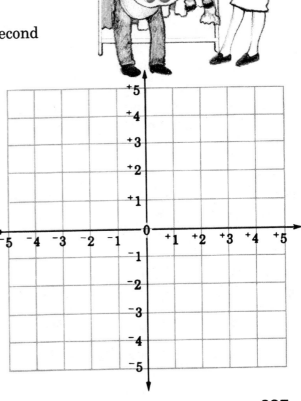

337

Practice

Complete the table and graph and connect the ordered pairs on the coordinate plane.

1.

Add ⁻2			
x	⁻3	0	⁺3
y			

2.

Subtract ⁺3			
x	⁻2	0	⁺2
y			

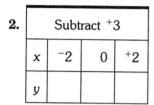

Complete the table and graph and connect the ordered pairs on the coordinate plane.

3.

Multiply by ⁺3			
x	⁻2	0	⁺2
y			

4.

Multiply by ⁻2			
x	⁻2	0	⁺2
y			

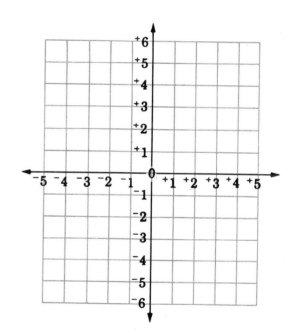

Complete the table and graph and connect the ordered pairs on the coordinate plane.

5.

Add ⁻3			
x	⁻1	0	⁺2
y			

6.

Subtract ⁻3			
x	⁻5	0	⁻1
y			

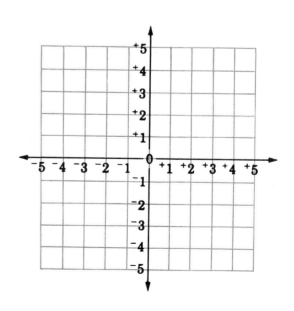

Review

The four-step plan can help us to be better problem solvers.

WALDEN SCHOOL
PROBLEM SOLVERS
CLUB

Dues: 5 solved problems

★ **SEE**

We state what the problem actually is.
We state all the facts we know that will help us to solve that problem.

★ **PLAN**

We think about the important facts and choose a plan or plans to help solve the problem.
Among the plans that will help us to solve a problem are:
Drawing a picture or diagram
Making a model with manipulatives or on paper
Acting the problem out
Making a systematic listing or a table
Making a tally or graph
Looking for a pattern
Determining missing data
Collecting needed data
Selecting appropriate notation
Writing an open sentence
Using a formula
Guessing and checking
Working backwards
Solving a simpler but related problem
Identifying a subgoal
Restating the problem in our own words
Making a flow chart

★ **DO**

We carry out the plan and reach a solution to the problem.

★ **CHECK**

We check the problem for careless errors.
We see if the solution is reasonable.
We look for another way to solve the problem.

Apply

Use the four-step plan to help solve these problems.

1. A bottle of ink spills on your homework paper and the blotch doubles in size every three seconds. How much of the paper will be covered three seconds before it gets completely covered with ink?

2. You are cutting two logs into pieces for your fireplace. One log can be cut into five pieces, and the other into six pieces. If it takes 60 seconds to cut the first log, how long will it take to cut the other log?

3. Tom and Inga are taking turns throwing bean bags at two targets, one marked 7 points and the other marked 3 points. List all the scores, less than 11, that it would be impossible to get in one turn.

4. How many different segments can be formed using the eight points below as endpoints?

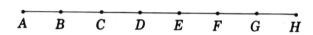

$A \quad B \quad C \quad D \quad E \quad F \quad G \quad H$

5. Mr. Pennypincher gave half of his fortune to his brother, $18,000 to his sister, half of what was left to the university, and the remaining $2,000 to the zoo. How much money did Mr. Pennypincher start with?

6. A rectangular sheet of paper can be rolled to create a cylinder. What shape of paper could be rolled to form a slanted cylinder? Hint: First make a cylinder, then dip both ends into water at an angle. Open up the paper and cut along the water line.

7. Does $^+7 + {}^-9$ equal $^-9 + {}^+7$? Support your answer.

8. The sum of two integers is negative. What do you know about the two integers?

9. There are two different numbers that make the following sentence true even though both n's represent the same number in the sentence. What are the two numbers?

$$n \times n = {}^+25$$

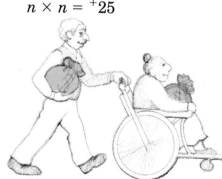

Add.

1. $^+3 + {}^+9 = $ ____

2. $^-6 + {}^-5 = $ ____

3. $^-3 + {}^-4 = $ ____

4. $^+7 + {}^+2 = $ ____

5. $^+5 + 0 = $ ____

6. $^-7 + {}^-3 = $ ____

7. $0 + {}^-3 = $ ____

8. $^-2 + {}^-3 = $ ____

9. $^-3 + {}^+5 = $ ____

10. $^+7 + {}^-8 = $ ____

11. $^+6 + {}^-3 = $ ____

12. $^-8 + {}^-9 = $ ____

13. $^-4 + {}^+3 = $ ____

14. $^-6 + {}^+5 = $ ____

15. $^-9 + {}^+3 = $ ____

16. $^+4 + {}^-8 = $ ____

Subtract.

17. $^+9 - {}^+8 = $ ____

18. $^-7 - {}^-3 = $ ____

19. $^-6 - {}^+4 = $ ____

20. $^-6 - {}^-8 = $ ____

21. $^+4 - {}^+6 = $ ____

22. $^-5 - {}^+7 = $ ____

23. $0 - {}^-3 = $ ____

24. $^+5 - {}^-3 = $ ____

25. $^-8 - {}^+2 = $ ____

26. $^-3 - {}^-8 = $ ____

27. $^+2 - {}^-4 = $ ____

28. $^+8 - {}^-7 = $ ____

Multiply.

29. $^-3 \times {}^+8 = $ ____

30. $^-7 \times {}^-7 = $ ____

31. $^+5 \times {}^-4 = $ ____

32. $^-1 \times {}^-9 = $ ____

33. $^+4 \times {}^+6 = $ ____

34. $^-2 \times {}^+3 = $ ____

35. $^-8 \times {}^-9 = $ ____

36. $^+5 \times {}^+6 = $ ____

Give the coordinates of each point.

37. $A(\underline{\quad}, \underline{\quad})$

38. $B(\underline{\quad}, \underline{\quad})$

39. $C(\underline{\quad}, \underline{\quad})$

40. $D(\underline{\quad}, \underline{\quad})$

41. $E(\underline{\quad}, \underline{\quad})$

42. $F(\underline{\quad}, \underline{\quad})$

Graph and label each point.

43. $X(^+3, {}^-4)$

44. $Y(^-4, 0)$

45. $Z(^+3, {}^-5)$

46. $L(^+2, 0)$

47. $M(^-5, {}^-4)$

48. $N(^-3, {}^+2)$

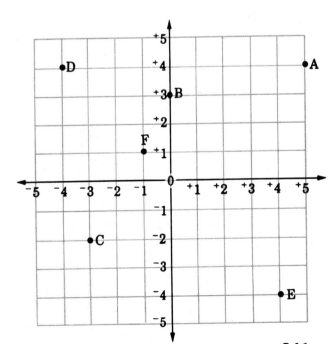

CUMULATIVE REVIEW

Circle the letter of the correct answer.

1 $4\frac{7}{8}$
$+ 3\frac{1}{3}$

a $7\frac{5}{24}$

b $7\frac{8}{11}$

c $8\frac{5}{24}$

d NG

2 $8\frac{2}{3} - 1\frac{4}{5}$

a $6\frac{13}{15}$

b $7\frac{2}{15}$

c $7\frac{13}{15}$

d NG

3 $3\frac{1}{5}$
$\times 2\frac{1}{2}$

a $\frac{1}{8}$

b $6\frac{1}{10}$

c 8

d NG

4 $4\frac{1}{2} \div 3\frac{3}{4}$

a $\frac{5}{6}$

b $1\frac{1}{5}$

c $16\frac{3}{4}$

d NG

5 $12.2 + 4.83$

a 16.03

b 17.03

c 60.5

d NG

6 $12 - 3.08$

a 8.92

b 9.02

c 9.08

d NG

7 0.09×0.06

a 0.54

b 0.054

c 0.0054

d NG

8 $6.08 \div 0.4$

a 1.52

b 15.2

c 152

d NG

9 Find the area.

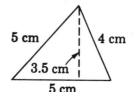

a 8.75 cm²

b 12.5 cm²

c 10 cm²

d NG

10 35% of 180

a 63

b 630

c 6,300

d NG

11 Both spinners are spun at the same time. What is $P(b$, odd number)?

a $\frac{2}{12}$

b $\frac{1}{12}$

c $\frac{3}{12}$

d NG

 score

342

ALTERNATE CHAPTER TEST

Add.

1. $7 + 9 =$ ____

2. $8 + 5 =$ ____

3. $4 + 6 =$ ____

4. $9 + 3 =$ ____

5. $\begin{array}{r} 8 \\ + 7 \\ \hline \end{array}$

6. $\begin{array}{r} 6 \\ + 6 \\ \hline \end{array}$

7. $\begin{array}{r} 5 \\ + 0 \\ \hline \end{array}$

8. $\begin{array}{r} 7 \\ + 4 \\ \hline \end{array}$

9. $\begin{array}{r} 2 \\ + 8 \\ \hline \end{array}$

10. $\begin{array}{r} 1 \\ + 9 \\ \hline \end{array}$

Add or subtract.

11. $17 - 9 =$ ____

12. ____ $+ 8 = 14$

13. $7 +$ ____ $= 12$

14. $11 - 8 =$ ____

15. $9 +$ ____ $= 14$

16. $15 - 7 =$ ____

17. ____ $+ 3 = 11$

18. $8 -$ ____ $= 0$

Subtract.

19. $\begin{array}{r} 9 \\ - 0 \\ \hline \end{array}$

20. $\begin{array}{r} 15 \\ - 9 \\ \hline \end{array}$

21. $\begin{array}{r} 8 \\ - 1 \\ \hline \end{array}$

22. $\begin{array}{r} 14 \\ - 5 \\ \hline \end{array}$

23. $\begin{array}{r} 16 \\ - 8 \\ \hline \end{array}$

24. $\begin{array}{r} 13 \\ - 6 \\ \hline \end{array}$

Multiply.

25. $2 \times 0 =$ ____

26. $9 \times 6 =$ ____

27. $8 \times 8 =$ ____

28. $5 \times 7 =$ ____

29. $\begin{array}{r} 6 \\ \times 1 \\ \hline \end{array}$

30. $\begin{array}{r} 3 \\ \times 4 \\ \hline \end{array}$

31. $\begin{array}{r} 9 \\ \times 5 \\ \hline \end{array}$

32. $\begin{array}{r} 7 \\ \times 6 \\ \hline \end{array}$

33. $\begin{array}{r} 8 \\ \times 7 \\ \hline \end{array}$

34. $\begin{array}{r} 7 \\ \times 9 \\ \hline \end{array}$

Divide.

35. $27 \div 3 =$ ____

36. $48 \div 6 =$ ____

37. $81 \div 9 =$ ____

38. $42 \div 7 =$ ____

39. $8\overline{)32}$

40. $4\overline{)20}$

41. $7\overline{)63}$

42. $9\overline{)27}$

43. $8\overline{)40}$

44. $6\overline{)54}$

Solve for n.

45. $5 + 4 \times 8 = n$

46. $35 \div 5 + 2 = n$

47. $6 + 2 \times 4 = n$

48. $30 \div 6 + 8 = n$

Write as standard numbers.

49. $5^3 =$ ____

50. $7 \times 10^2 =$ ____

51. $2^3 =$ ____

52. $4 \times 10^3 =$ ____

Write the place value for each red digit.

1. 7,439   2. 856,427   3. 381,562   4. 59,783

_____   _____   _____   _____

Write < or > between the numbers.

5. 678 ◯ 786   6. 3,871 ◯ 3,781   7. 5,436 ◯ 5,426   8. 29,541 ◯ 29,542

Round to the nearest thousand and again to the nearest ten thousand.

9. 15,100   10. 87,500   11. 256,603   12. 724,499

_____   _____   _____   _____

_____   _____   _____   _____

Write the place value for each red digit.

13. 133,209,645   14. 6,874,396   15. 352,175,439   16. 2,468,972,311

_____   _____   _____   _____

Add.

17. 8,549
  + 28,187

18. $249.75
  +   61.08

19. 315,755
  + 972,649

20. 229,463
     758,103
  + 653,974

Subtract.

21. 30,754
  − 8,979

22. 28,002
  − 9,467

23. 856,273
  − 394,198

24. $7,607.52
  − 3,296.94

Estimate by rounding to the nearest thousand.

25. 8,463
  + 9,742

26. 39,000
  − 21,433

27. 78,436
  + 25,841

28. 6,012
  − 2,476

29. 37,242
  + 18,387

30. 31,938
  − 26,099

Multiply. Use estimation to check the answers.

1. 76
    × 8

2. 49
    × 5

3. 123
    × 7

4. 908
    × 3

5. 69
    × 9

6. 54
    × 6

7. 286
    × 5

8. 405
    × 4

9. 5,162
    × 4

10. $39.87
    × 6

11. $805.46
    × 9

12. 289.597
    × 8

13. 7,492
    × 2

14. $63.59
    × 3

15. $602.75
    × 7

16. 125,624
    × 2

17. 84
    × 35

18. $6.07
    × 92

19. 415
    × 73

20. 7,936
    × 86

21. 75
    × 91

22. $6.43
    × 95

23. 388
    × 45

24. 2,976
    × 58

25. 929
    × 452

26. 5,138
    × 865

27. 37,294
    × 517

28. $860.26
    × 349

29. 893
    × 415

30. 6,347
    × 624

31. 52,468
    × 796

32. $508.38
    × 934

Divide and check.

1. $4\overline{)374}$ 2. $6\overline{)468}$ 3. $3\overline{)763}$ 4. $5\overline{)\$9.15}$

5. $8\overline{)4,539}$ 6. $2\overline{)8,379}$ 7. $7\overline{)\$91.42}$ 8. $9\overline{)27,530}$

9. $65\overline{)342}$ 10. $29\overline{)261}$ 11. $91\overline{)739}$ 12. $57\overline{)435}$

13. $36\overline{)779}$ 14. $74\overline{)292}$ 15. $82\overline{)386}$ 16. $59\overline{)496}$

17. $21\overline{)2,121}$ 18. $49\overline{)\$7,644.49}$ 19. $65\overline{)24,982}$

20. $593\overline{)4,962}$ 21. $472\overline{)293,885}$ 22. $914\overline{)\$33,589.50}$

23. $37\overline{)4,772}$ 24. $72\overline{)15,148}$ 25. $83\overline{)211,348}$

Write the LCM and GCF for each set of numbers.

1. 8, 10

LCM ___

GCF ___

2. 6, 24

LCM ___

GCF ___

3. 3, 11

LCM ___

GCF ___

4. 6, 10

LCM ___

GCF ___

Prime factor each number using exponents.

5. 24 _____

6. 45 _____

7. 75 _____

8. 90 _____

9. 35 _____

10. 32 _____

11. 48 _____

12. 36 _____

Find the equivalent fraction.

13. $\frac{6}{8} = \frac{}{24}$

14. $\frac{4}{} = \frac{36}{63}$

15. $\frac{}{8} = \frac{16}{32}$

16. $\frac{21}{28} = \frac{}{4}$

17. $\frac{15}{25} = \frac{}{5}$

18. $\frac{2}{7} = \frac{}{42}$

19. $\frac{3}{11} = \frac{12}{}$

20. $\frac{}{6} = \frac{30}{36}$

Rename in simplest form.

21. $\frac{14}{63} =$

22. $\frac{28}{32} =$

23. $\frac{24}{42} =$

24. $\frac{18}{36} =$

25. $\frac{14}{35} =$

26. $\frac{12}{42} =$

27. $\frac{27}{45} =$

28. $\frac{24}{56} =$

Write <, = or > in the circle.

29. $\frac{7}{8} \bigcirc \frac{4}{5}$

30. $\frac{6}{15} \bigcirc \frac{4}{10}$

31. $\frac{12}{16} \bigcirc \frac{7}{9}$

32. $\frac{3}{5} \bigcirc \frac{2}{3}$

33. $\frac{6}{18} \bigcirc \frac{2}{3}$

34. $\frac{3}{7} \bigcirc \frac{4}{9}$

35. $\frac{2}{9} \bigcirc \frac{1}{2}$

36. $\frac{3}{4} \bigcirc \frac{3}{7}$

Rename each mixed number as a fraction.

37. $7\frac{2}{3} =$

38. $6\frac{8}{9} =$

39. $2\frac{3}{10} =$

40. $6\frac{5}{8} =$

41. $9\frac{3}{4} =$

42. $8\frac{2}{7} =$

43. $5\frac{3}{5} =$

44. $4\frac{3}{11} =$

Rename each improper fraction as a whole or mixed number.

45. $\frac{16}{7} =$ _____

46. $\frac{37}{8} =$ _____

47. $\frac{16}{2} =$ _____

48. $\frac{42}{5} =$ _____

49. $\frac{56}{7} =$ _____

50. $\frac{16}{12} =$ _____

51. $\frac{70}{10} =$ _____

52. $\frac{49}{3} =$ _____

Add. Simplify answers if necessary.

1. $\frac{2}{9} + \frac{1}{9} =$ ____

2. $\frac{7}{12} + \frac{11}{12} =$ ____

3. $\quad 8\frac{5}{16}$
$\quad + 7\frac{7}{16}$

4. $\quad 3\frac{13}{24}$
$\quad + 9\frac{8}{24}$

5. $\frac{2}{3} + \frac{3}{5} =$ ____

6. $\frac{2}{7} + \frac{14}{21} =$ ____

7. $\quad 5\frac{5}{12}$
$\quad + 13\frac{3}{8}$

8. $\quad 6\frac{1}{2}$
$\quad + 6\frac{3}{10}$

9. $\quad 11\frac{3}{4}$
$\quad + 14\frac{7}{12}$

10. $\quad 10\frac{5}{9}$
$\quad + 3\frac{8}{18}$

11. $\quad 18\frac{2}{8}$
$\quad + 17\frac{5}{6}$

12. $\quad 12\frac{5}{6}$
$\quad 17\frac{1}{4}$
$\quad + 14\frac{7}{9}$

Subtract. Simplify answers if necessary.

13. $\frac{9}{10} - \frac{4}{10} =$ ____

14. $\frac{5}{14} - \frac{3}{14} =$ ____

15. $\quad 10\frac{11}{15}$
$\quad - 6\frac{8}{15}$

16. $\quad 14\frac{5}{6}$
$\quad - 8\frac{1}{6}$

17. $\frac{3}{4} - \frac{3}{5} =$ ____

18. $\frac{9}{10} - \frac{5}{6} =$ ____

19. $\quad 22\frac{2}{3}$
$\quad - 19$

20. $\quad 16\frac{1}{9}$
$\quad - 14\frac{2}{3}$

21. $\quad 17$
$\quad - 8\frac{7}{10}$

22. $\quad 13\frac{1}{4}$
$\quad - 7\frac{5}{6}$

23. $\quad 14\frac{1}{3}$
$\quad - 6\frac{5}{7}$

24. $\quad 11\frac{3}{8}$
$\quad - 8\frac{4}{5}$

25. $\quad 16\frac{2}{7}$
$\quad - 8\frac{2}{3}$

26. $\quad 14\frac{5}{11}$
$\quad - 6\frac{3}{4}$

27. $\quad 27\frac{1}{4}$
$\quad - 16\frac{3}{5}$

28. $\quad 24\frac{1}{2}$
$\quad - 19\frac{4}{7}$

Multiply. Factor wherever possible.

1. $\dfrac{5}{6} \times \dfrac{3}{2} =$

2. $\dfrac{9}{10} \times \dfrac{7}{9} =$

3. $\dfrac{2}{3} \times \dfrac{3}{4} =$

4. $\dfrac{3}{8} \times \dfrac{4}{7} =$

5. $18 \times \dfrac{5}{9} =$

6. $\dfrac{5}{6} \times 9 =$

7. $64 \times \dfrac{7}{8} =$

8. $\dfrac{4}{5} \times 30 =$

9. $4\dfrac{1}{6} \times 12 =$

10. $3\dfrac{1}{8} \times 1\dfrac{3}{10} =$

11. $2\dfrac{1}{4} \times 9\dfrac{1}{3} =$

12. $2\dfrac{5}{8} \times 1\dfrac{3}{7} =$

13. $4\dfrac{2}{3} \times 6\dfrac{1}{2} =$

14. $7\dfrac{1}{5} \times 3\dfrac{2}{9} =$

Write the reciprocal.

15. $\dfrac{7}{9}$

16. $9\dfrac{3}{4}$

17. 15

18. $\dfrac{16}{3}$

19. $4\dfrac{1}{8}$

20. $5\dfrac{3}{11}$

Divide.

21. $\dfrac{5}{8} \div \dfrac{1}{2} =$

22. $\dfrac{9}{10} \div \dfrac{3}{5} =$

23. $\dfrac{4}{9} \div \dfrac{5}{9} =$

24. $\dfrac{1}{8} \div \dfrac{2}{3} =$

25. $8 \div \dfrac{4}{5} =$

26. $\dfrac{6}{11} \div 9 =$

27. $12 \div \dfrac{3}{7} =$

28. $\dfrac{2}{9} \div 16 =$

29. $6\dfrac{1}{4} \div 1\dfrac{2}{5} =$

30. $3\dfrac{2}{3} \div 2\dfrac{1}{6} =$

31. $4\dfrac{2}{7} \div 1\dfrac{6}{14} =$

32. $5\dfrac{5}{8} \div 2\dfrac{1}{4} =$

33. $7\dfrac{2}{3} \div 4\dfrac{1}{8} =$

34. $9\dfrac{5}{6} \div 3\dfrac{2}{3} =$

Write in the place value of the 5 in each number.

1. 83.19475

2. 79.54072

3. 7.46875

_____

_____

_____

4. 5.92

5. 153.48

6. 17.596

_____

_____

_____

Write <, = or > between the decimal numbers.

7. 5.478 ◯ 5.487

8. 9.36 ◯ 9.360

9. 6.1 ◯ 6.01

10. 3.411 ◯ 3.141

11. 8.7 ◯ 8.8493

12. 49.743 ◯ 49.599

Round to the nearest hundredth.

13. 9.4397 _____

14. 2.7839 _____

15. 16.1756 _____

Round to the nearest thousandth.

16. 10.5884 _____

17. 3.71263 _____

18. 18.46759 _____

19. 152.14109 _____

20. 3.84921 _____

21. 4.6689 _____

Estimate each sum and difference by first rounding the numbers to the nearest whole number.

22. $\begin{array}{r} 65.67 \\ + 49.47 \\ \hline \end{array}$

23. $\begin{array}{r} 13.45 \\ - 8.459 \\ \hline \end{array}$

24. $\begin{array}{r} 16.491 \\ - 10.983 \\ \hline \end{array}$

25. $\begin{array}{r} 17.4 \\ - 8.59 \\ \hline \end{array}$

Add.

26. $\begin{array}{r} 26.87 \\ + 49.09 \\ \hline \end{array}$

27. $\begin{array}{r} 18.472 \\ + 36.75 \\ \hline \end{array}$

28. $\begin{array}{r} 53.168 \\ + 13.9417 \\ \hline \end{array}$

29. $\begin{array}{r} 82.0495 \\ + 96.3865 \\ \hline \end{array}$

Subtract.

30. $\begin{array}{r} 71.93 \\ - 58.77 \\ \hline \end{array}$

31. $\begin{array}{r} 64.258 \\ - 17.96 \\ \hline \end{array}$

32. $\begin{array}{r} 43.516 \\ - 9.8724 \\ \hline \end{array}$

33. $\begin{array}{r} 95.3547 \\ - 20.4966 \\ \hline \end{array}$

Multiply.

1.	$\begin{array}{r} 7.2 \\ \times\ \ 9 \\ \hline \end{array}$	**2.**	$\begin{array}{r} 5.63 \\ \times\ \ 8 \\ \hline \end{array}$	**3.**	$\begin{array}{r} 49 \\ \times 1.7 \\ \hline \end{array}$	**4.**	$\begin{array}{r} 8.02 \\ \times\ \ 36 \\ \hline \end{array}$

5.	$\begin{array}{r} 6.47 \\ \times\ 0.5 \\ \hline \end{array}$	**6.**	$\begin{array}{r} 3.8 \\ \times 0.29 \\ \hline \end{array}$	**7.**	$\begin{array}{r} 2.516 \\ \times\ \ 4.8 \\ \hline \end{array}$	**8.**	$\begin{array}{r} 7.35 \\ \times\ 9.7 \\ \hline \end{array}$

9.	$\begin{array}{r} 0.006 \\ \times\ \ \ 18 \\ \hline \end{array}$	**10.**	$\begin{array}{r} 0.09 \\ \times 0.05 \\ \hline \end{array}$	**11.**	$\begin{array}{r} 0.007 \\ \times\ \ 0.8 \\ \hline \end{array}$	**12.**	$\begin{array}{r} 4.02 \\ \times 0.006 \\ \hline \end{array}$

Divide.

13. $5\overline{)23.5}$　　**14.** $2\overline{)1.38}$　　**15.** $9\overline{)3.465}$　　**16.** $6\overline{)51.6}$

17. $0.04\overline{)2.858}$　　**18.** $0.7\overline{)0.042}$　　**19.** $1.2\overline{)7.68}$　　**20.** $5.4\overline{)4.968}$

21. $9.5\overline{)57}$　　**22.** $0.6\overline{)0.3}$　　**23.** $0.047\overline{)9.4}$　　**24.** $8.8\overline{)704}$

Write each fraction as a decimal to the nearest thousandth.

25. $\frac{8}{9} \approx$ _____　　**26.** $\frac{5}{6} \approx$ _____　　**27.** $\frac{3}{11} \approx$ _____　　**28.** $\frac{4}{7} \approx$ _____

Add or subtract.

1.   7 hr 36 min
    + 2 hr 15 min

2.   43 min 38 sec
    + 19 min 27 sec

3.   8 hr 17 min
    − 3 hr 58 min

4.   10 ft 8 in.
    − 5 ft 9 in.

5.   7 yd 10 in.
    + 3 yd 27 in.

6.   9 ft 11 in.
    + 2 ft 9 in.

7.   16 min 52 sec
    − 8 min 59 sec

8.   5 hr 4 min
    − 2 hr 20 min

9.   11 yd 15 in.
    + 3 yd 24 in.

Find the perimeter or circumference.

10.
6 in. /\ 6 in.
    4 in.

11.
9 ft × 4 ft rectangle

12.
circle 8 yd

Add or subtract.

13.   7 gal 6 qt
    + 8 gal 4 qt

14.   14 pt 9 oz
    + 18 pt 3 oz

15.   11 lb 6 oz
    − 3 lb 10 oz

16.   14 lb 8 oz
    + 2 lb 15 oz

17.   3 gal 1 qt
    − 1 gal 2 qt

18.   13 pt 2 oz
    − 4 pt 6 oz

Find the missing numbers.

19. 84 mm = _____ cm

20. 0.75 dm = _____ mm

21. 537 km = _____ m

22. 7 m = _____ cm

23. 7.5 km = _____ m

24. 55 mm = _____ m

25. 64,500 mm = _____ km

26. 45 T = _____ kg

27. 0.01 g = _____ mg

28. 52 kg = _____ mg

29. 68 cm = _____ dm

30. 24 kg = _____ g

31. 6.55 km = _____ m

32. 0.01 T = _____ g

33. 0.0011 g = _____ mg

Name each figure.

1.

_____

2.

_____

3. N_____O

_____

Use a protractor to measure each angle. Classify each angle according to its size.

4.    _____

_____

5.   _____

_____

6.   _____

_____

Complete the statements.

7.

FE is perpendicular to ____.

8.

The radius is ____.

9. Copy angle R on $\overrightarrow{MN}$.

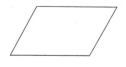

10. Bisect AB.

11. Identify the polygon. Draw a diagonal.

_____

12. Find m∠ MNO.

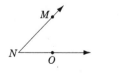

_____

13. The triangles are congruent. Name the angle congruent to ∠XYZ.

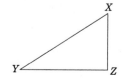

_____

14. Draw all possible diagonals.

Find the area of these rectangles.

1.
3 cm
7 cm

A = _____

2.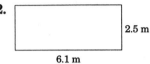
2.5 m
6.1 m

A = _____

3. l = 3.5 mm
w = 9.7 mm

A = _____

Find the area of these squares.

4.
7 m

A = _____

5.
17 mm

A = _____

6. s = 9.9 mm

A = _____

Find the area of these parallelograms.

7.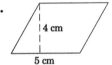
4 cm
5 cm

A = _____

8.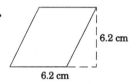
6.2 cm
6.2 cm

A = _____

9. b = 25.6 cm
h = 8.9 cm

A = _____

Find the area of these triangles.

10.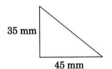
35 mm
45 mm

A = _____

11.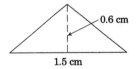
0.6 cm
1.5 cm

A = _____

12. b = 9 cm
h = 16 cm

A = _____

Find the area of these circles.

13.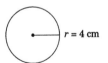
r = 4 cm

A = _____

14.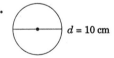
d = 10 cm

A = _____

15. r = 6.6 mm

A = _____

Find the surface area of each box.

16.
4 ft
3 ft
3 ft

surface area = _____

17.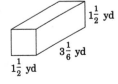
$1\frac{1}{2}$ yd
$3\frac{1}{6}$ yd
$1\frac{1}{2}$ yd

surface area = _____

Find the volume.

18.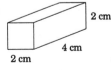
2 cm
4 cm
2 cm

V = _____

Write each ratio as a fraction.

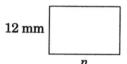

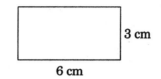

1. daisies to tulips ____

2. width to length ____

3. tulips to flowers ____

4. length to perimeter ____

Solve each proportion.

5. $\frac{6}{80} = \frac{n}{160}$

$n =$ ____

6. $\frac{6}{14} = \frac{3}{n}$

$n =$ ____

7. $\frac{3}{8} = \frac{18}{n}$

$n =$ ____

8. $\frac{28}{n} = \frac{4}{5}$

$n =$ ____

The figures are similar. Solve for n.

9.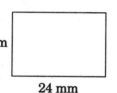

$n =$ _____

10.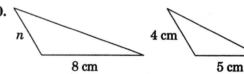

$n =$ _____

Use the scale to find the actual distance.

11.

4 cm

D E

Scale: 1 cm = 9 m _____

12.

5 cm

S T

Scale: 1 cm = 6 m _____

Write each fraction as a percent.

13. $\frac{7}{25} =$ _____

14. $\frac{3}{5} =$ _____

Write each percent as a fraction.

15. 85% = _____

16. 58% = _____

Find the percent of each number.

17. 60% of 82 = _____

18. 20% of 95 = _____

19. $4\frac{1}{2}$% of $82 = _____

20. 7.4% of $820 = _____

21. $6\frac{3}{4}$% of $108 = _____

22. $4\frac{3}{4}$% of 110 = _____

Use the double-bar graph to solve these problems.

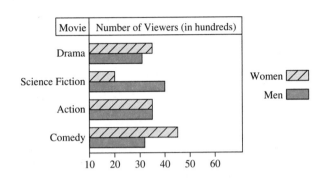

1. What type of movie appeals to men and women equally?

   _____

2. How many more men than women prefer science fiction movies?

   _____

3. Use the following data to draw a line graph.

Hours	Speed (mph)
1	43
2	35
3	46
4	57
5	52
6	60

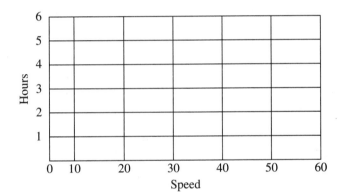

Use the circle graph to solve these problems.

4. What percent of people take the train to work?

   _____

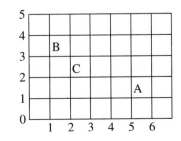

Use the graph to solve these problems.

5. Name point C. _____

6. Locate S (3,4).

7. Graph points A, B, and C.

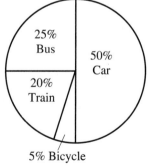

356

Add.

1. $^+4 + ^-8 =$ _____

2. $^+5 + ^+7 =$ _____

3. $^-6 + ^+2 =$ _____

4. $^-9 + ^-1 =$ _____

5. $^-7 + ^+4 =$ _____

6. $^+6 + 0 =$ _____

7. $^+8 + ^-3 =$ _____

8. $^+5 + ^+2 =$ _____

9. $^-3 + ^-1 =$ _____

10. $^-9 + ^-4 =$ _____

11. $^-2 + 0 =$ _____

12. $^+6 + ^-7 =$ _____

13. $^+8 + ^+3 =$ _____

14. $^+5 + ^-4 =$ _____

15. $^-2 + ^+9 =$ _____

16. $^-6 + ^-3 =$ _____

Subtract.

17. $^-5 - ^-9 =$ _____

18. $^+7 - ^+6 =$ _____

19. $^-8 - ^+2 =$ _____

20. $^+4 - ^-3 =$ _____

21. $^-2 - ^+6 =$ _____

22. $^-4 - ^-1 =$ _____

23. $^+3 - ^+5 =$ _____

24. $0 - ^-9 =$ _____

25. $^-8 - ^+4 =$ _____

26. $^-2 - ^-9 =$ _____

27. $^+7 - ^-9 =$ _____

28. $^+6 - ^-4 =$ _____

Multiply.

29. $^-6 \times ^-5 =$ _____

30. $^+2 \times ^-9 =$ _____

31. $^-8 \times ^-4 =$ _____

32. $^+7 \times ^+3 =$ _____

33. $^-4 \times ^+9 =$ _____

34. $^+1 \times ^-5 =$ _____

35. $^+8 \times ^+6 =$ _____

36. $^-7 \times ^-9 =$ _____

Give the coordinates of each point.

37. A (_____, _____)

38. B (_____, _____)

39. C (_____, _____)

40. D (_____, _____)

41. E (_____, _____)

42. F (_____, _____)

Graph and label each point.

43. X ($^+3$, $^-2$)

44. Y ($^-1$, $^+1$)

45. Z (0, $^-4$)

46. M ($^-2$, $^-4$)

47. N ($^+2$, $^+1$)

48. O ($^-3$, $^+2$)

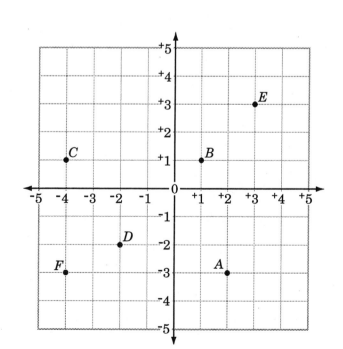

Glossary

Acute An angle which measure less than 90°. Also, a triangle having three acute angles.

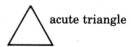
acute triangle

Addend A number that is added to another number.

In 3 + 4 = 7, 3 and 4 are both addends.

Angle The figure made by two straight lines that meet at one endpoint, or vertex.

vertex

Arc A part of a curved line as in a circle.

Area The measure of a surface surrounded by a boundary.

The shaded part of the square is its area.

Associative property When the grouping of 3 or more addends or factors is changed, the sum or product remains the same.

(2 + 5) + 1 = 2 + (5 + 1) or
(5 × 3) × 2 = 5 × (3 × 2)

Average The number obtained by adding two or more quantities and dividing by the number of quantities added.

The average of 2, 5, and 11 is 6;
2 + 5 + 11 = 18, 18 ÷ 3 = 6

Bar graph A representation of numerical facts using lengths of bars to show information.

Base two (See binary system)

Binary System The numeration system which uses only two symbols, 0 and 1.

Bisect To divide into two equal parts.

Central angle An angle whose vertex is the center of a circle.

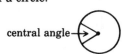
central angle

Chord A line segment that joins two points on a circle.

$\overline{AB}$ is a chord
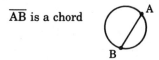

Circle graph A representation of numerical facts using parts or sections of a circle to show information.

Circumference The distance around a circle.

Common denominator A common multiple of two or more denominators.

The common denominator of $\frac{2}{3}$ and $\frac{3}{4}$ is 12.

Commutative property In addition or multiplication the order of the addends or factors can be changed without changing the sum or product.

5 + 7 = 7 + 5 or 3 × 4 = 4 × 3

Composite number A whole number greater than 1 which has more than 2 factors.

The factors of the composite,
12, are 1, 2, 3, 4, 6 and 12.

Congruent Figures, sides or angles having the same size and shape.

Constant key On a calculator, the equal key. It remembers the last operation and number entered.

Coordinates The ordered pair of integers used in graphing.

Cubic unit A unit for measuring volume.

Decimal A fractional part that uses place value and a decimal point to show tenths, hundredths and so on.

0.6 is the decimal equivalent for the fraction $\frac{3}{5}$.

Degree (of an angle) The unit for measuring angles.

Denominator The number below the line in a fraction.

In $\frac{3}{5}$, 5 is the denominator.

Diagonal A segment which connects two vertices of a polygon but is not a side.

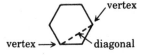
vertex
vertex
diagonal

Diameter A line or chord passing through the center of a circle.

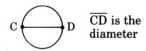
C   D $\overline{CD}$ is the diameter

Difference The answer in a subtraction problem.

In 14 − 2 = 12, 12 is the difference.

Discount An amount of money saved when an original price is lowered.

To find the discount of $\frac{3}{4}$ off $12,

multiply 12 by 3 and divide by 4.
The discount is $9.

359

Distributive property   The property that allows a factor to be multiplied by each addend whose sum is the other factor.

$$5 \times (2 + 3) = (5 \times 2) + (5 \times 3)$$
$$5 \times 5 \qquad = 10 \qquad + 15$$
$$25 \qquad = 25$$

Dividend   The number that is being divided in a division problem.

In $42 \div 7 = 6$, 42 is the dividend.

Divisor   The number that is being divided into the dividend.

In $42 \div 7 = 6$, 7 is the divisor.

Endpoint   A point at the end of a segment or ray.

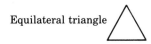

• A, • B and • C are endpoints.

Equilateral triangle   A triangle with 3 equal sides.

Equilateral triangle

Equivalent decimals   Decimals that name the same amount.

12.30, 12.3 and 12.300 are equivalent decimals.

Equivalent fractions   Fractions that name the same number.

$\frac{3}{4}$ and $\frac{9}{12}$ are equivalent fractions because both name $\frac{3}{4}$.

Exponent   A raised number that tells how many times the other number is to be used as a factor.

exponent
$$4^3 = 4 \times 4 \times 4$$

Factor   A number to be multiplied.

In $2 \times 3 = 6$, both 2 and 3 are factors.

Function   The operation and second number entered on a calculator when solving a mathematical equation.

$$15 \longrightarrow \boxed{\times 3} \longrightarrow 45$$

Function

Gram (g)   A basic metric unit of weight.

Greatest common factor (GCF)   The largest number that is a common factor of two or more numbers.

$12 = 3 \times 4$
$15 = 3 \times 5$ 3 is the GCF.

Improper fraction   A fraction whose numerator is larger in value than the denominator.

$\frac{6}{5}$ and $\frac{14}{13}$ are improper fractions.

Input   The first number entered on a calculator when solving a mathematical equation.

Input
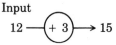

Integers   Any whole number including negative numbers, zero, and positive numbers.

-5, 0 and $+6$ are called integers

Interest   Money paid for the use of borrowed money. Rate of interest is expressed as a percentage per unit of time.

Inverse operation   Operations that are directly opposite of each other.

Addition and subtraction are inverse operations.

Isosceles triangle   A triangle with 2 equal sides.

isosceles triangle

Least common denominator (LCD)   The least common multiple (LCM) of the denominators of two or more fractions.

Least common multiple (LCM)   The smallest number that is a common multiple of two or more numbers.

The LCM of 4 and 6 is 12.

Line   A set of points whose straight path extends indefinitely in opposite directions.

C   D
line CD or $\overleftrightarrow{CD}$

Line graph   A representation of numerical facts using sets of points and lines on a grid.

Line of symmetry   A line which equally divides a figure to produce a mirror image.

line of symmetry

Line segment   A part of a line having two endpoints.

A _____ B   segment AB or $\overline{AB}$

Liter (L)   A basic unit of liquid measure.

1 liter = 1,000 milliliters

Meter (m)   A basic metric unit of length.

Minuend   A number or quantity from which another is subtracted.
   In 18 − 5 = 13, 18 is the minuend.

Mixed number   A fractional number greater than 1 that is written as a whole number and a fraction.
   $5\frac{2}{3}$ is a mixed number.

Multiple   The product of any given number and a whole number.
   10 × 3 = 30, 10 × 5 = 50
   30 and 50 are multiples of 10.

Negative number   An integer less than zero such as −1, −2, −3, −4 . . .

Numerator   The number above the line in a fraction.
   In $\frac{3}{5}$, 3 is the numerator.

Obtuse   An angle which measures between 90° and 180°. Also, a triangle having one obtuse angle.

obtuse triangle

One property   Any factor multiplied by one equals the original factor.
   4 × 1 = 4

Order of operations   The order for solving a mathematical problem:
   1. Multiply and divide starting at the left.
   2. Add and subtract starting at the left.
   3. Do any operations in parentheses before multiplying or dividing.

Ordered pairs   Two numbers that define one point on a grid; The first number names the distance across, and the second names the distance up.

Origin   The point on a grid represented by the ordered pair 0,0.

Output   The number appearing on a calculator screen after a mathematical equation has been entered.

4 —⊗× 5→ Output 20

Parallel   Lines in the same plane that do not intersect.

←——————→
←——————→

Parallelogram   A quadrilateral having two pairs of opposite, congruent, parallel sides.

Percent   A word meaning hundredths.
   37 percent is written 37%
   and means 0.37 or $\frac{37}{100}$.

Percent of a number   The product of a percent which has been renamed to a decimal, and a whole number.
   25% of 50 = .25 × 50 = 12.5

Perimeter   The distance around a figure that is the sum of the lengths of all of its sides.
   The perimeter of this rectangle is equal to 10 units.

   4
1 [   ] 1   4 + 1 + 4 + 1 = 10 units
   4

Perpendicular   Lines that form right angles where they interesect.

Pi (π)   The ratio of the circumference of a circle to its diameter, approximately 3.14.

Pictograph   A representation of numerical facts using pictures as symbols for multiples of a number.

Plane   A flat surface having infinite length and width.

Polygon   A closed plane figure having three or more angles or sides.

Polyhedron   A solid figure having faces made up of polygons.

Positive number   An integer greater than zero such as +1, +2, +3, +4 . . .

Power   The product of a number expressed in exponent form.
   Exponent form
   $2^3 = 2 × 2 × 2$
   8 is the third power of 2.

Prime factor   A factor that is a prime number.
   The prime factors for 60 = 2 × 2 × 3 × 5

Prime number   A counting number greater than one whose only factors are itself and 1.
   1 × 17 = 17
   1 × 3 = 3   17 and 3 are prime numbers.

Probability   A number which tells how likely it is that a certain event will happen.

Product   The answer to a multiplication problem.
   In 4 × 5 = 20, 20 is the product.

Proportion   An equation showing that two ratios are equal.
   $\frac{a}{b} = \frac{c}{d}$, then a × d = b × c

Quadrilateral   A polygon with 4 line segments joined to make 4 angles.

quadrilaterals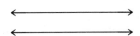

Quotient The answer to a division problem.

In $7\,\overline{)63}$, 9 is the quotient.

Radius A segment whose endpoints are the center of the circle and a point on the circle.

Radius $\overline{AB}$

Ratio A comparison of two quantities.
The ratio of 3 to 4 can be written $\frac{3}{4}$.

Ray A part of a line having one endpoint.

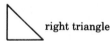 ray EF or $\overrightarrow{EF}$

Reciprocal When the product of two numbers is 1, they are called reciprocals of each other.
$\frac{5}{8}$ and $\frac{8}{5}$ are reciprocals
4 and $\frac{1}{4}$ are reciprocals

Repeating decimals Decimals that repeat themselves as single digits or as a pattern of digits. They can also be called non-terminating decimals.
$\frac{2}{3} = .6666\ldots$ $\frac{1}{11} = .090909\ldots$

Rhombus A parallelogram with all sides congruent.

 rhombus

Right angle An angle which measures exactly 90°.
In this square, all four angles are right angles.

 right angle

Right triangle A triangle having one 90° angle.

right triangle

Rounding Estimating a number's value by raising or lowering any of its place values.
To round to the nearest ten, look at the ones digit. If it is 4 or less, the tens digit stays the same, and the ones digit is replaced by zero. If the ones digit is 5 or more, the tens digit is raised by one, and the ones digit is replaced by zero. 34 rounded to the nearest 10 is 30, but 35 rounded to the nearest 10 is 40.

Scale A ratio between the dimensions of a representation and the actual object.

Scalene triangle A triangle with no sides the same length and no angles the same measure.

Similar polygon Plane figures that have the same shape but not necessarily the same size or position.

Figures A and B are similar

Simplest form A fraction or mixed number whose numerator and denominator cannot be divided by any common factor other than 1.

simplest form   simplest form
$\frac{12}{36} = \frac{1}{3}$ or $\frac{34}{6} = 5\frac{4}{6} = 5\frac{2}{3}$

Straight angle An angle which measures 180°.

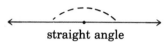
straight angle

Subtrahend The number that is subtracted from the minuend.
In $18 - 5 = 13$, 5 is the subtrahend.

Sum The answer to an addition problem.
In $8 + 9 = 17$, 17 is the sum.

Symmetrical A relationship between equal halves of a figure having the same size, shape and position.

Transversal A line that intersects two or more parallel lines in the same plane.

 Transversal

Trapezoid A quadrilateral having one pair of parallel sides.

Trapezoid

Vertex (pl. vertices) The point at which two sides of an angle, two sides of a plane figure, or three or more sides of a solid figure meet.

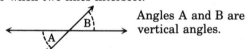 vertex

Vertical angles Angles which are opposite each other when two lines intersect.

 Angles A and B are vertical angles.

Volume The number of cubic units needed to fill a solid figure.

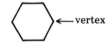 The volume of this cube is 8 cubic units.

Zero property If an addend is zero, the sum is the non-zero addend. If a factor is zero, the product is zero.

Addend   Factor
    ↓   ↓
$5 + 0 = 5$ and $2 \times 0 = 0$

TABLE OF MEASURES
Metric System

Metric Prefixes

Prefix	Multiplication Factor
kilo	1,000
hecto	100
deka	10
deci	0.1 or 1/10
centi	0.01 or 1/100
milli	0.001 or 1/1000

Common Equivalents

	Unit	Symbol	Relationship
Length	kilometer	km	1 km = 1,000 m
	meter	m	1 m = 10 dm
			100 cm
			1,000 mm
	decimeter	dm	1 dm = 0.1 m
			10 cm
	centimeter	cm	1 cm = 0.01 m
			10 mm
	millimeter	mm	1 mm = 0.001 m
Mass	kilogram	kg	1 kg = 1,000 g
	gram	g	1 g = 1,000 mg
			0.001 kg
	milligram	mg	1 mg = 0.001 g
	metric ton	T	1 T = 1,000 kg
Capacity	liter	L	1 L = 1,000 mL
	milliliter	mL	1 mL = 0.001 L
Volume	cubic centimeter	cm^3	$1\ cm^3 = 1\ mL$
	cubic decimeter	dm^3	$1\ dm^3 = 1\ L$
	cubic meter	m^3	$1\ m^3 = 1,000\ L$

Temperature

Water freezes at 0° Celsius (C)
Water boils at 100° Celsius (C)

TABLE OF MEASURES
Customary System

Common Equivalents

	Unit	Symbol	Relationship
Length	foot	ft	1 ft = 12 inches (in.)
	yard	yd	1 yd = 3 ft
			36 in.
	mile	mi	1 mi = 5,280 ft
			1,760 yd
Weight	pound	lb	1 lb = 16 ounces (oz)
	ton	T	1 T = 2,000 lb
Liquid Measure	tablespoon	tbs	1 tbs = 3 teaspoons (tsp)
	fluid ounce	fl oz	1 fl oz = 2 tbs
	cup	c	1 c = 8 fl oz
	pint	pt	1 pt = 2 c
			16 fl oz
	quart	qt	1 qt = 2 pt
			32 fl oz
	gallon	gal	1 gal = 4 qt
			8 pt
Dry Measure	quart	qt	1 qt = 2 pt
	peck	pk	1 pk = 8 qt
	bushel	bu	1 bu = 4 pk

Temperature

Water freezes at 32° Fahrenheit (F)
Water boils at 212° Fahrenheit (F)

Common Fraction/Decimal Equivalents

1/8 = 0.125	1/2 = 0.5
1/4 = 0.25	3/4 = 0.75
3/8 = 0.375	1/5 = 0.20
1/20 = 0.05	7/20 = 0.35

Time Equivalents

Unit	Symbol	Relationship
minute	min	1 min = 60 seconds (sec)
hour	h	1 h = 60 min
day	d	1 d = 24 h
week	wk	1 wk = 7 d
month	mo	1 mo = approximately 4 wk 28, 29, 30 or 31 d
year	yr	1 yr = 12 mo 365 d 366 d in a leap year
decade		10 yr
century		100 yr

Roman Numeral Equivalents

I = 1	VI = 6	XI = 11	L = 50	CD = 400
II = 2	VII = 7	XIX = 19	LX = 60	D = 500
III = 3	VIII = 8	XX = 20	XC = 90	CM = 900
IV = 4	IX = 9	XXX = 30	C = 100	M = 1,000
V = 5	X = 10	XL = 40	CC = 200	$\bar{V}$ = 5,000

Measurement Formulas

Measurement	Formula	Method
Circumference of a circle	$C = D\pi$	Multiply the diameter by 3.1416
Perimeter of a square	$P = 4S$	Multiply the length of one side by 4.
Perimeter of a rectangle	$P = 2(L+W)$	Multiply the sum of the length and width by 2.
Perimeter of a triangle	$P = S_1 + S_2 + S_3$	Add the length of the 3 sides.
Area of a rectangle	$A = LW$	Multiply the length by the width.
Area of a circle	$A = R^2\pi$	Multiply the square of the radius by 3.1416.
Area of a square	$A = S^2$	Multiply one side by itself.
Area of a trapezoid	$A = \frac{1}{2}A(B+B)$	Add the length of the two parallel sides, multiply by the altitude and divide by 2.
Area of a triangle	$A = \frac{1}{2}(AB)$	Multiply the altitude by the base and divide by 2.
Volume of a cube	$V = S^3$	Use the length of one edge as a factor 3 times.
Volume of a rectangular prism	$V = LWH$	Multiply the length by the width by the height.

Index